Making the most of Lamb & Pork

ROBERT CARRIER'S KITCHEN

Making the most of
Lamb & Pork

Marshall Cavendish   London Sydney & New York

Editor	Grizelda Wiles
Editorial Staff	Carey Denton
	Felicity Jackson
	Carol Steiger
Designer	Ross George
Series Editor	Pepita Aris
Production Executive	Robert Paulley
Production Controller	Steve Roberts

Photography
Bryce Attwell: 30, 38, 78, 86
Theo Bergstrom: 28, 104
Paul Bussell: 15, 32, 35, 37, 59, 60, 64, 68, 75
Laurie Evans: 27, 31, 39, 73, 76, 81, 107
Robert Golden: 62
Jon Harris: 25
James Jackson: 18, 20, 70
Chris Knaggs: 11, 23, 63, 74, 82, 83, 85
David Levin: 16, 17
Peter Myers: 21, 29, 67, 71, 84, 88, 110
Paul Webster: 9, 22, 24, 33, 66
Paul Williams: 13, 42, 87, 92
Cover picture: **Chris Knaggs**

Weights and measures
Both metric and imperial measurements are given. As these are not exact equivalents, please work from one set of figures or the other. Use graded measuring spoons levelled across.

Time symbols
The time needed to prepare the dish is given on each recipe. The symbols are as follows:

 simple to prepare and cook

 straightforward but requires more skill or attention

 time-consuming to prepare or requires extra skill

 must be started 1 day or more ahead

On the cover: Redcurrant-glazed loin chops, page 21

This edition published 1985
© Marshall Cavendish Limited 1984, 1985

Printed in Italy by
L.E.G.O. S.p.a. Vicenza

Typeset by Performance Typesetting, Milton Keynes

Published by Marshall Cavendish House
58 Old Compton Street
London W1V 5PA
ISBN 0 86307 264 X (series)

Contents

ROASTING LAMB

Lamb makes a delicious roast, whether it is a whole leg, stuffed shoulder or crown roast. It is economical as well as spectacular, tender and moist and, best of all, so easy to cook.

Roast lamb is delicious cooked either very plainly to emphasize the full flavour of the succulent meat or with added ingredients and flavourings. A sweet/sour fruit stuffing is a tasty combination, or add garlic or herbs such as oregano or the traditional, and delicious, rosemary.

Choosing lamb for roasting

Look for a fine-textured meat, lean and lightly pink. The fat should be firm and white, with a pink blush, and there should be a high proportion of meat to bone and fat. Always ask the butcher to turn the joint over so that you can examine it from all sides. Check that the fat is evenly distributed and not too thick.

Leg of lamb is expensive, but economical too, thanks to its leanness and the high proportion of meat to bone. To make the best use of the thin end of the leg where the meat tapers away to the bone, pare the meat away from the tip of the bone with a sharp knife, then cut off the bare protruding bone with a cleaver (about 15 cm/6 in should be enough). Tuck in the ends of the meat neatly and secure with skewers or a few stitches of strong thread. A butcher will do this boning for you in minutes if you do not feel like coping with it yourself.

A leg may be partially boned to take a stuffing, or completely boned and stuffed. A boned leg can also be rolled and tied – a good idea for spit-roasting and barbecueing.

As the year advances and the joints of lamb are larger, you need only half a leg – the fillet half or knuckle half – when cooking for a small number of people. Allow 225–375 g/8–12 oz (uncooked weight) meat on the bone per person.

Loin makes one of the finest and most delicately flavoured roasts. The loin divides into two parts, the middle loin and the chump end. A 'saddle' or double loin, which is the loins from both sides of the animal attached to each other by the backbone, makes a spectacular presentation for a large dinner party.

To avoid carving problems ask the butcher to chine the loin or chop through the backbone between the ribs. Chining entails sawing through the bone that runs along the length of the joint, so that when the meat has been cooked the bone can be removed, leaving the server with the easy job of running a knife down between the rib bones to separate them (*page 17*). If the butcher chops through the backbone this again makes carving easier but each serving will have a larger piece of bone with it. For stuffing or rolling ask the butcher to bone the loin completely. Allow 225–375 g /8–12 oz (uncooked weight) meat on the bone per person.

Best end of neck, sometimes known as rack, is cheaper than loin. It provides

delicate little cutlets, sweet and succulent. A best end makes an excellent roast, either one side on its own, or two sides cooked together, shaped into a crown with the cavity in the centre filled with stuffing to make a crown roast. You can also serve two best ends with the tips of the bones interlocked and the space between the bones stuffed to make a guard of honour – perfect for a special dinner party.

Like loin, a best end should be chined, and the tips of the cutlet bones scraped clean of any meat, which would otherwise char during roasting. It is also very easy to completely bone a best end for stuffing, or

simply for rolling and roasting. Just take a sharp knife down the cutlet bones and across the bottom and lift out the bones.

Shoulder is preferred to leg by many people for its delicate flavour. It can be plainly roasted, but it is easier to carve if it has been boned and stuffed (*page 15*).

Breast is a very cheap cut, supremely tender and full of flavour, but inclined to be fatty. You can have it boned for stuffing and rolling, but it is infinitely simpler to sandwich two small unboned breasts, fat side outwards, with a delicious stuffing, and tie them tightly together with string. Allow 275–350 g /10–12 oz (uncooked weight) meat on the bone or 150–175 g /5–6 oz (uncooked weight) boned meat per person.

Storing lamb for roasting

When you get your joint of lamb home, you should unwrap it, cover it loosely with greaseproof paper or foil and store it in the coldest part of your refrigerator. If your butcher has not 'hung' the lamb, keep it in

the refrigerator for 2 or 3 days to age it. It can be kept for 4-5 days in all.

It is very important to let the meat come to room temperature before you put it in the oven, or it will spend some of the cooking time losing its chill, rather than roasting.

Preparing lamb for roasting

Remove the joint from the refrigerator about 2 hours before you intend to roast it. Wipe it clean with a damp cloth. Cut away any lumps of excess fat, but leave the meat covered with a thin even layer. Pare off any official marks that have been stamped on. The 'fell', or tough papery outer skin, can be left on when roasting to keep the joint in shape. Remove the skin, though, if you are coating the lamb in breadcrumbs.

Next, the meat should be seasoned. The simplest way to do this is to rub the joint all over vigorously with a cut clove of garlic and season it generously with a little salt and freshly ground black pepper. Spread the joint generously with softened butter.

Roasting lamb

Roasting times for lamb vary according to the cut and method of preparation – a boned, stuffed joint will always need longer than one on the bone. All the following recipes give individual times and oven temperatures best suited to the dish. However, there are some general rules which will ensure good results if you are not following a particular recipe.

Cook the lamb in a moderate oven, 180C/ 350F/gas 4. For boned and stuffed joints allow 1 hour per kg/30 min per lb plus 30 mins for both, and for meat on the bone allow 45–50 mins per kg /20–25 mins per lb plus 20 mins. If you are using a meat thermometer, when it is inserted into the thickest part of the meat (but not touching the bone) it should register a temperature of 77C/170F for pink meat and 80C/176F for well done.

Serving roast lamb

Transfer the roast lamb to a very hot serving platter and let it stand in a warm place for 10–15 minutes before carving: at the front of the turned-off oven with the door open, in the warming compartment of your oven or on top of the stove. This allows the meat juices to 'settle' which makes the meat easier to carve thinly and neatly.

Make gravy with the skimmed pan juices. Any bones and scraps of meat that were trimmed off before the joint was roasted can be boiled up, while the meat is in the oven, to make a stock with which to make the gravy. Failing this, use a light beef stock or wine diluted with stock or water. Add this liquid to the skimmed pan juices, then bring the mixture to the boil, stirring. Thicken with a little *beurre manié* (twice the weight of butter to flour mashed to a smooth paste, which is stirred into the gravy in tiny pieces). Bring the mixture to the boil, simmer for 2–3 minutes until thickened, and serve in a well-heated sauce-boat. Remember to have thoroughly hot plates ready – lamb should be eaten very hot or very cold, but never lukewarm.

Lamb with apricots

2 hours soaking and standing, then 2¾ hours

Serves 6–8

1.6–2 kg./3½–4½ lb shoulder of lamb, boned
100 g/4 oz dried apricots, chopped
1 small onion, chopped
15 g /½ oz butter
75 g /3 oz fresh breadcrumbs
15 ml /1 tbls freshly chopped parsley
50 g /2 oz walnuts, chopped
2.5 ml /½ tsp ground cinnamon
salt and freshly ground black pepper
30 ml /2 tbls lemon juice
juice of 2 oranges
300 ml /10 fl oz beef stock, home-made or
  from a cube
15 ml /1 tbls cornflour

1 Pour 50 ml /2 fl oz water over the apricots and leave to soak for 2 hours. Bring the lamb to room temperature.
2 Sauté the onion in the butter, then mix with the apricots, breadcrumbs, parsley, walnuts and cinnamon. Season to taste. Heat the oven to 200C /400F /gas 6.
3 Lay the boned shoulder *(page 15)* skin side down and season. Push the stuffing into the hole left by the bones. Draw the meat in and secure the ends with skewers.
4 Mix the lemon and orange juices and pour over the lamb. Roast, uncovered, for 30 minutes, basting occasionally. Reduce the heat to 180C /350F /gas 4 and continue cooking for 1½ hours, basting every 15 minutes.
5 Lift the lamb onto a warmed serving dish and remove the skewers. Leave to 'settle' while you make the sauce: pour off the fat from the pan juices and add the stock. Blend the cornflour with a little water and stir this into the pan. Season to taste and bring to the boil. Boil, stirring, until thickened. Garnish the lamb with watercress and serve with new potatoes and the sauce.

Lamb with apricots

Mustard roast leg of lamb

20 minutes, 4 hours marinating, $1\frac{1}{2}$–$1\frac{3}{4}$ hours roasting plus settling

Serves 6 – 8
1.8 kg /4 lb leg of lamb
freshly ground black pepper
2 garlic cloves, finely chopped
60 ml /4 tbls Dijon mustard
5 ml /1 tsp ground ginger
20 ml /4 tsp soy sauce
30 ml /2 tbls olive oil
salt
2 bunches of watercress

1 Using a sharp knife, carefully remove the lamb's outer skin. Discard. Season generously with ground black pepper.
2 In a bowl, combine the finely chopped garlic, Dijon mustard, ground ginger and soy sauce. Stir until well blended with a fork or small wire whisk, then beat in the olive oil drop by drop.
3 Place the lamb on a rack in a roasting tin. Brush the mustard mixture all over the meat. Cover and leave to marinate for 4 hours in a cool place.
4 Heat the oven to 170C /325F /gas 3.
5 Just before cooking, season the lamb generously with salt.
6 Cook the lamb in the oven for 1 hour 30 minutes for pink meat, or 1 hour 45 minutes for well-done lamb. Turn the lamb twice during cooking, so that it is browned evenly all over. This will also prevent the mustard coating from forming a brown crust.
7 Transfer the roast lamb to a heated dish and leave in a warm place for 10–15 minutes to settle before carving.
8 Meanwhile, wash the watercress in cold water, removing and discarding the stems. Drain and pat dry with a clean tea-towel or absorbent paper.
9 To serve, make a bed of watercress leaves on a heated serving dish and lay the Mustard roast leg of lamb on top.

Roast loin of lamb with rosemary and oregano

10 minutes, 2 hours standing, 1–$1\frac{1}{2}$ hours roasting plus settling

Serves 6–8
1.4 kg /3 lb loin of lamb, chined
1–2 fat garlic cloves, slivered
5 ml /1 tsp dried rosemary, crushed
2.5 ml /$\frac{1}{2}$ tsp dried oregano
juice of 1 lemon
75 g /3 oz softened butter
pinch of freshly grated nutmeg
freshly ground black pepper

1 Remove the lamb from the refrigerator about 2 hours before you intend to roast it and leave it to come to room temperature. Cut small slits in the lamb with the point of

Mustard roast leg of lamb

a sharp knife, and insert the slivers of garlic into the slits.
2 Combine the rosemary and oregano with the lemon juice, softened butter, nutmeg and freshly ground black pepper to taste. Spread the mixture evenly over the fleshy side of the loin. Heat the oven to 170C /325F /gas 3.
3 Stand the lamb on a rack in a roasting tin and roast in the oven for 1 hour for pink meat or up to $1\frac{1}{2}$ hours for well-done meat, basting occasionally.
4 Transfer the roast lamb to a heated serving platter and leave in a warm place for 10–15 minutes, to settle before carving. To carve, remove the chined backbone and cut down between the ribs.

Indonesian lamb

20 minutes, overnight marinating, 30–35 minutes plus settling

Serves 4
1 best end of neck of lamb (8 ribs), weighing about 800 g /1$\frac{3}{4}$ lb, chined, with the rib bones trimmed
For the Javanese saté sauce
1 Spanish onion, finely chopped
10 ml /2 tsp salt
1 garlic clove, finely chopped
15 ml /1 tbls curry powder
2.5 ml /$\frac{1}{2}$ tsp each powdered turmeric, coriander and pure powdered chilli (not cayenne pepper or chilli seasoning)
90 ml /6 tbls lemon juice
15–30 ml /1–2 tbls clear honey
freshly ground black pepper

1 Cut the best end into 4 portions to make 4 double cutlets. In a large shallow dish combine the ingredients for the Javanese saté sauce. Lay the double cutlets in this sauce and marinate in a cool place for 12 hours or overnight. Turn the meat over once or twice during the marinating time.
2 Heat the oven to 190C /375F /gas 5. Remove the lamb from the marinade and wrap the rib bones in foil to prevent them burning. Place the lamb on a rack set over a roasting tin and spoon over all the marinade mixture. Roast in the oven for 30–35 minutes, turning the lamb over after 15 minutes, and basting now and then with the marinade and drippings in the roasting tin.
3 When the lamb is cooked, transfer it to a well-heated serving platter. Strain the marinade and meat drippings in the roasting tin into a heated sauce-boat and serve.

Crown roast of lamb

The stuffing for this classic dish combines a slightly sweet fruitiness with a hint of sharpness, which compliments the lamb perfectly.

2 hours standing, 45 minutes, then roasting and settling time

Serves 6–8
2 best end joints, each with 6–8 cutlets
salt
freshly ground black pepper
30 ml /2 tbls fresh rosemary, crushed
25 g /1 oz butter
watercress, to garnish
1 segmented orange, to garnish

For the stuffing
425 g / 15 oz canned apricot halves, drained
grated zest and juice of 1 orange
2 oranges, peeled and segmented
grated zest and juice of 1 lemon
225 g / 8 oz cooked rice
100 g / 4 oz white breadcrumbs
1 medium-sized onion, finely chopped
2.5 ml / ½ tsp ground cinnamon
salt
freshly ground black pepper

1 Bring the best ends to room temperature. Cut off the skin from the best ends, then trim the meat from the tops of the bones, scraping them clean with a knife. Weigh the joints and calculate the cooking time at 44 min per kg / 20 min per lb.
2 Sew one end of each joint together, sewing around the last bone of each joint. Stand the tied joints upright and bend them round until the other ends meet. Stitch these together to form a crown. Then tie around the base to hold the crown in shape. Season the lamb inside and out with salt and pepper and sprinkle a little of the rosemary inside. Heat the oven to 190C /375F /gas 5.
3 Reserve 12 apricot halves. Chop the rest and mix with the rest of the stuffing ingredients; season with salt and pepper.
4 In a roasting tin, melt the butter with the rest of the rosemary, then place the lamb in the tin. Spoon the stuffing loosely into centre of the crown. Cover bone ends with foil and roast for the calculated time, basting occasionally and covering stuffing with foil if it becomes too brown.
5 Place the lamb on a warmed serving dish. Remove string and foil and place cutlet frills on the bones. Leave to settle in a warm place for 10–15 minutes, then garnish with apricots, watercress and orange segments.

Savoury roast lamb with gravy

〰 2 hours standing,
1½–1¾ hours roasting plus settling

Serves 6
1.8 kg / 4 lb leg of lamb
100 g / 4 oz softened butter
5 ml / 1 tsp crushed dried rosemary
5 ml / 1 tsp dried thyme
juice of 1 lemon
freshly ground black pepper
For the gravy
300 ml / 10 fl oz beef stock, home-made or
   from a cube
15–30 ml / 1–2 tbls tomato purée
15 g / ½ oz butter
15 ml / 1 tbls flour
salt and freshly ground black pepper

1 Remove the lamb from the refrigerator about 2 hours before you intend to roast it.

Using a fork, beat the softened butter with the rosemary and thyme. Gradually beat in the lemon juice, then continue to mix until smooth. Season generously with freshly ground black pepper. Spread the seasoned butter over the entire surface of the joint. Leave it to stand at room temperature until it has lost its chill. Heat the oven to 170C / 325F /gas 3.
2 Place the lamb, fat side up, on a rack set over a roasting tin. Roast in the oven for 1½ hours for pink meat, or about 1¾ hours for well done. Baste the meat occasionally.
3 Transfer the roast lamb to a well-heated serving platter and leave it to stand in a warm place for 10–15 minutes to settle before carving.
4 Meanwhile, make the gravy. Skim the excess fat from the drippings in the roasting tin. Place the tin over direct heat, add the beef stock and tomato purée and bring the mixture to the boil, stirring and scraping the bottom and sides of the tin with a wooden spoon to dislodge the crusty bits.
5 Make a beurre manié with the butter and flour by mashing them together to a smooth paste. Add to the boiling liquid in tiny pieces, stirring until they have dissolved into the gravy. Simmer for a further 2–3 minutes, until the gravy has thickened. Season, strain the gravy into a heated sauceboat and serve with the lamb.

Crown roast of lamb

Roast rack of lamb with Italian breadcrumb topping

Ask your butcher to chine the best end. This will make carving much easier, as you can carve down between the cutlets. To save time and trouble you can also ask him to trim the top of the ribs.

🔪🔪 2 hours standing, then about 1¼ hours plus settling

Serves 4
2 best ends of neck of young lamb, weighing about 500 g /1 lb each, chined, with the rib bones trimmed
salt and freshly ground black pepper
65–75 g /2½–3 oz softened butter
75 g /3 oz fresh white breadcrumbs
45 ml /3 tbls freshly grated Parmesan cheese
2.5 ml /½ tsp dried marjoram
2.5 ml /½ tsp dried thyme
1.5 ml /¼ tsp dried oregano
finely grated zest of ½ lemon
1 small egg, beaten
For the garnish
4 tomatoes
sprigs of watercress

1 Remove the lamb from the refrigerator 2 hours before you intend to roast it. Strip off the skin that covers the fat. Season the fat with salt and freshly ground black pepper, then leave the meat to stand at room temperature until it has lost its chill. Heat the oven to 200C /400F /gas 6.
2 Heat a frying-pan, lay the lamb in it, fat side down, and sear over a high heat until the fat takes on a little colour.
3 Spread 25 g /1 oz of the softened butter over the best ends. Stand them up in a roasting tin, cover the rib bones with foil, and roast in the oven for 20 minutes. Remove the tin from the oven and leave the meat aside while you prepare the topping. Do not switch off the oven.
4 Prepare the topping: mix together the breadcrumbs, Parmesan cheese and dried herbs, then add the grated lemon zest, beaten egg and the rest of the softened butter and make a paste. Use half of this mixture to coat the fatty side of each best end. Return the best ends to the oven, again covering the rib bones with foil, and roast for a further 30 minutes for pink meat, or 40 minutes for well done. Baste the lamb occasionally towards the end of the cooking time with the fatty juices. Meanwhile, heat the grill to moderate.
5 When the lamb is cooked, transfer it to a well-heated serving platter. Leave to settle in a warm place for 10–15 minutes. While it settles, grill the tomatoes. Transfer the tomatoes to the serving platter, garnish with sprigs of watercress and serve. Carve down between the bones and serve each person 2 cutlets.

● For an alternative topping omit the oregano and the Parmesan cheese and replace these with finely chopped parsley.

Leg of lamb in pastry

This is one instance where a roasted lamb joint should not settle before carving – the pastry might become soggy.

🔪🔪 2 hours standing, 1 hour roasting, cooling, then 1 hour

Serves 4–6
1.4 kg /3 lb leg of young lamb, boned
400 g /14 oz made-weight puff pastry
4 lambs' kidneys
50 g /2 oz butter
100 g /4 oz button mushrooms, thinly sliced
50 g /2 oz fresh white breadcrumbs
good pinch of dried thyme
good pinch of chopped dried rosemary
salt and freshly ground black pepper
30 ml /2 tbls brandy
50 g /2 oz liver pâté
1 medium-sized egg, lightly beaten

1 Remove the lamb from the refrigerator about 2 hours before you intend to roast it. Remove most of the fat from the lamb, leaving a thin layer of fat to cover the meat. Leave to stand at room temperature until it has lost its chill. If you are using frozen pastry, allow it to defrost during this time.
2 Meanwhile, clean the kidneys, remove the skins and cores, then cut the kidneys into 5 mm /¼ in dice. Melt half of the butter in a heavy frying-pan and sauté the kidneys for 1 minute, stirring so that they brown all over. Drain off most of the fat, then add to the pan the sliced mushrooms, the breadcrumbs, herbs and salt and freshly ground black pepper to taste. Sauté for a further 3–4 minutes, until the breadcrumbs are golden. Remove the pan from the heat. Pour the brandy over the kidney mixture and, standing well back, set it alight with a match. Let the flames burn themselves out, then leave the mixture until lukewarm.
3 Blend the pâté into the kidney mixture, then leave until cold.
4 Heat the oven to 190C /375F /gas 5. When the meat has lost its chill, press the

Roast rack of lamb with Italian breadcrumb topping

kidney mixture into the space left by the bone. Ease the joint back into shape. Tie it up securely, or sew along the seams with a trussing needle and thread.

5   Place the stuffed leg of lamb on a rack set in a roasting tin and place in the oven for 45–60 minutes, depending on how well cooked you like your lamb. The lamb will only be partly cooked at this stage. Remove it from the oven and cool completely.

6   Heat the oven to 230C /450F /gas 8. Remove the string or thread from the cold lamb and spread the lamb with the remaining butter. Roll the pastry to a rectangle, about 35 × 40 cm /14 × 16 in. Lay the lamb on the pastry, then fold the pastry up over the lamb to enclose it, sealing the edges together with a little beaten egg.

7   Transfer the pastry-wrapped lamb to a lightly dampened baking sheet, joins downward. Make 2 or 3 holes in the top of the parcel, about 20 mm /¾ in in diameter, to allow the steam to escape. Decorate around

the holes with leaves made from pastry trimmings, attaching them with a little beaten egg. Lightly brush the pastry all over with cold water.

8   Carefully place some aluminium foil over the pastry leaves so that they do not get too brown in the oven, then bake in the oven for 10 minutes. Remove the foil, brush the pastry all over with beaten egg and bake for a further 10 minutes, until the pastry is puffed and golden. Serve hot.

Port-glazed loin of lamb

For special occasions, port gives an extra touch of flavour.

2 hours standing,
then 1¼ hours plus settling

Serves 4
about 1 kg /2¼ lb loin of lamb, boned, rolled and tied, reserving the bone
1 medium-sized carrot, sliced
1 bouquet garni
salt
freshly ground black pepper
8 small onions, peeled
30 ml /2 tbls port
30 ml /2 tbls redcurrant jelly
25 g /1 oz lard
about 25 g /1 oz butter
15 ml /1 tbls flour
flat-leaved parsley, to garnish

1   Remove the lamb from the refrigerator about 2 hours before you intend to roast it. Meanwhile, make the stock. Put the bone in a saucepan with the carrot, bouquet garni, 500 ml /18 fl oz water and a little salt and pepper. Bring to the boil, cover and simmer the stock for 30 minutes.

2   Strain the stock into a clean pan, add the onions, bring to the boil, cover and cook for 5 minutes. Remove the onions and reserve. Boil the stock until it is reduced to 300 ml / 10 fl oz, then reserve.

3   Heat the oven to 190C /375F /gas 5. Put the port and redcurrant jelly in a small pan and add 30 ml /2 tbls stock. Whisk the mixture over a moderate heat until smooth.

4   Use the lard to grease a small roasting tin, then put in the joint with the join underneath. Surround it with the onions and put a small piece of butter on each onion. Brush the joint with the glaze. Put the tin in the oven and roast for 1 hour, brushing the joint generously with the glaze twice more during this time. The second time also brush the onions with glaze.

5   Transfer the joint and onions to a warm serving dish and leave to settle in a warm place while you make the gravy.

6   Stir the flour into the fat in the roasting tin, put it over moderate heat and cook for 1 minute, stirring. Gradually add the reserved stock and bring to the boil, scraping up any sediment and juices in the pan. Simmer for 3 minutes, then season to taste with salt and pepper. Strain into a warm sauce-boat.

7   Carve the meat, garnish with flat-leaved parsley and serve with the gravy.

Glazed saddle of lamb

This cold lamb dish makes a spectacular centrepiece for a big family occasion, or when you have a crowd of friends round in the summer. The recipe tells you how to garnish and present the saddle of lamb so that it looks as well as tastes its very best.

standing, cooking vegetables, 2 hours, cooling, 1 hour decorating

Serves 8–10
3.2 kg /7 lb saddle of lamb
salt and freshly ground black pepper
25 g /1 oz butter, softened
30 ml /2 tbls redcurrant jelly
50 ml /2 fl oz port
75 ml /3 fl oz dry white wine
2 shallots, finely chopped
grated zest of ½ orange
grated zest of ½ lemon
To serve
1 kg /2 lb cold, cooked new potatoes
45 ml /3 tbls olive oil
15 ml /1 tbls wine vinegar
225 g /8 oz cold, cooked green beans
15 ml /1 tbls finely chopped parsley
sprigs of fresh mint

1   Ask the butcher to remove the tough outer skin from the saddle. Remove the lamb from the refrigerator about 2 hours before you intend to roast it to allow it to come to room temperature.

2   Heat the oven to 220C /425F /gas 7.

3   Place the saddle of lamb on a rack in a roasting tin. Season with salt and freshly ground black pepper and spread with the softened butter. Cook in the oven for 10 minutes. Reduce the heat to 170C /325F / gas 3 and cook the lamb for a further 1½–2 hours. Remove from the oven and allow to cool completely.

4   When cold, remove the meat carefully from the bone in 2 long fillets; use a sharp knife to do this, following the shape of the bones carefully. Trim the fat from the top of each one right down to the meat. Leave the outer edge with its fat to add flavour. Cut each fillet into 8 diagonal slices.

5   Replace the slices on the bone upside-down, so that the fat is underneath and the slices stand almost upright along each side of the backbone.

6   In a saucepan, combine the redcurrant jelly, port and white wine with the finely chopped shallot and grated zest from the orange and lemon. Bring to the boil and cook for 10 minutes or until it is syrupy. Spoon the glaze over the meat.

7   Place the saddle on an oval serving platter and put the cold new potatoes at each end of the meat.

8   Just before serving, beat together the oil and vinegar to form an emulsion, pour over the green beans and toss until well coated. Arrange the beans in piles on either side of the saddle. Sprinkle the potatoes with finely chopped parsley and garnish the saddle with sprigs of fresh mint. Serve at once.

Roast stuffed shoulder of lamb

It is well worth boning this shoulder of lamb to add the tasty celery stuffing and make it easy to carve.

standing and marinating,
1¾–2¼ hours plus settling

Serves 8
1.6 kg / 3½ lb boned shoulder of lamb
1 garlic clove, finely chopped
30 ml / 2 tbls olive oil
freshly ground black pepper
salt
celery leaves, to garnish
For the stuffing
100 g / 4 oz bread, cubed
75 g / 3 oz butter
½ onion, finely chopped
4 celery stalks, finely chopped
salt
freshly ground black pepper
30 ml / 2 tbls finely chopped parsley
1.5 ml / ¼ tsp cayenne pepper

1   Remove the lamb from the refrigerator about 2 hours before you intend to roast it. In a small bowl, combine the finely chopped garlic with olive oil and season generously with freshly ground black pepper. Brush the lamb with the marinade inside and out and leave to marinate for at least 1 hour.
2   Meanwhile, prepare the stuffing. Heat the grill to high.
3   Spread the bread cubes on a baking tray and grill for 4–5 minutes until evenly browned all over, turning them constantly and being careful that they do not burn.
4   In a medium-sized saucepan, melt the butter. Sauté the onion and celery for 10 minutes, or until soft, turning occasionally with a wooden spoon. Season to taste with salt and freshly ground black pepper. Leave to cool a little.
5   Add the toasted bread cubes, chopped parsley and cayenne pepper to the onion and celery and stir until well mixed.
6   Heat the oven to 170C / 325F / gas 3. Lay the lamb on a board, skin side down. Insert the stuffing into the hole left by the removed bones and tuck in any scrappy ends of meat. Draw the meat in and secure the blade and shank ends with skewers. Season generously with salt and freshly ground black pepper.
7   Line a roasting tin with foil. Place the joint in it and bring up the sides of the foil, without completely enclosing the meat.
8   Roast for about 1¼ hours for pink meat, or up to 1¾ hours for well done, basting occasionally with the meat juices. Increase the temperature to 200C / 400F / gas 6. Open out the foil and roast the lamb uncovered for the last 30 minutes, or until golden brown and cooked through.
9   Remove the skewers from the lamb and transfer it to a heated serving platter. Leave to settle in a warm place for 10–15 minutes before carving. Garnish the shoulder of lamb with celery leaves and serve.

Roast stuffed shoulder of lamb

Tunnelling a shoulder

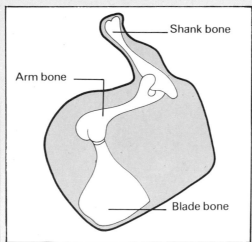

Here we show you how to remove all the bones from a shoulder, but you can remove the blade alone if you want to retain more of the original shape and are short of time.

Starting with the thin blade end, scrape the meat from both sides of this flat bone, turning the shoulder over if it helps. Work until you meet the next bone.

Twist the blade bone to loosen it at the joint. Cut through the sinews to free the blade and pull it out. Turn the shoulder, skin side up and shank end towards you.

Slice through the skin along the shank bone, and, keeping the knife close to the bone, cut the meat away up to the joint. Grip the shank, cut the sinews and work free.

Continue working to halfway along the arm bone. Turn the shoulder round, skin side down, and scrape the rest of the meat from the bone. Pull the arm bone out.

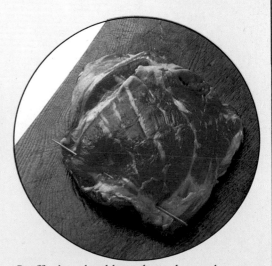

Stuff the shoulder, then draw the meat together at the blade end, and secure by threading with a skewer. Tuck in and skewer the shank end.

Carving roast lamb

Carving a joint of meat into neat slices makes it look more appetizing and stretch further than a joint merely hacked into portions. Being able to do this at the table will add to the sense of occasion.

To the uninitiated the prospect of carving the meat quickly and neatly before an expectant audience can appear daunting. It is, however, a skill which is not difficult to acquire. Make sure you have the right equipment, familiarize yourself with the joint of meat and follow the step-by-step guide.

The cook's job is to:
● make the joint a neat shape for carving – if necessary, by tying it
● time the cooking so that the meat has a chance to 'firm up' before carving, by standing for 10–15 minutes in a warm place
● serve the joint on a large spiked serving dish or board that will prevent the meat from slipping, preferably one with grooves to collect the meat juices
● wrap any knuckle bone in foil or a white cloth ready for the carver to grasp
● provide very hot dinner plates.

The carver needs to:
● make sure before the meal that the carving knife is really sharp
● use the finger guard on the fork to avoid accidents
● know the anatomy of the joint so that carving is done between or towards the bones, if any
● carve across the grain of the meat
● arrange the carved slices on individual plates so each portion looks generous and appetizing.

Carving a leg of lamb

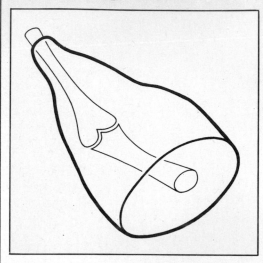

Arrange the leg on a carving dish with the rounded side uppermost. Carve a thin wedge-shaped slice from the centre of the leg, cutting right down to the bone. Continue carving slices from either side of the first cut (see picture below), slanting the knife to obtain the largest slice you can.

Turn the joint over, hold firmly by the shank and carve thin horizontal slices from along the leg (see picture above).

Hold the joint by the shank and angle it so that the remaining meat from the sides can be sliced off.

Carving a shoulder of lamb

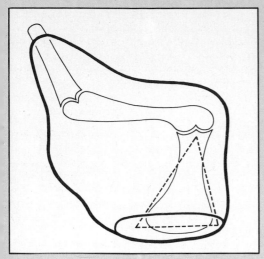

Here is a clever way to carve a shoulder of lamb neatly and economically.

Before cooking, cut round the blade bone to loosen (see dotted line in diagram).

Roast the joint well. Grasp the exposed blade bone, twist until free, then pull out.

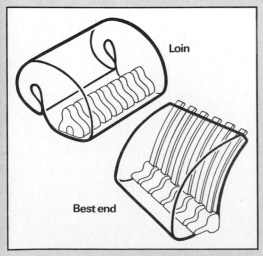

Slice the meat downwards in 5 mm /¼ in slices, until the remaining bone is reached.

Turn the joint and slice until the bone is reached again.

Finally, keep turning and carving until all the meat is removed.

Carving a loin and best end of lamb

Loin

Best end

Loin: ask the butcher to chine it or to chop through the backbone *between* the ribs. This will help when you are carving.
Best end: ask the butcher to chine the joint.

Image shown with Loin being carved.

Loin: when cooked, carve the meat by cutting between the rib bones, dividing the joint into chops which are about 10 mm /½ in thick.

Best end: when it is cooked, remove the chine bone entirely. Carve the joint by cutting downwards between the rib bones into cutlets.

GRILLING LAMB

Lamb is a rewarding meat to grill; whether you choose the cheaper or more expensive cuts, its flavour and tenderness are almost guaranteed if you grill it with care and serve it with imagination.

There can be few things more tempting than a tender lamb cutlet or a thick, juicy lamb steak with a crisply browned surface and a succulent pink centre, eaten straight from the grill.

One of the great advantages of grilling meat is that it is so quick; it will cook in the time that it takes you to toss a salad and set the table. And of course grilling is a perfect way to cook meat for the weight conscious — you can trim any fat off the meat itself before grilling.

What lamb to grill?

The lamb that you buy from the butcher will be either fresh and home-produced or frozen and imported. Home-produced lamb is usually more expensive because it is considered superior in both quality and flavour, although this can vary according to the time of year.

The younger the lamb, the more tender it will be: signs that indicate a young animal are pale pink, finely grained flesh and firm creamy or white fat. Look for freshly cut meat: the surfaces will have a slightly moist appearance.

The following cuts of lamb are ones that are particularly suitable for quick grilling.

Loin chops: as their name suggests, these chops are cut from the loin of the lamb. They have a lean eye of meat surrounded by fat. They weigh about 125 g /4 oz and are usually 25 mm /1 in thick.

Chump chops: these are cut from between the loin and the leg. They are meatier than a loin chop but also have a larger bone. Chump chops weigh about 175 g /6 oz and are usually 20 mm /$\frac{3}{4}$ in thick.

Cutlets: these are also known as best end chops because they are cut from the best end of neck. The tenderest and cheapest of the chops, they are also tiny; you will probably need 3 per person. You can buy them ready-prepared or buy a best end of neck and do it yourself. Make sure that the chine bone has been removed (this requires a saw, but your butcher will probably do it quite happily). Skin the best end of neck and divide it up into cutlets by cutting down between the bones with a sharp knife. Trim any excess fat off each cutlet, following the shape of the meat, and scrape the meat away from the end of the bone.

Leg steaks: lean, tender slices from the very top of the leg, lamb steaks are often sold with the small round bone removed. Leg steaks weigh about 250 g /9 oz and are about 20 mm /$\frac{3}{4}$ in thick.

Shoulder and leg: These can both be boned and cubed and used for kebabs or brochettes. A shoulder weighing 1 kg /2 lb will make about 700 g /1$\frac{1}{4}$ lb of boned meat. Leg steaks or the top (meatier) half of the leg are also ideal for brochettes.

Kidneys: lamb's kidneys are an essential part of a traditional mixed grill, and are also delicious served for breakfast. Allow 2 or 3 kidneys per person.

Sweetbreads: these are glands from either the throat or pancreas of the lamb. They are sold in pairs which weigh 50–100 g /2–4 oz or you can buy them in 450 g /1 lb packs.

How to prepare lamb for grilling

Marinating: lamb benefits enormously from being marinated before grilling. Try olive oil and lemon juice with a little chopped onion and plenty of garlic and herbs. The marinade will tenderize the lamb and add to the flavour as well. Cubed lamb for brochettes should be marinated for at least 4 hours before cooking. Chops and

Sweetbread kebabs and
Garlic lamb kebabs

steaks will absorb the most flavour if marinated overnight. Remember to take the meat, in its marinade, out of the refrigerator at least 2 hours before you wish to grill it so that it comes to room temperature.

When you are ready to grill it remove the meat from the marinade, draining off any excess. Reserve the marinade to baste the meat while it is grilling.

Pat meat that has not been marinated dry with absorbent paper before preparing it for cooking.

Trimming the fat: leave a small border of fat around the edge of large steaks and chops to help keep them moist while cooking. Slash the fat at intervals with a sharp knife to stop the fat curling up while it cooks. With cutlets and loin chops just trim the fat to follow the shape of the meat and neaten it in appearance.

Seasoning: when you remove the meat from the refrigerator to bring it to room temperature, season it well with freshly ground black pepper and sprinkle with herbs if using. This allows plenty of time for the flavours to permeate the meat. Just before you are ready to grill the lamb season it again with salt and brush it with a half-and-half mixture of melted butter and oil.

Preparing kidneys: nick the membrane that covers the kidney with the point of a sharp knife; it should then pull off in one go. If you are cutting the kidneys completely in half, first trim out the core in a V-shape with a pair of scissors. Cut the kidneys in half horizontally from the curved side. The other method of preparing a kidney is to spatchcock it: don't trim out the core as above but cut the kidney in half horizontally almost to the core: it should still be joined together when opened out flat. Metal skewers are used to keep the kidneys flat while they are grilled.

Preparing sweetbreads: remove the membrane that covers the sweetbreads and soak them in cold water for 1–2 hours to remove all the blood. Change the water frequently during this soaking time. Drain the sweetbreads, rinse under cold running water and put them in a saucepan, cover them with cold, salted water and add 5–10 ml / 1–2 tsp lemon juice to acidulate the water. Bring the water to the boil and simmer the sweetbreads for 1–2 minutes. Drain the sweetbreads quickly and refresh them under cold running water to stop the cooking process. They are now ready to use as instructed in the recipe.

Timing for grilling lamb steaks and chops

Cut	Weight	Thickness	Distance from heat	Time each side	Result
Loin chop	125 g /4 oz	25 mm /1 in	7.5 cm /3 in	4 minutes	rosé
				6 minutes	well-done
Best end cutlet	75 g /3 oz	25 mm /1 in	7.5 cm /3 in	4 minutes	rosé
				6 minutes	well-done
Chump chop	175 g /6 oz	20 mm /$\frac{3}{4}$ in	7.5 cm /3 in	3 minutes	rosé
				5 minutes	well-done
Leg steak	250 g /9 oz	20 mm /$\frac{3}{4}$ in	7.5 cm /3 in	3 minutes	rosé
				5 minutes	well-done

Grilling lamb

Heating the grill: heat the grill to maximum before you start cooking so that it will sear the meat immediately, sealing in the juices. If you leave the grill pan under the grill while it is heating be sure you do not leave the grid in it. The grid should be cold when the meat is placed on it or the meat will begin to cook from both sides. The grid should be about 7.5 cm /3 in from the source of heat.

Cooking times: the cooking time depends on how you like your lamb cooked. Rosé

Trimming a cutlet

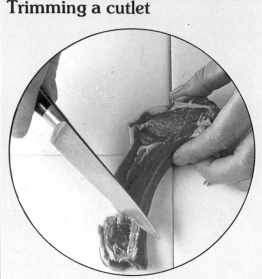

Trim the fat and taper it into the bone 3 cm/ 1½ in from the end. Scrape the bone clean below this point.

means that the meat is brown on the outside but still slightly pink inside. If you prefer it well done the meat should be beige all the way through to the centre. For perfect results preheat the grill to maximum, follow my chart and time your lamb carefully on each side.

To check whether the chops or steak are done to your liking, slip the point of a sharp knife down between the meat and the edge of the bone – this is the part that takes the longest to cook – and look at the colour of the meat.

Turning: turn the chops or steak only once during their cooking time and always use tongs or two wooden spoons – turning them with a fork might puncture the chops and allow the juices to escape, which makes the meat tough.

Grilling brochettes: cook the brochettes 7.5 cm /3 in from the heat for 4–6 minutes, depending on the size of the cubes of meat and how you like them done. Turn the skewers during the cooking time so that the brochettes cook evenly.

Don't forget, if you have marinated them, to baste the brochettes with the reserved marinade while they are cooking. This will keep them moist and succulent and make full use of the marinade. In some recipes you can heat the reserved marinade and use it as a flavourful sauce.

Sweetbread kebabs

🍴 soaking the sweetbreads 1–2 hours,
then 25 minutes

Serves 6 as a starter
225 g /8 oz lamb sweetbreads
5 ml /1 tsp lemon juice
3 leeks, trimmed
2 red peppers, seeded
salt and freshly ground black pepper
olive oil

1 Remove the membranes from the sweetbreads. Soak them in a bowl of cold water for 1–2 hours, changing the cold water frequently.
2 Drain the sweetbreads. Place them in a saucepan and cover with cold water. Add the lemon juice, bring to the boil and simmer for 1–2 minutes. Remove from the heat and plunge the sweetbreads into cold water. Drain and cut them into 24 pieces.
3 Heat the grill without the grid to high.
4 Put the leeks in a saucepan and cover them with cold water. Bring to the boil and blanch for 2 minutes. Drain and refresh under cold running water. Cut into 18 × 15 mm /½ in lengths.
5 Cut the red peppers into 18 × 15 mm /½ in cubes.
6 Thread each of 6 skewers with a piece of sweetbread, leek and red pepper. Repeat twice more and finish with a piece of

Honey and lemon loin chops

sweetbread. Season with salt and freshly ground black pepper. Brush the kebabs with olive oil.
7 Brush the grill grid with olive oil and place the kebabs on the grid. Grill 5 cm /2 in from the heat for 4 minutes, turning them frequently so they cook evenly. Serve the kebabs hot.

Honey and lemon loin chops

Serve one loin chop per person for a family meal and 2 each for dinner parties or special occasions. Serve with a creamy purée of swedes.

🔪 marinating the chops 4 hours,
then 8–12 minutes

Serves 4–8
8 loin chops, 25 mm /1 in thick, weighing
*   about 125 g /4 oz each*
salt and freshly ground black pepper
olive oil
For the marinade
150 ml /5 fl oz olive oil
45 ml /3 tbls lemon juice
15 ml /1 tbls clear honey
1 garlic clove, crushed
2 bay leaves, crushed

1 Wipe the chops with absorbent paper and trim off any excess fat, leaving a narrow border only. Season the chops generously with freshly ground black pepper and arrange them side by side in a shallow dish just large enough to take them in a single layer.
2 In a small bowl, whisk together the marinade ingredients until thoroughly combined. Pour the marinade over the chops, turn them to coat, and leave to marinate for at least 4 hours, turning them occasionally to ensure they remain coated. If you are marinating them in the refrigerator, remove them well before cooking to allow them to come to room temperature.
3 Heat the grill without the grid to high.
4 Brush the grill grid with olive oil. Remove the chops from the marinade and place them on the grid. Grill 7.5 cm /3 in from the heat until they are cooked to your taste (see chart), turning them once. Brush the chops from time to time with the marinade.
5 Arrange the chops on a heated serving platter, season with salt and freshly ground black pepper and serve immediately.

Garlic lamb kebabs

Marinate cubes of lamb shoulder in a garlicky mixture of olive oil and white wine for tenderness and flavour, grill them on skewers with tomatoes and mushrooms, and serve with rice pilaff and green salad.

🔪 marinating the lamb 4 hours,
then 20–25 minutes

Serves 6
700 g /1½ lb boned shoulder of lamb
6 small tomatoes
18 mushroom caps
salt
olive oil
freshly ground black pepper
For the garlic wine marinade
120 ml /8 tbls white wine
120 ml /8 tbls olive oil
2–3 garlic cloves, finely chopped
2 small bay leaves, crumbled
freshly ground black pepper

1 Combine the marinade ingredients in a large bowl. Cut the meat into 24×25 mm / 1 in cubes. Add meat to the marinade and leave to marinate for at least 4 hours – overnight is best. If marinating for a longer period, refrigerate, then bring the meat back to room temperature before cooking.
2 Heat the grill without the grid to high.
3 Discarding the ends, cut each tomato into 3 even slices. Thread each of 6 skewers with a lamb cube, a tomato slice and a mushroom cap. Repeat twice more and finish with a piece of lamb. Season generously with salt.
4 Brush the grill grid with olive oil. Place the kebabs on the grid and grill, 7.5 cm /3 in from the heat, for 4–6 minutes according to your taste, turning the skewers and basting them from time to time with the marinating juices. Serve immediately.

Mixed grill

bringing to room temperature,
then 45 minutes

Serves 4

4 best end cutlets, 25 mm /1 in thick,
  weighing about 75 g /3 oz each
salt and freshly ground black pepper
4 slices back bacon
4 lambs' kidneys
4 chipolata sausages
olive oil
4 small, firm tomatoes, halved
melted butter

1 Trim the fat from the cutlets and scrape
the ends of the bones clean. Season with
ground black pepper and allow to come to
room temperature. The bacon, kidneys and
sausages should be at room temperature.
2 Heat the grill without the grid to high.
3 Remove the outer skins of the kidneys,
snip out the white cores with scissors and cut
in half. Remove the rind from the bacon.
Prick the sausages all over with a fork.
4 Brush the grill grid with olive oil and
place the sausages on it. Grill, 7.5 cm /3 in
from the heat, for 5 minutes.
5 Season the cutlets with salt and pepper.
Turn the sausages and place the cutlets on
the grid. Grill for 4 minutes.

6 Turn the sausages and cutlets and brush
with oil. Place the kidneys, cut side up, and
the tomatoes on the grid. Brush them with
melted butter and season with salt and
freshly ground black pepper. Place the
bacon on the grid. Cook for 2 minutes, then
turn the kidneys and bacon with a fish slice.
Brush the kidneys with butter and cook for a
further 1–2 minutes. The kidneys should be
cooked but still pink in the middle.
7 Arrange the mixed grill on a warmed
serving platter and serve immediately.

Redcurrant-glazed loin chops

20 minutes, bringing to room
temperature, then 45 minutes

Serves 4

4 loin lamb chops, 25 mm /1 in thick
salt and freshly ground black pepper
100 g /4 oz made-weight shortcrust pastry,
  defrosted if frozen
olive oil
60 ml /4 tbls redcurrant jelly
30 ml /2 tbls mint jelly
sprigs of mint, to garnish
finely snipped fresh chives, to garnish

Mixed grill

1 Trim the chops of excess fat, season
them with freshly ground black pepper and
allow them to come to room temperature.
2 Meanwhile, make the jelly tartlets: roll
the pastry out thinly and cut out 4 × 5 cm /2
in circles with a serrated round pastry
cutter. Press each circle into a 4 cm /1½ in
tartlet tin and leave to relax for 1 hour in
the refrigerator.
3 Heat the oven to 200C /400F /gas 6.
Prick the tartlet shells with a fork and bake
for 10 minutes, then lower the heat to 180C
/350F /gas 4 and bake for a further 3–5
minutes, checking often to make sure they
do not burn.
4 While the tartlet shells are baking, heat
the grill without the grid to high and brush
the grid with oil. Season the chops with salt
and more pepper and brush with oil. Place
them on the grid and grill, 7.5 cm /3 in from
the heat, until they are cooked to your taste
(see chart). Turn them once and brush from
time to time with oil. Meanwhile, gently
heat 30 ml /2 tbls redcurrant jelly.
5 Spoon 15 ml /1 tbls mint jelly into each
of 2 baked tartlet shells and garnish with
mint sprigs. Spoon 15 ml /1 tbls redcurrant
jelly into each of the remaining shells and
garnish with snipped chives.
6 Brush the cooked chops on both sides
with the redcurrant glaze and place on a
heated serving platter with the tartlets.
Garnish with sprigs of mint and serve.

PAN FRYING LAMB

Pan frying is the perfect way to cook tender cuts of lamb. It leaves the meat with a crisp, brown outside and a tender, juicy centre, and is every cook's dream of the quick answer to a gourmet dinner.

For pan frying choose young, tender lamb from small animals. Larger, older lambs are better for slower cooking methods. Ask the butcher to cut the chops thickly. Thin chops are inclined to shrivel in the heat of the frying-pan and may also become hard, however tender the meat was when you started. Choose small cutlets from the best end of neck, slightly larger ones from the loin, or chump chops from the top of the leg, which are the meatiest of lamb chops. Lamb steaks are also cut from the leg – they are boneless and very lean.

Ask the butcher to trim off any sharp corners of bone, so that the chops will lie really flat in the pan and brown evenly. For medallions of lamb, ask him to bone the best end of neck completely, but not to roll it as you will want to trim off all the fat before doing this.

Preparing lamb for frying

If the lamb has been frozen, make sure it is completely thawed before cooking. Meat can be cooked from frozen if you choose a slow method, but for quick cooking it is best if it is completely thawed. Otherwise the meat is inclined to go hard.

When you take the meat out of the refrigerator, wipe it dry with absorbent paper. Trim chops well, but leave a thin layer of fat round the meat to keep it moist. Season the meat well with pepper, then leave it to come to room temperature. Just before cooking, season it with salt.

Noisettes of lamb (noisette is French for nut) are little round steaks, the equivalent of beef tournedos. They are made from the best end of neck of lamb. Ask the butcher to remove all the bones, then, when you are ready to prepare them, pull off all the skin and roll up the meat with the lean eye inside and the natural border of fat round the outside. Trim this to fit neatly, so that it just surrounds the noisette. Tie the roll securely along its length with pieces of string. Then cut the roll between the strings into round steaks about 4 cm /1½ in thick.

Medallions: a new, and to my mind much fresher and more interesting, idea is to make these little round steaks without their collar of fat. The noisette has a collar of fat to moisturize the lean meat as it cooks. But without the fat the meat is cooked more briefly, in the *nouvelle cuisine* manner.

To make medallions strip all skin and fat from the boned best end of neck with a very sharp knife. Roll the meat up firmly with the eye inside and tie it securely with fine string in several places. You can either cut the roll into medallions at this stage or sear the roll as it is before cutting. Heat a little butter and olive oil in a heavy frying-pan and sear the outside of the roll, turning it in the hot fat until well browned, about 4–6 minutes. Remove from the pan and cut between the

strings into 25 mm /1 in slices. You will need 2–3 medallions per person, depending on the dish, so allow 2–3 chops per person.

Pan frying lamb

Butter gives the best flavour for pan frying lamb, but add a little olive oil with the butter to prevent the butter burning. Alternatively, if you prefer to use less fat, use a little lamb fat. After you have trimmed the fat from the chops, spike this on a long fork, and wipe round the hot pan.

When the butter is melted and sizzling, or if you are using lamb fat, when the pan is thoroughly hot but not smoking, put the meat in the pan. Make sure the surface of the meat is flat against the pan and cook over high heat for 2 minutes on each side. Turn the meat with tongs or two wooden spoons, being careful not to puncture the meat as this will toughen it.

When the meat is well seared and brown, lower the heat to moderate and continue to cook until done to your taste, turning the meat once more. Use the chart as a guide to cooking times. If the lamb was marinated before cooking, blot it well with absorbent paper before frying and allow about 1 minute longer cooking on each side.

How people like their lamb cooked may well depend on their nationality. The French, for instance, are inclined to like it *rosé*, or still pale pink in the centre. The British normally prefer it well cooked right through.

Just before the meat is ready, unless the recipe tells you otherwise, add a small knob of extra butter to the pan. Let it melt and then turn the lamb over in it briefly. This will give it an attractive glaze.

Remove the cooked meat from the pan and keep it warm on a heated serving dish. To make a little sauce for the lamb, pour off any excess fat from the pan and deglaze the pan by adding 15–30 ml /1–2 tbls stock, water, wine or lemon juice to the fat and juices remaining. Stir well and heat until bubbling, then pour over the meat.

Medallions of lamb with almonds and Pan-fried herbed lamb chops

Making medallions of lamb

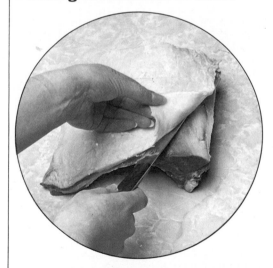 

Bone a best end of neck of lamb and strip off all the skin and fat using a sharp knife. Roll the meat up firmly with the eye inside.

Tie securely with fine string in several places. Cut between the strings to make 25 mm /1 in slices.

Cooking perfect lamb chops

*Marinated chops will take about 1 minute longer on each side.

Cut	Weight	Thickness	Cooking time each side*	Result
Chump chop	about 175 g /6 oz	25 mm /1 in	3–3½ minutes	rosé
			4 minutes	well-done
Loin chop	about 150 g /5 oz	25 mm /1 in	3 minutes	rosé
			4 minutes	well-done
Best end of neck cutlet	about 75 g /3 oz	25 mm /1 in	3 minutes	rosé
			4 minutes	well-done

*Including initial 2 minutes at high heat on each side.

Medallions of lamb with almonds

 bringing lamb to room temperature, then 25 minutes

Serves 4

1½ best ends of neck of lamb (8 chops), boned but not divided into chops
freshly ground black pepper
50 g /2 oz butter
45 ml /3 tbls olive oil
salt
60 ml /4 tbls slivered blanched almonds
90–120 ml /6–8 tbls Madeira
30 ml /2 tbls finely chopped parsley
fresh herbs, to garnish

1 Trim all the fat off the lamb with a sharp knife and season with freshly ground black pepper. Roll up each piece of meat firmly, with the thick side inside, and tie the rolls at intervals with fine string. Leave to come to room temperature.
2 Heat 25 g /1 oz butter and 30 ml /2 tbls olive oil in a heavy frying-pan and fry the rolls until well browned on all sides, about 4–6 minutes. Remove the rolls from the pan and cut between the strings into 8 medallions, approximately 25 mm /1 in thick. Season the medallions with salt and freshly ground black pepper.
3 Heat the remaining butter and olive oil in the same pan and fry the lamb medallions until lightly browned on both sides and cooked to your liking, 2–3 minutes on each side. Transfer to a heated serving dish, remove the strings and keep hot.
4 Pour off half the fat from the pan, add the slivered almonds and fry over a medium-high heat until golden brown, taking care not to burn them. Add the Madeira and stir rapidly over a medium heat, scraping with a wooden spoon, until sizzling.
5 Pour the almonds and sauce over the medallions, sprinkle with chopped parsley and serve, garnished with fresh herbs.

Lamb steaks with bearnaise sauce

🍴 1 hour

Serves 4

4 lamb leg steaks, about 175 g /6 oz each
salt and freshly ground black pepper
50 g /2 oz butter
30 ml /2 tbls olive oil
1 bunch of watercress
tomato waterlilies
tarragon leaves (optional)

For the bearnaise sauce

4–6 sprigs of fresh tarragon, coarsely chopped
4–6 sprigs of fresh chervil, coarsely chopped
15 ml /1 tbls chopped shallot
2 black peppercorns, crushed
30 ml /2 tbls tarragon vinegar
150 ml /5 fl oz dry white wine
3 large egg yolks
225 g /8 oz unsalted butter, diced into 10 mm /½ in cubes
salt
lemon juice
cayenne pepper

Lamb steaks with bearnaise sauce

1 Make the bearnaise sauce: place half of the coarsely chopped tarragon and chervil in a saucepan with the chopped shallot, crushed black peppercorns, tarragon vinegar and white wine. Bring to the boil and cook over high heat until the liquid has reduced to 30 ml /2 tbls. Remove the pan from the heat and set on one side.
2 Beat the egg yolks with 15 ml /1 tbls cold water, then place in the top pan of a double boiler, or a bowl set over a saucepan. Strain in the reduced liquid. Using a wire whisk, stir briskly and constantly over hot but not simmering water until the mixture is light and fluffy.
3 Whisk in the first piece of butter. When it has melted and been incorporated, add the second piece. Wait until each piece of butter has been completely incorporated before adding the next piece.
4 When the mixture begins to thicken, start adding a few pieces of butter at a time. Whisk thoroughly all the time, stirring from the bottom of the pan until the sauce is thick and smooth and all the butter pieces have been incorporated.
5 Remove the pan or bowl of sauce from the hot water. Season to taste with salt, lemon juice and cayenne pepper. Strain the sauce through a fine sieve to give it a good gloss and stir in the remaining chopped tarragon and chervil.
6 Keep the sauce warm, covered, in the top pan of a double boiler over warm water.
7 Trim the fat around the outside of the lamb steaks if necessary and then beat the steaks individually between cling film with a rolling pin or meat bat to double their size. Season both sides with salt and pepper.
8 Heat the butter and olive oil in a large frying-pan and sauté 2 of the lamb steaks at a time for 1 minute on each side for pink meat, 2–3 minutes for well-done. Transfer them to a heated platter and keep warm. Repeat with the remaining 2 steaks.
9 To serve, overlap the lamb steaks slightly down the centre of a serving platter and garnish with bearnaise sauce and bouquets of watercress on each steak. Decorate the plate with tomato waterlilies and more watercress or tarragon leaves. Serve immediately, accompanied by the rest of the bearnaise sauce.

● To make tomato waterlilies, cut around the middle of each tomato in a zig-zag pattern with a small, sharp knife.

Pan-fried herbed lamb chops

🔪 bringing chops to room temperature, then 10 minutes

Serves 4

8 thick loin lamb chops
salt and freshly ground black pepper
40 g /1½ oz butter
30 ml /2 tbls olive oil
15 ml /1 tbls dried oregano or marjoram
juice of 1 lemon
30 ml /2 tbls finely chopped parsley
fresh herbs, to garnish

1 Trim the chops but leave a small border of fat around the meat. Season them with salt and freshly ground black pepper.
2 Heat 25 g /1 oz butter and the olive oil in a large, heavy frying-pan over high heat and fry the chops for 2 minutes on each side. Sprinkle the chops with the dried oregano or marjoram. Reduce the heat to medium and cook for 1–2 minutes on each side.
3 About a minute before the chops are ready, add another 15 g /½ oz butter to the pan. When it has melted, turn the chops over in it briefly to give them a good glaze. Transfer them to a warmed dish. Keep hot while making the sauce.
4 Add the lemon juice and parsley to the juices in the frying-pan. Cook, scraping the pan, until the sauce is sizzling. Pour it over the cooked chops, garnish with fresh herbs and serve immediately.

Lamb cutlets italienne

🕙 2–4 hours marinating, then 15 minutes plus boiling potatoes

Serves 4
8 lamb cutlets, trimmed
60 ml /4 tbls olive oil
salt and freshly ground black pepper
2 garlic cloves, crushed
2.5 ml /½ tsp dried oregano
30 ml /2 tbls freshly chopped parsley
juice of 1 large lemon
30 ml /2 tbls capers, chopped
lemon wedges, to garnish
parsley sprigs, to garnish

For the sautéed potatoes
4 medium-sized potatoes, boiled until just tender, thinly sliced
40 g /1½ oz butter
15 ml /1 tbls olive oil
salt and freshly ground black pepper

1 Season the olive oil with freshly ground black pepper, add the garlic and spoon over the cutlets in a shallow dish. Cover and leave to marinate in a cool place for 2–4 hours, turning once.
2 Strain the marinade into a large frying-pan, add the herbs and place over a moderate heat. When hot, fry the cutlets quickly until lightly browned on each side, then lower the heat, cover the pan and cook gently for 12 minutes, turning the cutlets once during this time.
3 Meanwhile, sauté the potatoes: heat the butter and oil in a large frying-pan and add the sliced potatoes. Cook, turning often, until golden brown and crisp on all sides. Drain on absorbent paper, season and keep warm while you finish the cutlets.
4 Sprinkle the lemon juice and capers over the cutlets, season lightly with salt and pepper and heat through for 1–2 minutes.
5 Arrange the cutlets and potatoes on a hot serving dish and spoon the pan juices over them. Garnish with lemon wedges and parsley sprigs and serve at once.

Italian breaded lamb chops

🕙 25 minutes

Lamb cutlets italienne

Serves 4
8 baby lamb chops or 4 large cutlets, trimmed
salt and freshly ground black pepper
25 g /1 oz flour
25 g /1 oz day-old breadcrumbs
25 g /1 oz freshly grated Parmesan cheese
1 medium-sized egg
50 g /2 oz butter
30 ml /2 tbls olive oil
For the garnish
1 lemon, cut in wedges
finely chopped parsley
8 paper cutlet frills

1 Season the chops or cutlets to taste with salt and freshly ground black pepper, then dust with flour, shaking off any excess flour.
2 Mix together the breadcrumbs and freshly grated Parmesan cheese on a plate; lightly beat the egg on a second plate. Dip each chop in egg and then in the crumb and cheese mixture until thoroughly coated.
3 Heat the butter and olive oil in a large frying-pan until very hot. Add the chops or cutlets and cook over high heat for 2 minutes each side, then lower the heat to moderate and cook until the coating is golden and the chops are done to your liking, carefully turning once more. Drain on absorbent paper.
4 Decorate the exposed bones with cutlet frills, and serve at once, garnished with lemon wedges and finely chopped parsley.

● Alternatively, the chops or cutlets can be deep fried for 3–5 minutes in oil heated to 180C /350F.

CASSEROLING & POT-ROASTING LAMB

Lamb is a good choice for casseroles – the flavour blends well with a variety of herbs and spices, giving a wide repertoire of dishes from a basic theme, and the meat becomes meltingly tender.

Casseroling and stewing are flavoursome ways of cooking pieces of lamb or other meat gently in a little liquid, with added vegetables and herbs. Casseroling and stewing are virtually identical and the words have become interchangeable, but strictly a casserole is cooked in a slow oven and a stew on top of the cooker.

Types of meat
Almost any cut of lamb can be used for casseroles. Many lamb recipes, such as Lancashire hot pot or Dublin stew, are traditionally made with really bony cuts such as middle neck, scrag and breast of lamb. The flavour of these is excellent and a really tasty meal comes out of the pot. But for entertaining I prefer cuts with less bone in them and I usually go for shoulder meat, which the butcher will bone for you if you ask in advance, or for neck cutlets. Leg or loin make equally good casseroles, but these cuts are more expensive.

Making the casserole
In most cases when you are making a casserole, once the initial preparation has been done the dish can be left to cook unattended. There are two main methods of starting off the casserole – the cold start method and the fry start method. The cold start method is best for tough cuts such as neck and scrag chops. Bring the lamb slowly to simmering point and cook very gently, covered, for about 2 hours on the top of the cooker or in the oven at 150C /300F /gas 2.

The fry start method is used for cubes of shoulder meat or neck chops. The surfaces of the meat are sealed and browned by frying in hot fat. The meat can be tossed in seasoned flour and then browned in fat or it can be browned on its own. Then the meat is transferred to a tightly covered pan with flavouring vegetables, herbs, spices and liquid and cooked very gently at 150C /300F /gas 2 until meltingly tender.

Pot-roasting and braising
Pot-roasting and braising are such similar methods that there is little to distinguish between them. Pot-roasting is carried out in a covered pan – a flameproof casserole is ideal – either on top of the stove or in the oven at 170C /325F /gas 3, for a minimum of 1½ hours, allowing 80 minutes per kg /40 minutes per lb for lamb joints. Traditionally there should be very little or no liquid in a pot-roast, the moisture from the meat providing most of the liquid for cooking.

A braise is cooked in much the same way but there is usually a little more liquid added to form the cooking liquid and sauce. Braising is suitable for chunks of meat, leg, shoulder, chump chops or whole joints. Leg of lamb is particularly good boned and stuffed before braising.

Browning the meat
For both pot-roasting and braising the meat is first browned on top of the cooker. Use either olive oil or butter, or good dripping, preferably from the same type of meat as the one being cooked. If the joint is a fatty one trim off some of the fat and render it down in a frying-pan. Discard any crisp remains of skin and use the liquid to brown the meat.

If flavouring vegetables are to be added to the pot-roast or braise they can be browned in the same fat, or they can be added raw. If being browned, remove the meat from the pan while you brown the vegetables to avoid overcrowding. Traditionally the vegetables for a braise are made into a mirepoix – all evenly diced to the same size and browned well in the dripping. The vegetables then form a bed on which the meat rests while it is cooking. Other flavourings such as diced fat salt pork, bacon and herbs can be included.

Adding the liquid
When both the meat and the vegetables have been browned, return the meat to the pan and add the liquid. Choose a good stock and add a little wine for extra flavour if wished.

Whichever liquid you choose, always bring it to the boil before adding it to the meat in the casserole dish. If you add the liquid to the pot cold and bring it to the boil with the meat, it will then extract flavour and moisture from the meat.

Controlling the cooking
Whether you cook on top of the cooker or in the oven, cover the casserole tightly and control the heat to keep it just at a gentle simmer. If the liquid is allowed to boil the meat will harden and the liquid is likely to boil away before cooking is complete.

Lamb with limes

45 minutes, 1 hour cooking, then 10 minutes

Serves 4
900 g–1.2 kg /2–2½ lb boned shoulder of
lamb, in 25 mm /1 in cubes
salt and freshly ground black pepper
25 g /1 oz butter
30 ml /2 tbls olive oil
1 Spanish onion, finely chopped
1 garlic clove, finely chopped
300 ml /10 fl oz chicken stock
grated zest and juice of 2 limes
150 ml /5 fl oz thick cream
1 large egg yolk
peeled segments of 1 lime, to garnish

1 Heat the oven to 150C /300F /gas 2. Season the lamb with salt and pepper.
2 In a flameproof casserole, heat the butter and olive oil. When the foaming subsides, add enough lamb to cover the base of the casserole and sauté until golden brown on all sides; remove with a slotted spoon. Sauté the remaining lamb and remove.
3 To the fat remaining in the pan add the finely chopped onion and garlic and sauté for 2–3 minutes until transparent.
4 Add the stock, bring to the boil and stir to remove the sediment from the base of the pan. Return the sautéed lamb to the casserole and add the grated zest and juice of 2 limes. Season with salt and freshly ground black pepper to taste, cover and cook in the oven for 1 hour or until tender.
5 In a small bowl, beat the thick cream and egg yolk together. Remove the casserole from the oven and add a little of the sauce to the cream and egg yolk mixture, mix thoroughly, then slowly add the liaison to the casserole. Continue to cook, stirring, over a low heat until the mixture has thickened. Do not allow to boil. Correct the seasoning and garnish with lime segments. Serve the casserole immediately.

Lamb korma

This casserole in the Indian tradition is marinated in a spicy yoghurt mixture.

30 minutes, 1 hour marinating, then 1¾ hours

Serves 6–8

1.4 kg /3 lb boned shoulder of lamb
300 ml /10 fl oz yoghurt
2.5 ml /½ tsp ground cardamom
5 ml /1 tsp ground cumin
7.5 ml /1½ tsp ground turmeric
125 g /4 oz desiccated coconut
25 g /1 oz butter
300 ml /10 fl oz milk
60–90 ml /4–6 tbls olive oil
1 Spanish onion, finely chopped
2 garlic cloves, crushed
5 ml /1 tsp ground ginger
5 ml /1 tsp dry mustard
1.5 ml /¼ tsp cayenne pepper
1.5 ml /¼ tsp ground cinnamon
1.5 ml /¼ tsp ground cloves
2 medium-sized tomatoes, blanched, peeled, seeded and diced
salt and freshly ground black pepper
10 ml /2 tsp lemon juice

1 Cut the shoulder of lamb into 25 mm /1 in cubes, trimming off any excess fat and gristle on the joint.
2 In a large bowl, mix the yoghurt with the ground cardamom, cumin and turmeric. Add the pieces of lamb and toss until each cube is thoroughly coated in the yoghurt and spice mixture. Cover the bowl and leave the meat to marinate for 1 hour in a cool place.
3 Meanwhile, place the desiccated coconut, butter and milk in a heavy-based saucepan and bring to the boil over a moderate heat, stirring until the butter has melted. Simmer for 15 minutes. Strain through a fine sieve, pressing the coconut against the sides of the sieve with a spoon to extract all its flavour. Put the desiccated coconut and the strained coconut milk aside in separate bowls.
4 In a flameproof casserole heat half the oil. When hot add the pieces of lamb, together with the yoghurt and spice marinade, and cook over a high heat, stirring, for about 5 minutes. Remove the pan from the heat.
5 Heat the remaining oil in a frying-pan and sauté the finely chopped onions and garlic for 10–12 minutes until soft and golden. Remove the pan from the heat; add the remaining spices and mix well. Return

the pan to the heat and cook, stirring, for 2 minutes longer to blend and bring out the flavours.
6 Add the spiced onion mixture to the lamb, together with the diced tomato flesh, the strained coconut milk and a little salt to taste. Bring the mixture to the boil over a low heat, stirring occasionally; then cover the casserole and simmer very gently for about 30 minutes.
7 Uncover the casserole and then continue cooking over low heat for another 30 minutes or until the lamb is very tender and the sauce is rich and thick, stirring very occasionally to prevent the lamb sticking to the bottom of the pan.
8 Just before serving, stir in the lemon juice and season with a little more salt and freshly ground black pepper if necessary. If the sauce seems too thin add some of the reserved coconut and simmer for 2–3 minutes longer.

● Serve the Lamb korma with the usual curry accompaniments: a selection of chutneys, poppadoms, preserved kumquats, thinly sliced raw onion rings and boiled rice.

Lamb with limes and
Lamb korma

Spiced best end of neck of lamb

 2 hours

Serves 6
1 neck of lamb joint, consisting of 2 best ends still joined, about 1.4 kg /3 lb, with 6 cutlets each side, trimmed and chined
1 small piece fresh root ginger, cut in narrow strips
1.5 ml /¼ tsp dried thyme
salt and freshly ground black pepper
40 g /1½ oz butter
30 ml /2 tbls olive oil
2 medium-sized onions, quartered
2 garlic cloves, finely chopped
850 ml /1½ pt beef stock
a pinch of saffron strands, soaked in 15 ml / 1 tbls boiling water
2.5 ml /½ tsp ground cinnamon
10 ml /2 tsp paprika
1.5 ml /¼ tsp cayenne pepper
5 ml /1 tsp ground ginger
2 small lemons, quartered
watercress, to garnish

1   With a sharp knife, cut deep slits in the lamb and insert the strips of ginger. Rub with thyme and season with salt and pepper.
2   Heat the butter with the olive oil in a flameproof casserole large enough to take the double joint of lamb. When the foaming subsides, brown the lamb, fat side down first, for 4 minutes on each side. Remove the meat from the casserole and keep hot.
3   Add the quartered onions and finely chopped garlic and cook over low heat for 7–10 minutes, or until the onion is soft.
4   Add the beef stock, saffron with the soaking water, cinnamon, paprika, cayenne pepper, ground ginger and lemons. Season to taste with salt and freshly ground black pepper. Bring to the boil. Return the lamb, fat side down, to the casserole. Cover and simmer for 45 minutes or until the lamb is tender, basting frequently.
5   Turn the joint over and cook for a further 10 minutes, to ensure that the neck of lamb is cooked evenly. Transfer the lamb to a serving platter, arranging it like an arch, and keep hot.
6   Remove the lemons from the casserole with a slotted spoon and discard. Place casserole over high heat and boil until the liquid is reduced to half the original quantity (about 425 ml /15 fl oz). Pour the sauce into a sauce-boat. Garnish the lamb with watercress, tucking it under the arch at each end. Serve immediately. To carve, cut down between the cutlets.

Irish stew

This world-famous lamb dish is often made very badly. It should be thick and creamy, not swimming in juice, with a pure lamb flavour.

2¾ hours

French spring lamb

This is a colourful and fresh-tasting casserole of spring lamb combined with a selection of tender vegetables. Its French name is *Navarin printanier*.

2½ hours

Serves 4
700 g /1½ lb boneless lean shoulder of lamb, cut in 25 mm /1 in cubes
25 g /1 oz butter
15 ml /1 tbls oil
10 ml /2 tsp sugar
15 ml /1 tbls flour
salt and freshly ground black pepper
450 ml /15 fl oz hot chicken stock, home-made or from a cube
15 ml /1 tbls tomato purée
1 clove garlic, crushed
bouquet garni of bay leaf, sprig each of thyme and parsley, tied together
8 button onions, peeled
8 baby carrots, scraped
12 tiny new potatoes, scraped
150 g /5 oz shelled peas or young broad beans

French spring lamb

1   Heat the butter and oil in a flameproof casserole (with a lid) large enough to hold all the ingredients.
2   When hot, fry the meat briskly, in 2 batches, stirring frequently, until lightly browned. Strain off excess fat and return all the meat to the pan. Sprinkle in the sugar and stir until lightly caramelized.
3   Heat the oven to 150C /300F /gas 2.
4   Add the flour and generous seasonings of salt and pepper to the meat, lower the heat and stir for a minute or two until the flour is lightly coloured. Add the stock, tomato purée, garlic and bouquet of herbs and stir until simmering.
5   Cover the casserole tightly; transfer to the centre of the oven. Cook for 1 hour.
6   Skim excess fat from the surface of the casserole, then add the onions, carrots and potatoes, pushing them under the surface of the sauce. Cover and cook for a further 40 minutes.
7   Stir in the peas or broad beans, cover and cook for another 15 minutes or until all the ingredients are tender.
8   Skim off any surface fat, discard the bouquet of herbs and check the seasoning. Serve from the casserole.

Serves 4–6

1.5 kg /3 lb 5 oz best end of neck
salt and freshly ground black pepper
1 kg /2 lb potatoes, sliced fairly thinly
25 g /1 oz freshly chopped parsley
5 ml /1 tsp fresh thyme, chopped, or 2.5 ml /
½ tsp dried thyme
450 g /1 lb onions, sliced fairly thinly
butter for greasing

1 Bone the lamb and put the meat and the bones in a large saucepan, cover with water and season with salt and freshly ground pepper. Place the pan over medium heat and boil gently for 30 minutes.
2 Drain off the liquid and reserve, allowing it to cool so any fat can be skimmed off the top. While the stock is cooling, cut the meat into fairly large pieces.
3 Heat the oven to 130C /250F /gas ½. Put a thickish layer of potatoes in a casserole, sprinkle with parsley and thyme, add a layer of meat, then onions, seasoning each layer well with salt and freshly ground pepper. Repeat until all the ingredients are used, ending with a layer of potatoes.
4 Pour over the reserved liquid, cover the casserole with greased foil and a lid and place in the oven for 1½ hours or until the potatoes are tender, adding a very little more liquid if the ingredients seem to be drying up. Serve immediately.

Pot-roasted lamb provençal

🔪 1¾ hours

Serves 6

1.4–1.8 kg /3–4 lb shoulder of young lamb
2 garlic cloves
salt and freshly ground black pepper
60 ml /4 tbls olive oil
2 Spanish onions, finely chopped
1 carrot, chopped
300 ml /10 fl oz beef stock, home-made or
from a cube
3 large, ripe tomatoes, blanched, skinned,
seeded and finely chopped
30 ml /2 tbls tomato purée
2.5 ml /½ tsp dried crushed thyme
75–125 g /3–4 oz black olives, stoned
flat-leaved parsley, to garnish

1 Peel the garlic cloves and cut them into thin slivers. With the point of a sharp knife make slits all over the shoulder of lamb and push in the garlic slivers as deeply as possible. Season the joint generously.
2 Heat the olive oil in a large, flameproof casserole and brown the shoulder of lamb on all sides. Remove the joint. To the remaining fat, add the chopped onions and carrot and sauté until golden.
3 Add the stock, chopped tomatoes and tomato purée, and season the vegetables to taste with salt and pepper. Bring to the boil. Return the shoulder of lamb to the casserole and sprinkle with thyme.
4 Cover the casserole and simmer gently until the lamb is tender, about 1 hour for medium rare.

5 About 10 minutes before the end of cooking time, add the stoned olives.
6 When the lamb is tender, transfer it to a heated serving dish. Skim the fat from the sauce and spoon the vegetables and sauce around the lamb. Garnish, then serve hot.

Lamb casserole with caramelized onions

🔪🔪 3½ hours

Serves 4

900 g /2 lb boned shoulder of lamb
15 ml /1 tbls olive oil
40 g /1½ oz butter
1 Spanish onion, thinly sliced
550 g /1¼ lb very starchy potatoes, sliced
salt and ground black pepper
bouquet garni
2 leeks, washed and sliced
about 2.3 L /4 pt boiling water
8 small potatoes, trimmed into regular, oval
shapes
16 white button onions, blanched
30 ml /2 tbls caster sugar
30 ml /2 tbls finely chopped parsley
Worcestershire sauce, to serve

1 Cut the lamb into squares weighing about 50 g /2 oz each, discarding any fat or gristle. In a large flameproof casserole, heat the olive oil and 15 g /½ oz butter. Add enough meat to cover the base and sauté until evenly browned all over, then remove with a slotted spoon and reserve. Repeat with the remaining lamb.
2 In the casserole, arrange alternate layers of lamb, sliced onion and sliced potatoes, seasoning to taste with salt and freshly ground black pepper between each layer. Add the bouquet garni, the sliced leek and sufficient boiling water to cover. Bring to the boil, cover and simmer for 30 minutes.
3 With a slotted spoon, remove the meat and reserve. Allow to cool a little, then purée the vegetables and cooking juices in a blender, in batches if necessary.
4 Return to the casserole and boil rapidly for about 45 minutes, or until reduced to 1.4 L /2½ pt of liquid.
5 Add the trimmed potatoes and simmer for a further 20–30 minutes, or until potatoes are cooked but not too soft.
6 While the potatoes are cooking, heat the remaining butter in a medium-sized saucepan. Add the onions, sugar and 150 ml /5 fl oz water, then simmer for 15 minutes, or until the onions are caramelized and tender, turning frequently with a wooden spoon.
7 When the potatoes are cooked, return the meat to the casserole and add the caramelized onions and their juices. Reheat very gently over a low heat until the meat is hot (reheating over a high heat tends to toughen it).
8 Transfer to a heated deep serving dish. Sprinkle with chopped parsley and serve with Worcestershire sauce.

Pot-roasted lamb provençal

Lamb in a blanket

Tender chunks of lamb are covered with a 'blanket' of delicately flavoured sauce.

20 minutes, 12 hours soaking, then 2¼ hours

Serves 6

1.2 kg /2¾ lb boned lamb shoulder or breast
juice of 1½ lemons
about 1L /2 pt veal or chicken stock, home-made or from a cube
salt and freshly ground black pepper
1 Spanish onion, stuck with 1 clove
2 carrots
1 leek
bouquet garni
12 button onions
12 tight white button mushrooms
about 50 g /2 oz butter
30 ml /2 tbls flour
2 medium-sized egg yolks
125 ml /4 fl oz thick cream
pinch of freshly grated nutmeg
fresh parsley, finely chopped

1   Cut the lamb into 25 mm /1 in cubes and put them in a bowl. Cover with water acidulated with the juice of ½ lemon and leave in the refrigerator to soak for 12 hours or overnight, changing the water 2 or 3 times. This soaking makes the meat white and delicate.
2   Drain the meat and place it in a deep, flameproof casserole with enough stock to cover, 5 ml /1 tsp salt and pepper to taste. Bring to the boil, skimming off the scum.
3   Add the onion, carrots, leek and bouquet garni, cover and simmer very gently for 1½ hours, until tender. Alternatively, put it into an oven at 150C /300F /gas 2.
4   Ten minutes before the lamb is done, simmer the button onions in a little water until just firm, drain and keep warm. Cook the button mushrooms in a little butter until tender, adding a sprinkling of lemon juice to preserve their colour. Keep warm.
5   When the lamb is tender, melt 25 g /1 oz butter in a heavy saucepan. Stir in the flour off the heat, then simmer for a minute or two, stirring constantly, to make a pale *roux*. Gradually add 600 ml /1 pt stock ladled from the lamb and bring to the boil,

Hearty hotpot

stirring. Lower the heat and simmer for 15 minutes, stirring occasionally.
6   Beat the egg yolks with cream and the juice of ½ lemon. Remove the sauce from the heat and add the egg and cream mixture. Stir over a low heat until the sauce thickens.
7   Drain the lamb, discarding any pieces of bone or fat. Rinse and dry the casserole and return the meat to it.
8   Strain the white sauce through a fine sieve onto the meat. Carefully fold in the onions and button mushrooms and correct the seasoning, adding a pinch of freshly grated nutmeg and more salt or pepper if necessary. Garnish with the finely chopped parsley and serve at once.

Hearty hotpot

This is a simple and economical dish of middle neck of lamb and lambs' kidneys.

30 minutes, then 2 hours cooking

Serves 4

1 kg /2¼ lb middle neck of lamb, chopped
  into large pieces
30 ml /2 tbls flour
salt and freshly ground black pepper
25 g /1 oz dripping or lard
3–4 lambs' kidneys, thickly sliced
100 g /4 oz mushrooms, quartered if large
1 large onion, thinly sliced
450 ml /15 fl oz beef stock, home-made or
  from a cube
750 g /1½ lb potatoes, thinly sliced

1   Heat the oven to 170C /325F /gas 3.
Season the flour with salt and pepper, then
coat meat in the flour. Reserve left-over
flour.
2   Heat the fat in a large saucepan and fry
the meat, in batches, until browned.
Transfer to a hotpot and scatter over the
kidneys and mushrooms.
3   Fry the sliced onion gently in the fat left
in the saucepan for a few minutes, then
transfer to the hotpot. Add the remaining
flour to the pan and stir until browned. Stir
in the stock and bring to the boil. Check the
seasoning and simmer for a few minutes,
until slightly thickened.
4   Cover the meat with overlapping potato
slices. Pour the sauce over the potatoes,
cover the hotpot and cook in the oven for 1½
hours. Uncover the pot and cook for a
further 30 minutes until the meat is tender
and the potatoes are browned, then serve the
hot pot at once.

Lamb bourguignon

1½ hours, 3½–4 hours cooking,
then 15 minutes

Serves 4–6

1.4 kg /3 lb boned shoulder of lamb
90 ml /6 tbls seasoned flour
45 ml /3 tbls olive oil
65 g /2½ oz butter
salt and freshly ground black pepper
60 ml /4 tbls brandy
2 carrots, coarsely chopped
1 leek, coarsely chopped
4 shallots, coarsely chopped
1 Spanish onion, coarsely chopped
1 garlic clove, coarsely chopped
1 calf's foot, split (optional)
bouquet garni
850 ml /1½ pt hot beef stock
300 ml /10 fl oz red Burgundy, heated
16 button onions
10 ml /2 tsp sugar
15 ml /1 tbls lemon juice
12 button mushrooms
beurre manié, made from 15 ml /1 tbls flour
  and 15 g /½ oz butter
30 ml /2 tbls freshly chopped parsley

1   Heat the oven to 150C /300F /gas 2.
2   Cut lamb into 5cm /2 in squares, removing any fat and gristle. Toss the meat in
seasoned flour, shaking off the excess.
3   In a large flameproof casserole, heat 30
ml /2 tbls olive oil and 25 g /1 oz butter.
Sauté the lamb in batches, just enough to
cover the bottom of the casserole each time,
for about 3 minutes each side, or until well

browned all over. Transfer to a plate with a
slotted spoon. Once all the meat is browned,
return to the casserole and season to taste.
4   Put the brandy into a metal ladle and
warm it gently. Standing well back, ignite it
with a taper and pour it over the lamb.
When the flames die out, transfer the lamb
to a heated plate. Keep warm.
5   Add the chopped vegetables and garlic to
the fat in the casserole and cook, stirring, for
about 4 minutes or until lightly browned.
6   Return lamb to the casserole with the
calf's foot, if wished, bouquet garni and
stock. Reserve 60 ml /4 tbls red Burgundy
and add the rest to the casserole. Cover and
cook for 3½–4 hours.
7   Meanwhile, heat the remaining olive oil
and 15 g /½ oz butter in a saucepan and add
the button onions. Sprinkle with sugar and
cook for 5 minutes, or until well browned all
over, shaking continuously. Add reserved
wine. Cover and cook gently for 15–20
minutes. Remove from the heat; keep warm.
8   In a frying-pan, melt the remaining
butter. Add the lemon juice and sauté the
mushrooms for 8 minutes, or until tender.
9   Remove the calf's foot and bouquet
garni from the casserole. Add the beurre
manié in small pieces, stirring it in carefully
until the sauce thickens.
10   Correct the seasoning, and add the
onions and mushrooms, sprinkle the
casserole with chopped parsley and serve.

Lamb and tomato bredie

Lamb and tomato bredie

1½ hours

Serves 4

900 g /2 lb boned leg of lamb
60 ml /4 tbls vegetable oil
2 large onions, thinly sliced
700 g /1½ lb tomatoes, skinned and sliced
2–3 chillies, seeded and chopped
3 cloves
2 garlic cloves, crushed
4 cm /1½ in piece root ginger, finely chopped
salt and freshly ground black pepper
a pinch of cayenne pepper
5 ml /1 tsp sugar

1   Heat the oil in a large flameproof
casserole over a medium heat, add the
onions and sauté until deep golden brown
but not burned, about 15–20 minutes.
2   Add the tomatoes in a layer over the
onions, sprinkle over the chillies, cloves,
crushed garlic and root ginger. Bring to
boiling point, then put the meat on top of
the tomatoes. Season to taste with salt and
pepper. Add the cayenne pepper and sugar.
3   Put on a tightly fitting lid, turn down the
heat and simmer gently for 50–60 minutes
or until the meat is really tender.
4   Check the seasoning and serve.

LAMB OFFAL

Lamb offal ranges from homely but delicious hearts to elegant, and expensive, sweetbreads. Learn how to make the most of them, and liver, kidneys and brains too.

Offal is often looked on as 'unfashionable' or simply ignored, but many offal dishes can be found among the world's classic recipes.

All offal should be very fresh when you buy it, and is best eaten on the day of purchase, though it can be kept up to 24 hours in the refrigerator, loosely covered (brains, hearts and sweetbreads are best blanched first).

Liver

Lamb's liver is very economical, as there is virtually no waste, and you need only about 100 g /4 oz per portion. Avoid any liver that looks dull, dry or bluish, or has an unpleasant smell.

Preparing: wash in cold water and pat dry. If the liver is in one piece, remove any outer skin, then slice evenly along the length of the lobe. Cut out any large veins.

Cooking: liver contains very little natural fat and will easily become unpalatable if overcooked. The most successful ways of cooking it are lightly grilling or frying.

To grill, cut the liver into even, 10 mm /½ in slices. Heat a little oil in a shallow flameproof dish large enough to hold the liver in a single layer. Turn each slice in the hot fat, then place under a grill heated to moderate for 1–2 minutes. Season lightly, then turn and cover completely with thin slices of bacon. Grill for 2–3 minutes, until the liver is just cooked and the bacon crisp. Serve with the pan juices poured over.

To fry, cut the liver into slices 5–10 mm / ¼–½ in thick and coat with well-seasoned flour. Heat a little fat or oil in a shallow frying-pan. When sizzling, fry the liver over moderate heat for 2–3 minutes, just until beads of blood appear on the surface. Turn and cook another 2–3 minutes, and serve with a sauce made with the pan juices.

Kidneys

Lamb's kidneys weigh 25–50 g /1–2 oz each. Look for plump, firm ones; if they are encased in suet, it should be firm and white.
Preparing: cut through the suet and pull it

away. Then nick the membrane that covers the kidney on the rounded side. Draw the skin back until it is only attached at the core. With scissors, cut a deep V-shape on either side of the core so that you can remove the core and the skin together. Rinse the kidneys under cold water and pat dry.

Spatchcock kidneys are grilled by slicing horizontally from the curved side towards the core without cutting through completely. Then open out and take a 'stitch' through the middle with metal skewers or cocktail sticks to hold them flat.

Cooking: overcooking toughens kidneys, so time carefully. Fresh kidneys are excellent grilled, while frozen kidneys, which tend to be softer, are better fried.

To grill, heat the grill to high. Lay the spatchcocked kidneys, cut side uppermost, in a flameproof dish and smear with softened butter. Grill for 3–4 minutes, depending on size. Season lightly, turn, spread with butter and grill for another 3–4 minutes until pink but not bloody inside. Remove skewers or cocktail sticks, pour the pan juices over and top with a knob of chive or garlic butter.

To fry, halve the kidneys if they are small; slice them if they are large. Fry the kidneys briskly in a mixture of butter and oil, tossing frequently, for 2 minutes. Add crushed garlic and chopped parsley and

Kidneys dijonnaise

chives and simmer 2 minutes, then stir in 30 ml /2 tbls lemon juice or wine and a large knob of butter and cook a further 2 minutes, until the kidneys are tender but still slightly pink inside, and the sauce is syrupy.

Brains

Because of their whiteness, light texture and delicate flavour, brains are considered a luxury by the discerning French.

Buy one set of brains per person. They should be shiny, plump and moist, and greyish pink in colour.

Preparing: as soon as you can, wash in cold water to remove blood clots, then refrigerate in a bowl of cold water for 1–2 hours before cooking. Remove the covering membrane by pulling gently, and remove any white matter. Soak again in fresh cold water until you are ready to use them.

Blanching: unless you are poaching the brains, you must blanch them before cooking. Place in cold water with 15 ml /1 tbls vinegar or lemon juice and 5 ml /1 tbls salt for each 1 L /2 pt water. Add a small onion and a bay leaf for flavour. Bring slowly to the boil, simmer gently for 15 minutes, then put them in a bowl of cold water to firm up.

Cooking: shallow frying is probably the most common way to cook brains. Slices can be floured, if wished, and fried lightly in butter, or coated with egg and breadcrumbs and fried in oil, for 3–4 minutes each side. Alternatively, coat the sliced brains in batter and deep fry in oil heated to 180C /350F.

Brains can also be poached, whole, in a winey court bouillon or other flavourful cooking liquid. The brains are sliced to serve and the cooking liquid reduced to make a sauce to accompany them.

Sweetbreads

Sweetbreads come from the thymus gland and pancreas of the lamb – those from the thymus are the 'true' sweetbreads and are finer. Sweetbreads should be pale, creamy and plump. Allow 100 g /4 oz per person – one or two pairs.

Soak in cold water for at least 1 hour, changing the water several times, until no traces of blood remain. Drain and rinse under the cold tap.

Blanching: just cover with cold water, add 15 ml /1 tbls lemon juice and 5 ml /1 tsp salt and bring slowly to the boil. Simmer gently for 10 minutes, drain and plunge into cold water to firm. Remove the tubes and outer membrane.

Pressing: for a neat shape, place blanched sweetbreads between two plates, cover with a weight and leave in a cool place for several hours, until firmed up.

Cooking: to braise, just cover the blanched sweetbreads with stock, add sliced onion and carrot and a bouquet garni, bring slowly to the boil and simmer for 30–40 minutes. Remove the sweetbreads with a slotted spoon and keep warm while you reduce the stock and make a sauce from it.

Pressed and blanched sweetbreads can also be brushed with melted butter and grilled, or floured or egg-and-breadcrumbed and shallow fried in butter, then served with a sauce.

Stir-fried liver

Heart

Heart should be moist and firm, with a pleasant smell. Allow one heart per person.

Preparing: wash thoroughly in cold running water to remove any blood clots. Trim off all excess fat, then snip out the artery and vein stubs. Soak in cold, salted water for 1–8 hours.

Blanching: place in a saucepan, cover with fresh cold water, bring to the boil and simmer 2 minutes, then drain and rinse. The hearts are now ready for cooking.

Cooking: lamb's heart is good braised, casseroled or pot-roasted, either sliced, or whole and stuffed. Or thread small pieces on skewers with vegetables, marinate and then grill slowly, basting with marinade.

Tongue

Lambs' tongues are not as easy to find as ox tongues. They are smaller, varying in size from 100–275 g /4–10 oz each. They are best soaked overnight in salted water, then simmered slowly, in stock or water flavoured with vegetables or herbs, for 1½–2½ hours.

Kidneys dijonnaise

Tender kidneys in a creamy, mustard-flavoured sauce are quickly prepared.

🔪 45 minutes

Serves 4
550 g /1¼ lb lambs' kidneys
10 ml /2 tsp flour
50 g /2 oz butter
50 g /2 oz shallots or onion, finely chopped
150 ml /5 fl oz dry white wine or dry vermouth and water mixed
15 ml /1 tbls lemon juice
150 ml /5 fl oz thick cream
25 ml /1½ tbls Dijon mustard
salt and freshly ground black pepper
freshly chopped parsley, to garnish
boiled rice, to serve

1   Skin and halve the kidneys lengthways, removing the core. Dust lightly with the flour.

2   Melt the butter in a large, shallow frying-pan. When sizzling put in the kidneys and fry fairly briskly for 2–3 minutes, turning them so that they seal and change colour on each side. Remove the kidneys with a slotted spoon and reserve.

3   Add the shallots or onion and fry very gently, 2 minutes if using the shallots or 5 minutes for the onion.

4   Add the wine and lemon juice and boil rapidly until they are reduced to one quarter of their original quantity.

5   Off the heat stir in the cream and mustard. Return the kidneys and their juices to the pan and season lightly with salt and pepper. Reheat gently without boiling, stirring frequently, for 5 minutes. Serve immediately, sprinkled with the parsley, on a bed of plain boiled rice.

Stir-fried liver

🔪 40 minutes

Serves 4
450 g /1 lb lamb's liver
15 ml /1 tbls cornflour
5 ml /1 tsp salt
5 ml /1 tsp ground ginger
15 ml /1 tbls medium sherry
5 ml /1 tsp oil
50 g /2 oz lard or dripping
1 large garlic clove, crushed
25 ml /1½ tbls coarsely chopped spring onion
    tops
boiled rice, to serve
For the sauce
25 ml /1½ tbls soy sauce
15 ml /1 tbls medium sherry
15 ml /1 tbls tomato purée
25 ml /1½ tbls wine vinegar
25 ml /1½ tbls chicken stock, home-made or
    from a cube
5 ml /1 tsp sugar

1 Trim away skin and veins from the liver. With a sharp knife cut the liver into 3 mm /⅛ in thick slices and then cut these into 25 mm /1 in strips.
2 In a bowl combine the cornflour, salt and ginger. Blend in 30 ml /2 tbls water, the sherry and oil and mix until smooth.
3 Add the liver slices and turn gently to coat with the cornflour mixture. Leave to stand for 15 minutes.
4 In a mixing bowl combine all the sauce ingredients until well blended.
5 Heat the lard or dripping in a frying-pan over moderate heat. When sizzling add the liver, spreading the pieces evenly over the pan. Increase the heat and cook briskly, stirring, for 30 seconds.
6 Sprinkle in the garlic and spring onions and continue stir-frying for another 30 seconds. Pour the sauce mixture into the pan, bring to the boil and cook, stirring constantly, for a further 30 seconds. Serve immediately, with boiled rice.

Orange and lemon hearts

🕐 🍴 soaking, overnight marinating, then 2 hours

Serves 4–8
4 lambs' hearts, trimmed, soaked, blanched
    and thinly sliced
flour for dusting
30 ml /2 tbls olive oil
15 ml /1 tbls brandy
600 ml /1 pt or more beef stock, home-made
    or from a cube
10 ml /2 tsp ground coriander
2 garlic cloves, crushed
grated zest of 1 lemon
grated zest of 1 oramge
24 button onions
4–8 large croûtons
orange and lemon slices, to garnish
sprigs of flat-leaved parsley, to garnish

Orange and lemon hearts

For the marinade
juice of 1 lemon
juice of 1 orange
30 ml /2 tbls olive oil
150 ml /5 fl oz red wine
12 coriander seeds
freshly ground black pepper
For finishing the sauce
125 g /4 oz button mushrooms, very finely
    chopped
40 g /1½ oz butter
7.5 ml /½ tbls flour
15 ml /1 tbls port
salt and freshly ground black pepper

1 Put the sliced hearts in a bowl and cover with the marinade ingredients. Stir, cover the bowl and leave in a cool place overnight.
2 The next day, remove the heart slices, reserving the marinade, and pat them dry with absorbent paper. Roll them in the flour and shake off any excess.
3 Heat the oil in a large, heavy-based frying-pan or flameproof casserole, then brown the hearts over a medium-high heat.
4 Pour the brandy into a ladle, warm it,

ignite it and pour it into the pan, then add the marinade and let it bubble for 2–3 minutes. Add the beef stock, coriander, garlic and grated zests. Cover and simmer gently for 30 minutes.
5 Add the onions. If they are not covered by the cooking liquid, add a little more stock. Cover and simmer for a further 45 minutes, until the hearts can easily be pierced with a fork.
6 Arrange the croûtons on a large, warmed serving platter. Using a slotted spoon, remove the heart slices from the pan and arrange on croûtons. Place the onions around the edge of the dish. Keep warm.
7 To finish the sauce, sauté the mushrooms in 25 g /1 oz of the butter until they are soft and dark brown.
8 Combine the remaining butter and the flour to make a *beurre manié* and reserve.
9 Strain the cooking liquid over the mushrooms, stirring, over a medium-high heat. Add the *beurre manié* and stir constantly for 3–4 minutes, until the sauce is thickened. Stir in the port, then season.
10 Pour the sauce over the hearts, garnish the platter with the orange and lemon slices and parsley and serve at once.

Sweetbread vol-au-vents

Small vol-au-vents make ideal party food or an impressive first course. In France they are called *bouchées à la reine* because Louis XV's wife was fond of them. Larger ones make a main course.

🔪🔪 defrosting pastry, 1 hour soaking and blanching, then 1¾ hours

Makes 4 medium or 20 small vol-au-vents
225 g /8 oz puff pastry, defrosted if frozen
1 medium-sized egg, beaten
450 g /1 lb lambs' sweetbreads, soaked and
*   blanched*
275 ml /10 fl oz chicken stock, home-made
*   or from a cube*
30 ml /2 tbls dry sherry
50 g /2 oz butter
100 g /4 oz mushrooms, wiped and sliced
5 ml /1 tsp lemon juice
25 g /1 oz flour
60 ml /4 tbls thick cream
1 slice cooked ham, diced
salt and freshly ground black pepper

1 Roll out the pastry 15–20 mm /¼–¾ in thick. Use a 10 cm /4 in round cutter if the vol-au-vents are for a main course, or a 5 cm /2 in cutter for small ones. Cut out twice the appropriate number of rounds, then use a smaller cutter to make a hole 3 cm /1¼ in wide in half the small rounds or 8 cm /3¼ in wide in half the larger rounds. You now have bases, borders and lids. Brush each base with beaten egg, place a border on top and press lightly. Brush the lids with egg. Place on a dampened baking sheet and refrigerate.
2 Heat the oven to 180C /350F /gas 4. Cut the sweetbreads into small pieces and place in an ovenproof dish. Add stock and sherry.
3 Melt 25 g /1 oz butter in a small pan and sauté the sliced mushrooms for 2–3 minutes. Add to the sweetbreads and cook in the oven for 15 minutes. Remove the dish from the oven but don't turn the oven off.
4 Drain the sweetbreads and reserve the liquid. Sprinkle the sweetbreads with the lemon juice. Melt the remaining butter in a saucepan over a low heat. Add the flour and cook for about 2 minutes, stirring, until it froths. Add the reserved liquid and whisk until smooth. Boil for 1 minute, remove from the heat and stir in the cream, ham, sweetbreads and mushrooms. Adjust seasoning and keep warm.
5 Remove the vol-au-vent cases from the refrigerator and bake in the centre of the oven for about 20 minutes. When the pastry has risen and is golden brown, remove from the oven and scrape out any soft pastry from the centre. Fill with the braised sweetbreads, top with the lids and serve.

● The vol-au-vents can be prepared several days in advance, cooled on a wire rack and kept in an airtight tin, then reheated.
● Fill vol-au-vents just before serving, otherwise the pastry will become soggy.

Liver and bacon brochettes

🔪 20 minutes

Serves 4
450 g /1 lb lambs' liver
freshly ground black pepper
pinch of dried sage
8–10 slices bacon
30–45 ml /2–3 tbls unsalted or clarified
*   butter*

1 Cut the slices of liver into 16–20 strips, about 4 cm /1½ in long and 15 mm /½ in thick. Season with pepper and sage to taste.
2 Cut the bacon slices across in half. Wrap half a slice of bacon around each strip of liver, then thread on 4 short metal skewers.
3 Place a large, heavy-based frying-pan over a moderate heat. When the pan is hot, add the butter. When the butter is sizzling hot, arrange the liver and bacon brochettes in the pan, spacing slightly apart. Cook for 5–7 minutes, turning once, then serve.

Brains with black butter

🔪🔪 1 hour 20 minutes soaking and blanching, then 15 minutes

Serves 4
450 g /1 lb lambs' brains, soaked and
*   blanched*
salt and freshly ground black pepper
150 g /5 oz butter
30 ml /2 tbls chopped parsley
15 ml /1 tbls wine vinegar

1 Drain the brains, dry on absorbent paper, cut them into slices and season well.
2 Heat 25 g /1 oz butter in a frying-pan. When the foaming subsides fry the brains until golden on both sides. Remove to a warm serving dish.
3 Add the remaining butter to the pan and allow it to turn golden brown. When it is just beginning to smoke, add the chopped parsley, then quickly pour over the brains.
4 Warm the vinegar slightly, sprinkle over the brains and serve immediately.

USING LEFTOVER LAMB

Cooked lamb, left over from a roast joint, can be turned into so many different dishes that it is well worth buying a larger joint than you require for one meal just for the possibilities of the second meal.

With a little imagination and ingenuity, seemingly ordinary ingredients can be added to leftover shoulder or leg of lamb to create many exciting dishes. Often the addition of just one spice or herb is enough to create an interesting new flavour, or an unusual but simple combination can produce an unexpectedly delicious dish. Forget about shepherd's pie, and start inventing!

All the dishes given here can be cooked from scratch with raw meat, but they are often improved by using already cooked meat. This is particularly true in the case where the meat is to be minced, as you get a smoother texture. For the best results with leftovers, roast the lamb until just pink.

Use leftover lamb sliced, cubed or minced. It is generally best to use the leg meat for mincing as it is less fatty than the shoulder. However, the shoulder meat is often the sweeter and many people prefer it. If mincing a shoulder joint, trim off excess fat first.

Storing leftover lamb

To store the cooked meat, let it cool thoroughly, then wrap it tightly in foil and put it in the refrigerator where it will keep well for up to 4 days. Do not mince or cube the meat until you actually want to cook with it or it will go dry and hard. You can freeze cooked lamb for up to 2 months, but avoid freezing sliced lamb, as it tends to be dry when reheated.

The bones and trimmings should be used immediately to make stock. Refrigerate it when cool and use within 4 days, or freeze for up to 6 months, removing the fat just before you use the lamb.

Italian sauté of lamb

 30 minutes

Serves 4
500 g /1 lb cooked lamb, cut into strips
6 large, firm tomatoes
60 ml /4 tbls olive oil
salt and freshly ground black pepper
2 garlic cloves, finely chopped
90 ml /6 tbls spring onions, thinly sliced
90 ml /6 tbls finely chopped parsley
grated zest of 1 lemon

1 Lower the tomatoes into boiling water for about 30 seconds, then remove them with a slotted spoon. Skin them at once and cut them into quarters. Remove the seeds and juice from each quarter with a teaspoon, a small knife, or simply with your finger. Cut the remaining outer shell and membranes of each quarter into thin strips.

2 Heat the olive oil in a large, thick-bottomed frying-pan. Add the lamb strips and cook over a high heat until well browned on all sides. Season generously with salt and freshly ground black pepper, and stir in half of the finely chopped garlic. Add the tomato strips and continue to cook, stirring continuously, for about 1 minute.

3 Add the thinly sliced spring onions and finely chopped parsley. Toss well over the heat, then sprinkle with the grated lemon zest and the remaining finely chopped garlic. Cover the pan and allow the aromatics to heat through for 3 minutes before serving.

Lamb with black peppercorns

This is ideal for a dinner party as it can all be prepared in advance and the sauce gently reheated just before serving. Broad beans and new potatoes tossed in melted butter and chopped parsley are good accompaniments.

30 minutes

Serves 4
8–12 slices cooked lamb, slightly pink if possible
40 g /1½ oz butter
2 medium-sized onions, finely chopped
1 garlic clove, finely sliced
30 ml /2 tbls flour
300 ml /10 fl oz left-over gravy or concentrated lamb stock
30 ml /2 tbls dry white wine
10 ml /2 tsp black peppercorns, slightly crushed
5 ml /1 tsp Dijon mustard
30 ml /2 tbls soured cream

1 Melt the butter over low heat in a large heavy-bottomed saucepan. Add the onions and garlic and cook till soft and golden. Sprinkle over the flour and stir well. Let it brown slightly over moderate heat, but take care not to burn it.

2 Gradually pour in the gravy or stock, a little at a time, stirring constantly. Continue to stir until the sauce thickens, about 5 minutes. Add the white wine and stir for a further 3–4 minutes.

3 Add the black peppercorns and mustard, mixing well. Put the meat carefully in the pan, coat with the sauce and simmer for 5–10 minutes to heat the meat through.

4 Remove the meat with a slotted spoon and arrange on a warmed serving dish. Increase the heat under the pan to high and quickly stir in the soured cream. Stir once or twice to mix in well and pour immediately over the lamb slices.

Coriander meat balls with yoghurt

These delicately spiced meat balls can be served as a delicious and unusual appetizer or as a snack with drinks.

1 hour marinating, then 45 minutes plus chilling

Makes 16 meat balls
250 g /8 oz cooked lamb
1 medium-sized onion
2.5 ml /½ tsp dried mint
5 ml /1 tsp ground coriander
1 garlic clove, crushed
75 ml /5 tbls olive oil
100 g /4 oz cooked rice
1 small egg
For the sauce
½ medium-sized cucumber
250 ml /9 fl oz yoghurt
10 ml /2 tsp dried mint
30 ml /2 tbls olive oil
salt and freshly ground black pepper

1 Mince the lamb finely and place it in a large bowl. Grate the onion into the bowl and add the mint, coriander, garlic and 15 ml /1 tbls olive oil. Cover the bowl and leave to marinate for 1 hour.

2 Meanwhile, make the sauce. Peel and

Spiced lamb loaf

2 hours
including marinating

Serves 4
275 g /10 oz cooked lamb
1 large onion
15 ml /1 tbls tomato purée
30 ml /2 tbls chopped fresh coriander leaves
   or watercress
2.5 ml /½ tsp chilli powder
2.5 ml /½ tsp ground fenugreek seeds
2.5 ml /½ tsp ground ginger
2.5 ml /½ tsp cumin seeds
1 garlic clove, crushed
salt and freshly ground black pepper
2 large aubergines
120 ml /8 tbls olive oil
1 medium-sized egg
butter for greasing
sprigs of fresh coriander leaves or
   watercress, to garnish

For the tomato-chilli sauce
30 ml /2 tbls olive oil
1 medium-sized onion, finely chopped
1 garlic clove, crushed
400 g /14 oz canned tomatoes
2.5 ml /½ tsp sugar
3 cloves
15 ml /1 tbls tomato purée
2 small red chillies, seeded and chopped
salt and freshly ground black pepper

1   Finely mince the lamb into a large bowl. Grate in the onion and add the tomato purée, coriander leaves or watercress, chilli powder, fenugreek, ginger, cumin seeds and garlic. Mix thoroughly, season with salt and pepper and leave to marinate for at least 30 minutes.
2   Wipe the aubergines with a damp cloth but do not peel. Cut them into thin slices crossways, put on a plate in one layer, sprinkle generously with salt and leave to drain for 30 minutes.
3   Heat the oven to 180C /350F /gas 4. Wash the aubergine slices in running water and pat dry. Heat the olive oil in a large frying-pan. When nearly smoking add the aubergines and fry till golden on both sides, about 5 minutes each side. You may need to do this in 2 batches. Drain the aubergines on absorbent paper and reserve.
4   Stir the egg into the minced lamb mixture to bind it. Grease a 850 ml /1½ pt loaf tin and put in half the lamb, pressing it down well. Place the aubergines on top in an even layer, and cover with the rest of the lamb. Bake for 30–40 minutes. Test to see if the loaf is done by piercing it with a skewer – it should come out clean.
5   Meanwhile, make the sauce: heat the oil in a large, heavy-bottomed pan over moderate heat. Add the onion and garlic and sauté till soft and golden. Add the tomatoes, sugar, cloves, tomato purée and chillies. Season and simmer over low heat while the loaf is baking. Stir it from time to time to prevent it sticking to the pan.
6   When the loaf is done, turn it out onto a serving dish, pour over the tomato sauce, garnish with sprigs of fresh coriander leaves or watercress and serve immediately.

---

grate the cucumber into a bowl. Drain off any excess moisture. Add the yoghurt, mint and olive oil. Season to taste, stir thoroughly and put in the refrigerator to chill.
3   Add the cooked rice to the lamb and beat in the egg to bind.
4   Using 10 ml /2 tsp of the mixture at a time, form small round balls, patting them firmly but gently into shape.
5   Heat the remaining oil in a large frying-pan over low heat. When the oil is hot, put in the meat balls. Cook for 20 minutes, turning them regularly, then turn up the heat and cook for a further 4 minutes, turning. Remove with a slotted spoon and drain on absorbent paper. Serve immediately, with the sauce handed round separately.

● This dish can also be served as a main course for two people with rice and a tomato and basil salad.

Baked lamb with cheese crust

This is the perfect dish for a cold winter's day, especially if served with potatoes baked in their jackets.

1¼ hours

Lamb with black peppercorns

Serves 4
275 g /10 oz cooked lamb, cut into 2 cm /¾
   in cubes
200 g /7 oz butter
2 medium-sized onions, thinly sliced
5 ml /1 tsp dried thyme
3 bay leaves
salt
freshly ground black pepper
400 g /14 oz canned tomatoes
75 g /3 oz fresh breadcrumbs
150 g /5 oz Cheddar cheese, grated

1   Heat the oven to 180C /350F /gas 4. Melt 50 g /2 oz butter in a large frying-pan over moderate heat. Add the onions and sauté them until golden and soft.
2   Put the onions in the bottom of a casserole dish, place the lamb on top and sprinkle in the thyme. Put in the bay leaves and season with salt and freshly ground black pepper. Pour in the tomatoes with their juice.
3   Melt the remaining butter in a large frying-pan, add the breadcrumbs and stir until the breadcrumbs are nicely browned and have absorbed all the butter.
4   Mix the breadcrumbs with the grated cheese and spread evenly over the tomatoes. Bake for 40 minutes, or until the top is crusty and all the cheese melted. Serve the casserole immediately.

LAMB FOR THE FAMILY

Lamb can be cooked in a variety of ways – as patties, loaves or on skewers – and with the addition of herbs, spices or a sauce to create interesting new flavours. Try some of these ideas for family-style dishes.

Tournedos-style lamb patties

 1¼ hours

Serves 6
600 g /1 lb 6 oz lean minced lamb
1 Spanish onion, finely chopped
1 garlic clove, finely chopped
25 g /1 oz butter
30 ml /2 tbls olive oil
50 g /2 oz fresh white breadcrumbs
45–60 ml /3–4 tbls milk
45 ml /3 tbls freshly chopped parsley
1.5 ml /¼ tsp dried oregano
10 ml /2 tsp Worcestershire sauce
1 large egg, lightly beaten
salt and freshly ground black pepper
flour for coating
about 6 fat bacon slices
watercress sprigs, to garnish

Lamb with cider

1 Simmer the chopped onion and garlic in half the butter and oil until soft, then cool. Soak the breadcrumbs in the milk, then squeeze out the excess moisture. Heat the grill to high.
2 Place the lamb in a large bowl. Add the onion and garlic, breadcrumbs, herbs, Worcestershire sauce and egg, and mix well. Season with salt and black pepper.
3 Divide mixture into 6. Shape each portion into a ball, then roll in flour and flatten into patties 7.5 cm /3 in in diameter.
4 Stretch each bacon slice thinly with the back of a knife to meet round the middle of each patty. If a slice does not reach, use an extra slice. Tie securely with string. Grill the patties for 2–3 minutes on each side to seal them.
5 Heat the remaining butter and oil in a large frying-pan, or 2 smaller pans, and fry the patties slowly on all sides for about 30 minutes until cooked through.
6 Discard the strings, transfer the patties to a heated serving dish and serve very hot, garnished with watercress.

Lamb with cider

2 hours standing, then 2¼ hours

Serves 6–8
1.8 kg /4 lb leg of lamb
1 garlic clove, slivered
25 g /1 oz butter, melted
salt and freshly ground black pepper
5 ml /1 tsp flour
75 ml /3 fl oz oil
1 large carrot, scraped
sprig of thyme or rosemary
300 ml /10 fl oz dry cider
1 medium-sized onion, peeled
5 ml /1 tsp cornflour
150 ml /5 fl oz thick cream
15 ml /1 tbls freshly chopped parsley

1 Remove the lamb from the refrigerator about 2 hours before you intend to roast it. Heat the oven to 200C /400F /gas 6. With a sharp knife make slits in the leg and insert the garlic slivers into the slits. Brush the leg with butter and season with salt and pepper to taste. Sprinkle the leg with flour.
2 Heat the oil in a roasting tin and add the lamb. Brown the leg on all sides for 10 minutes. Add the carrot and sprig of thyme or rosemary to the tin.
3 Transfer the lamb to the oven and roast for 30 minutes, then reduce the temperature to 180C /350F /gas 4. Remove the tin from

the oven and add 150 ml /5 fl oz cider to the
tin. Baste the lamb with the cider, then add
the whole peeled onion and return to the
oven for 45–60 minutes depending on how
you want the meat cooked.

4 Remove the lamb from the oven,
transfer to a heated serving dish and leave in
a warm place to settle.

5 Remove and discard the carrot, onion
and herb sprig and add the remaining cider
to the tin. Place tin over a high heat and boil
down for 3 minutes. Mix the cornflour with
30 ml /2 tbls water and add to the reduced
sauce. Bring back to the boil and simmer,
stirring, for 2 minutes. Remove the tin from
the heat and stir in cream. Reheat gently.

6 Carve the lamb and arrange the slices on
the serving dish. Pour a little of the sauce
over the slices and sprinkle with parsley.
Serve the rest of the sauce separately.

Curried baked lamb loaf

🔪 1¾ hours

Serves 6
1 kg /2 lb minced lamb
15 ml /1 tbls curry powder
2.5 ml /½ tsp ground ginger
2.5 ml /½ tsp ground turmeric
2.5 /½ tsp ground coriander
a pinch of paprika
a pinch of cayenne pepper
15 ml /1 tbls flour
salt and freshly ground black pepper
1 large egg, lightly beaten
butter for greasing
sprig of flat-leaved parsley, to garnish
For the sauce
1 small onion, finely chopped
1.5 ml /¼ tsp paprika
1.5 ml /¼ tsp ground coriander
salt and freshly ground black pepper
150 ml /5 fl oz yoghurt

1 Heat the oven to 180C /350F /gas 4.
2 In a bowl, combine the minced lamb,
curry powder, ground ginger, turmeric,
coriander, paprika, cayenne pepper and
flour. Season with salt and pepper and mix
well. Stir in the beaten egg.
3 Butter a 1.7 L /3 pt loaf tin and fill it
with the lamb mixture, pushing it well into
the corners. Cover with foil and bake in the
oven for 1¼ hours, or until cooked.
4 Drain and reserve the fat from the loaf,
then turn the loaf out onto a heated serving
platter. Keep it warm.
5 Heat 30 ml /2 tbls of the reserved fat in
a saucepan and add the finely chopped
onion. Cook for 7–10 minutes or until transparent, stirring occasionally with a wooden
spoon. Stir in the paprika, ground coriander
and season with salt and freshly ground
black pepper to taste. Remove from the heat
and leave to cool slightly.
6 Stir the yoghurt into the onion mixture,
correct the seasoning and pour the sauce
over the curried baked lamb loaf. Garnish
with a sprig of flat-leaved parsley and serve
immediately.

Super lamb curry

🔪 1¾ hours

Serves 4–6
1.6 kg /3½ lb shoulder of lamb on the bone
salt and freshly ground black pepper
30 ml /2 tbls olive oil
25 g /1 oz butter
1 Spanish onion, finely chopped
2 celery stalks, finely chopped
1 green pepper, finely chopped
1 garlic clove, finely chopped
15 ml /1 tbls curry paste
1.5 ml /¼ tsp ground ginger
1.5 ml /¼ tsp ground turmeric
a large pinch of paprika
a large pinch of cayenne pepper
30 ml /2 tbls flour
300 ml /10 fl oz chicken stock, home-made
  or from a cube
60 ml /4 tbls sultanas
150 ml /5 fl oz yoghurt
juice of ½ lemon
boiled rice to serve

Curried baked lamb loaf

1 Cut the lamb from the bone into 4 cm /
1½ in cubes, discarding the gristle and a little
of the fat. Season generously with salt and
freshly ground black pepper.
2 In a flameproof casserole, heat the olive
oil and butter. Sauté the lamb in 2–3
batches, 1–1½ minutes each side, or until
lightly browned. Remove with a slotted
spoon to a plate and keep it warm. Repeat
with the remaining meat.
3 Add the finely chopped onion, celery,
pepper and garlic to the casserole and cook
over a moderate heat for 10–12 minutes or
until softened, stirring occasionally.
4 Add the curry paste, ginger, turmeric,
paprika, cayenne and flour to the softened
vegetables and blend with a wooden spoon.
Add the chicken stock and sultanas; bring to
the boil, stirring constantly. Simmer gently
for 10 minutes.
5 Return the lamb to the casserole, cover
with a lid and simmer gently for 1 hour, or
until tender, stirring occasionally.
6 Stir the yoghurt and lemon juice into the
curry. Heat through and serve with rice.

Barbecued riblets

1½ hours

Serves 4 as a starter
2 breasts of lamb
30 ml /2 tbls vinegar
boiling water, to cover
parsley sprigs and lemon slices, to garnish
For the sauce
30 ml /2 tbls tomato ketchup
30 ml /2 tbls clear honey
30 ml /2 tbls soy sauce
30 ml /2 tbls plum jam
15 ml /1 tbls dry mustard
10 ml /2 tsp Worcestershire sauce

1   Remove and discard the skin and excess fat, then put the breasts into a saucepan large enough to hold them both. Cover with boiling water and add the vinegar. Cover the saucepan and simmer for 15 minutes.
2   Mix all sauce ingredients together in a saucepan and heat gently, stirring.
3   Heat the oven to 180C /350F /gas 4. Drain the breasts, then cut between the ribs into 25 mm /1 in wide strips.
4   Arrange the riblets close together in a roasting tin, pour the sauce over and cook for 30 minutes, turning once.
5   Baste thoroughly, then increase the heat to 200C /400F /gas 6 and cook for a further 15–20 minutes until the riblets are crisp.
6   Garnish with parsley sprigs and lemon slices and serve with the remaining sauce.

Lamb chops with apple and potatoes

1 hour 40 minutes

Serves 4
4 × 225 g /8 oz lamb shoulder chops
salt and freshly ground black pepper
30 ml /2 tbls olive oil
50 g /2 oz butter
1½ Spanish onions, thinly sliced
500 g /1 lb potatoes, sliced
2 apples, peeled, cored and quartered
30 ml /2 tbls flour
300 ml /10 fl oz apple juice
150 ml /5 fl oz chicken stock, home-made or from a cube
50 g /2 oz Gruyère cheese, grated

1   Heat the oven to 190C /375F /gas 5.
2   Trim the chops. Season generously with freshly ground black pepper and allow them to come to room temperature. Just before cooking, season again with salt and freshly ground black pepper.
3   In a heavy-based frying-pan large enough to take the chops in one layer, heat 15 ml /1 tbls olive oil and 25 g /1 oz butter. When foaming subsides, sauté the chops for 2–3 minutes each side, or until lightly browned, turning them with a spatula. Remove with a slotted spoon to a plate and keep warm.
4   Add the thinly sliced onions to the pan

and sauté over a moderate heat for 10 minutes or until golden, stirring occasionally. Season with salt and freshly ground black pepper to taste. Remove with a slotted spoon to a separate plate and keep warm.
5   Add the remaining oil and butter to the frying-pan and sauté the potatoes for 7–10 minutes, or until lightly golden, turning them constantly with a spatula. Season with salt and pepper to taste.
6   In a casserole large enough to take the chops in one layer, spread half the onions on the bottom, then half the sautéed potatoes. Arrange the lamb chops in a single layer over the potatoes, and cover with the remaining onions and potatoes. Arrange apple quarters, end to end and rounded side up, around the edge of the casserole.
7   With a wooden spoon, blend the flour into the fat remaining in the frying-pan and cook over a low heat, stirring constantly for 2–3 minutes, to make a pale roux. Pour in the apple juice and chicken stock, whisking vigorously to prevent lumps forming. Simmer gently for 2 minutes, season with salt and pepper to taste and pour over the lamb and vegetables in the casserole.
8   Sprinkle with grated Gruyère cheese and bake in the oven for 45 minutes or until the lamb is tender and the cheese is golden brown. Serve at once, from the casserole.

Skewered mixed grill

1 Cut the meat from the bone and cut it into 4 cm /1½ in cubes, discarding any fat and gristle (you should have 800 g /1¾ lb meat). Sprinkle the flour onto a plate and season generously with salt and freshly ground black pepper. Toss each cube of lamb in the flour, shaking off the excess.
2 Heat the olive oil and butter in a heavy-based flameproof casserole. Sauté the lamb cubes in the hot fat for 1–2 minutes or until browned all over. Transfer the cubes to a plate with a slotted spoon and keep warm. Repeat with the remaining lamb cubes.
3 Put the sautéed lamb cubes back in the casserole. Pour in the stock, canned tomatoes and chopped garlic and season with salt and freshly ground black pepper. Bring to the boil, reduce the heat, cover the pan and simmer for 1 hour 20 minutes, or until nearly tender.
4 Meanwhile, peel the carrots, halve them lengthways and then cut them into 5 cm /2 in lengths. Peel the button onions, peel and halve the potatoes. Add the prepared vegetables to the lamb and tomato casserole and cook for a further 30 minutes or until just tender (the vegetables take longer to cook than usual because the liquid is just at a gentle simmer).
5 Finally, stir in the frozen peas and the finely chopped parsley. Simmer for 5 minutes. Correct the seasoning and serve.

Kidney stroganoff

 40 minutes

Serves 4
450 g /1 lb fresh lambs' kidneys
50 g /2 oz butter
30 ml /2 tbls oil
250 g /8 oz onion, thinly sliced
250 g /8 oz mushrooms, thinly sliced
60 ml /4 tbls dry vermouth
150 ml /5 fl oz soured cream
salt and freshly ground black pepper
boiled rice to serve
freshly chopped parsley, to garnish
4 lemon wedges, to garnish

1 Wash the kidneys under cold running water, drain and pat dry with absorbent paper. Peel off the thin membrane, if any, and snip out the central core with scissors. Cut the kidneys into thin slices.
2 Heat half the butter and half the oil in a large frying-pan. When sizzling fry the kidneys briskly for 2–3 minutes, stirring frequently. Remove from the pan and reserve.
3 Add the remaining butter and oil to the pan and, when hot, add the onion and sauté very gently for 10 minutes.
4 Increase the heat a little, add the mushrooms and fry for another minute or so, stirring constantly.
5 Return the reserved kidneys to pan, add vermouth, cover and simmer for 3 minutes.
6 Finally stir in the soured cream and generous seasonings of salt and pepper and heat very gently, without boiling, for another minute.
7 Serve kidneys on a bed of rice, garnished with parsley and lemon wedges.

Skewered mixed grill

1 hour marinating, then 30 minutes

Serves 4
225 g /8 oz boned shoulder of lamb
225 g /8 oz boned sirloin
225 g /8 oz fresh lambs' kidneys
60 ml /4 tbls olive oil, plus extra for greasing
60 ml /4 tbls lemon juice
1 garlic clove, finely chopped
2.5 ml /½ tsp dried thyme
2.5 ml /½ tsp dried sage
8 mushroom caps
8 small white onions, parboiled
rosemary sprigs, to garnish
lemon slices, to garnish

1 Cut the lamb and beef into 25 mm /1 in cubes. Cut the kidneys in half, skin them and remove the cores; cut each half into 4 pieces. Place the pieces of meat in a large shallow dish. Mix together the olive oil, lemon juice, finely chopped garlic and herbs and pour over the meat. Leave in a cool place for 1 hour, turning occasionally.
2 Heat the grill to medium-high. Meanwhile, remove the grid from the grill pan and line the pan with aluminium foil. Thread the pieces of meat onto 4 greased

Barbecued riblets

metal skewers, alternating with the mushroom caps and parboiled onions.
3 Lay the skewers across the grill pan. Grill about 7.5 cm /3 in from the heat, basting with the marinade and turning from time to time for about 20 minutes, until the meat is cooked. Garnish with rosemary and lemon and serve.

Lamb stew with tomatoes

2¾ hours

Serves 4
1.2 kg /2¾ lb leg of lamb
90 ml /6 tbls flour
salt and freshly ground black pepper
30 ml /2 tbls olive oil
25 g /1 oz butter
300 ml /10 fl oz hot chicken stock, home-made or from a cube
400 g /14 oz canned tomatoes
1 clove garlic, finely chopped
4 medium-sized carrots
8 button onions
4 small potatoes
225 g /8 oz frozen peas
30 ml /2 tbls finely chopped parsley

STAR MENUS & RECIPE FILE

Giving a dinner party can be a rewarding exercise, and yet far too many cooks tend to stay with a small repertoire of their favourite party recipes. As a result they repeat the same dishes time and time again. It is more trouble to try your hand at new recipes – and of course you have to accept that you may not achieve complete success the first time – but your guests will be flattered that you have tried, and when the party proves a success your sense of achievement will also be much higher.

This lamb menu goes East for a three-course meal for a dinner party for six. We start the festivities with a refreshing appetizer of

Raw mushroom salad with a tangy soured cream and chive or watercress dressing. Garnish the salad with crisp lettuce leaves, tomato wedges or 'roses' – spirals of tomato peel – and black olives. Or serve the salad as a side dish with the main course, an aromatic Indian lamb curry. Accompany it with boiled rice and Chapatis, an unleavened Indian bread that provides the perfect foil for the hot curry flavours of the lamb and is perfect for soaking up the juices. To drink, a refreshing chilled lager will go best with this fiery meal.

After a hot, spicy meal a very light, cooling dessert, Nectarine water-ice, provides the perfect sweet touch.

*Raw mushroom salad
with soured cream*

Indian lamb curry
Chapatis
Devilled carrots

Nectarine water-ice

To drink: lager

Plan-ahead timetable

On the day before
Nectarine water-ice: make and freeze.

On the morning of the meal
Indian lamb curry: make the curry paste and add to the lamb, sauté the onions and the lamb, add the yoghurt mixture and simmer for 1–1¼ hours. Let cool, then refrigerate.

Two hours before the meal
Chapatis: make the dough and leave to rest. Divide into 12 and roll out.
Devilled carrots: prepare the carrots.

One and a half hours before the meal
Raw mushroom salad with soured cream: prepare the mushrooms, the dressing and the garnish.

One hour before the meal
Chapatis: fry the chapatis and keep warm.

Thirty minutes before the meal
Devilled carrots: cook and keep warm in a serving dish.
Boiled rice: cook, dish up and keep warm.
Indian lamb curry: put over a low heat to warm through.

Just before the first course
Raw mushroom salad with soured cream: toss the mushrooms in the soured cream dressing and garnish the salad.
Nectarine water-ice: transfer from the freezer to refrigerator.

Between the first and main course
Indian lamb curry: stir in the lemon juice, transfer to a serving dish, garnish and serve.
Devilled carrots: garnish and serve.

Between the main course and the dessert
Nectarine water-ice: scoop into glasses, garnish and serve.

Raw mushroom salad with soured cream

Serves 6
225 g /8 oz button mushrooms
275 ml /10 fl oz soured cream
60 ml /4 tbls milk
15 ml /1 tbls lemon juice
30 ml /2 tbls chopped chives or watercress leaves
salt and freshly ground black pepper
For the garnish
lettuce leaves
tomato wedges or tomato 'roses'
black olives

1   Trim off the mushroom stalks so that they are level with the caps. Wipe the caps with a clean, damp cloth.
2   In a bowl, stir together the soured cream and milk. Stir in the lemon juice and chopped chives or watercress. Season with salt and freshly ground black pepper to taste.
3   Slice the mushrooms finely and add them to the soured cream dressing, tossing with a fork so that the mushroom slices are evenly coated. Check the seasoning.
4   Pile the mushrooms into a shallow serving dish and garnish with crisp leaves of lettuce. Arrange tomato wedges, or 'roses' – made out of carefully cut tomato peel wound around in spirals – and black olives on the salad. Serve immediately.

● Do not combine the mushrooms and dressing until just before serving – the juice from the mushrooms will cause the dressing to run.

30 minutes

Indian lamb curry

Serves 6

2–2.3 kg /4½–5 lb shoulder of
  lamb, boned out flat
5–6.5 cm /2–2½ in piece of root
  ginger, peeled and chopped
3 garlic cloves, chopped
3 green chillies, seeded and
  chopped
4 ml /¾ tsp ground cardamom
22.5 ml /1½ tbls ground
  coriander
22.5 ml /1½ tbls ground cumin
2.5 ml /½ tsp ground cloves
5 ml /1 tsp saffron strands and
  45 ml /3 tbls boiling water or

a large pinch of saffron
  powder
75 g /3 oz butter
3 small onions, finely chopped
salt
freshly ground black pepper
425 ml /15 fl oz yoghurt
45 ml /3 tbls lemon juice
22.5 ml /1½ tbls freshly chopped
  coriander or parsley
1 lemon, thinly sliced
sprigs of coriander or flat-leaved
  parsley to garnish
boiled rice, to serve

1 Cut the lamb into 25 mm /1 in cubes, discarding a little of the outside fat. Put the cubes in a large bowl.
2 Put the chopped ginger, garlic and chillies with 125 ml /4 fl oz water in a blender and purée until the mixture is smooth. Transfer the mixture to a mortar. Add the ground cardamom, coriander, cumin and cloves and work with a pestle to a smooth paste. Add the spicy mixture to the meat cubes and mix well. Pour 45 ml /3 tbls boiling water over the saffron strands, if using, in a cup.
3 Melt 40 g /1½ oz butter in a large casserole over a gentle heat. Add the finely chopped onions and sauté, stirring occasionally with a wooden spoon, for 8–10 minutes or until golden. Remove the onions with a slotted spoon and keep warm.
4 Melt the remaining butter in the same casserole. Add half the spicy lamb cubes and sauté for 8–10 minutes or until light brown, stirring occasionally. Remove with a slotted spoon and keep warm. Sauté the second batch of lamb cubes. Return the first batch of lamb and sautéed onions to the casserole. Season with salt and freshly ground black pepper to taste.
5 Put the yoghurt in a bowl and pour in the saffron strands and their liquid or add the saffron powder. Stir to combine, then add the mixture to the casserole. Place over a low heat until the liquid is gently simmering. Cook uncovered, stirring occasionally, for 1–1¼ hours or until the lamb is tender.
6 Just before serving, stir the lemon juice into the casserole. Transfer the curry to a heated serving dish. Sprinkle with chopped coriander or parsley and garnish with lemon slices and coriander or parsley sprigs around the platter. Serve immediately with boiled rice.

 2½ hours   lager

Chapatis

Serves 6

225 g /8 oz wholewheat flour
2.5 ml /½ tsp salt
50 g /2 oz clarified butter or margarine
30 ml /2 tbls clarified or melted butter

1 Mix the flour and salt in a large bowl. Add the clarified butter or margarine and rub into the flour with your fingertips until it resembles fine breadcrumbs. Make a well in the centre and pour in 75 ml /3 fl oz water. Mix the flour into the liquid with your fingers, gradually adding another 50 ml /2 fl oz water. Bring the dough together to form a ball.
2 Put the dough on a floured surface and knead it for 10 minutes, or until it is smooth and elastic.
3 Put the dough into a bowl. Cover it with a clean cloth and leave to stand for 30 minutes at room temperature.
4 Divide the dough into 12 portions. Roll out each portion on a floured surface into a thin round.
5 Heat a heavy iron frying-pan over a moderate heat. Place a round of dough in the hot pan. When small blisters appear on the surface press the chapati with a fish slice to flatten it. Turn the chapati over and cook it until it is pale and golden in colour.
6 Remove the chapati from the pan and brush with a little clarified butter (or melted butter). Place the chapati on a warmed plate and keep warm until all the chapatis are cooked in the same way. Serve warm.

● A chapati is an unleavened Indian bread, traditionally served with curries. In India *ghee* is used for making the dough and for serving. The nearest equivalent to this is clarified butter, but margarine can be used for making the dough.
● To make clarified butter, melt the butter over very low heat. It will foam and then the foam will sink leaving the butter clear like oil. Pour off the butter, leaving the white sediment in the pan.

 50 minutes including resting,
then 30 minutes

Devilled carrots

Serves 4–6
1 kg /2 lb small carrots
90 ml /6 tbls olive oil
1 garlic clove, finely chopped
½ Spanish onion, finely chopped
15 ml /1 tbls wine vinegar
15 ml /1 tbls dry mustard
4 ml /¾ tsp powdered cumin
4 ml /¾ tsp paprika
4 ml /¾ tsp cayenne pepper
salt and freshly ground black pepper
30 ml /2 tbls finely chopped parsley
20 ml /4 tsp lemon juice

1   Peel the carrots with a vegetable peeler and slice thinly.
2   Heat the olive oil in a saucepan. Add the finely chopped garlic
and onion and sauté, stirring constantly, for 4–5 minutes or until
they are soft. Add the sliced carrots and continue to cook, stirring
all the time, for 3 minutes.
3   Add 90 ml /6 tbls water, the wine vinegar, dry mustard,
powdered cumin, paprika and cayenne pepper. Season with salt and
freshly ground black pepper to taste and simmer gently for 20–25
minutes or until the carrots are tender. Stir occasionally. Transfer
to a heated serving dish.
4   Sprinkle the carrots with finely chopped parsley and add a little
lemon juice just before serving.

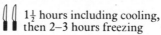
45 minutes

Nectarine water-ice

Serves 6
4 large nectarines
boiling water
juice of 1 lemon, strained
2–3 drops of almond essence
red food colouring (optional)
3 black grapes, seeded and halved
For the syrup
225 g /8 oz sugar
juice of ½ lemon

1   If you are using the freezer compartment of the refrigerator
rather than a freezer, set the refrigerator at its lowest temperature
(the highest setting) 1 hour before you make the water-ice.
2   To make the syrup, combine the sugar and 600 ml /1 pt water in
a saucepan. Bring the mixture slowly to the boil, stirring constantly,
until all the sugar has dissolved. Boil for 10 minutes and then add
the lemon juice. Set aside to cool.
3   Pour boiling water over the nectarines and allow them to stand
for 10 seconds, then skin and stone them. Rub the flesh through a
fine nylon sieve until you have 300 ml /10 fl oz purée.
4   Add the syrup to the purée and flavour with the strained lemon
juice and almond essence to taste. Tint the mixture slightly with red
food colouring if you like. Allow it to become completely cold.
5   Transfer the mixture to a freezer container, cover and freeze.
6   Stir the water-ice vigorously with a fork every ½ hour, until half
frozen. Leave it for at least 2 or 3 hours until frozen hard.
7   About 1 hour before serving, transfer the water-ice from the
freezer to main compartment of your refrigerator.
8   When you are ready to serve, scoop the nectarine water-ice into
wine glasses and arrange a halved black grape on each serving.

● Once the nectarines have been skinned and stoned, it is important
to prepare the purée as quickly as possible without interruption as
the fruit will otherwise turn brown. Regular beating is necessary to
prevent large crystals forming in the ice.
● If you cannot buy nectarines, fresh peaches could be used instead.

1½ hours including cooling,
then 2–3 hours freezing

STAR MENU 2

Belgian chicken liver pâté

Rack of lamb persillé
Harem pilaff
Green beans à la grecque

Pineapple Bavarian cream

Wine: Pisse-Dru or another beaujolais

Plan-ahead timetable

The day before or earlier in the day
Belgian chicken liver pâté: prepare pâté and chill in refrigerator.
Pineapple Bavarian cream: prepare cream and chill in refrigerator.

Three hours before the meal
Rack of lamb persillé: remove lamb from refrigerator.

One hour before the meal
Green beans à la grecque: prepare beans and tomato sauce.
Harem pilaff: prepare tomatoes, mushrooms and onions.

Forty-five minutes before the meal
Green beans à la grecque: simmer beans and sauce.
Rack of lamb persillé: place lamb in oven and prepare coating.
Harem pilaff: make the pilaff and place in oven. Prepare filling.

Twenty-five minutes before the meal
Pineapple Bavarian cream: unmould and decorate the dessert.
Rack of lamb persillé: coat the lamb and return to the oven.

Five minutes before the first course
Harem pilaff: make the rice ring and fill the centre. Keep warm in the oven.
Green beans à la grecque: dish up the beans and keep warm.
Rack of lamb persillé: move the lamb to a serving dish, turn off the oven, leave the door open and leave the lamb to settle.
Belgian chicken liver pâté: make toast and cut into fingers.

There is nothing like a rack of spring lamb for a dinner party to remember. Two whole best ends of neck of succulent lamb are roasted with a savoury coating, and the combination of crisply browned breadcrumbs and herbs and the moist pink lamb is hard to beat. If you want to serve them arranged like a guard of honour, interlock the bones and roast the racks in position.

Belgian chicken liver pâté

Serves 6
500 g /1 lb chicken livers
salt
250 g /8 oz butter
60 ml /4 tbls finely grated Spanish onion
10 ml /2 tsp dry mustard
2.5 ml /½ tsp freshly grated nutmeg
1.5 ml /¼ tsp ground cloves
freshly ground black pepper
hot toast, to serve

1   Cover the livers with salted water. Bring to the boil, then simmer, covered, for 20 minutes. Drain the livers, pat them dry with absorbent paper and put twice through the finest blade of a mincer, or liquidize to a paste in a blender.
2   Return the paste to the saucepan and beat with a spoon over a moderate heat for 1 minute to evaporate the excess moisture.
3   Work the butter with a wooden spoon until soft and creamy. Flavour it with finely grated onion, dry mustard, freshly grated nutmeg and ground cloves. Then beat in the minced livers. Season to taste with salt and freshly ground black pepper. If you prefer an absolutely smooth texture, rub the mixture through a fine sieve.
4   Pack the pâté firmly into a small earthenware pot or terrine and chill until needed.
5   Serve with fresh fingers of hot toast: trim off all crusts and cut the toast into thin strips.

● This deliciously rich but simple chicken liver pâté is a convenient one because it can be stored for up to a week in the refrigerator.

 40 minutes,
plus chilling

The accompanying pilaff is simmered in butter, stock and wine and then tossed just before serving with a 'harem' garnish of diced avocado pear, mushrooms, chicken livers and tomato. It is as beautiful to look at as it is to eat. Green beans à la grecque, beans cooked in the Greek manner with tomato purée and onion, adds another interesting colour and flavour complement to the lamb.

Rack of lamb persillé

Serves 6
2 best ends of neck of baby lamb, 6 cutlets each, chined
salt and freshly ground black pepper
10–15 ml /2–3 tsp dry mustard
15 ml /1 tbls dry white wine
90 ml /6 tbls fresh breadcrumbs
45 ml /3 tbls finely chopped parsley
2.5 ml /½ tsp finely chopped garlic
15 g /½ oz butter, diced small
parsley sprigs, to garnish

1 Remove the meat from the refrigerator at least 2 hours before roasting.
2 Heat the oven to 200C /400F /gas 6. With a sharp knife make light cuts through the fat on top of both joints in 2 directions for a diagonal effect. Season the trimmed racks of lamb generously with salt and freshly ground black pepper. Roast in the oven for 20 minutes.
3 Mix together the dry mustard and dry white wine to form a paste. Brush this all over the racks of lamb. Mix together the breadcrumbs, finely chopped parsley and garlic and pat the mixture over the fatty side of the lamb. Dot with butter. Return the meat to the oven and roast for 20–30 minutes for pink meat.
4 Remove lamb from oven and leave in a warm place to settle. If wished the exposed bones can be garnished with cutlet frills for serving. This makes carving much easier, as the carver can hold the lamb by the frill without getting greasy fingers while cutting down between the bones to free the chops. Garnish the racks with parsley sprigs and serve.

● A rack is an American and Australian term for a best end of neck, roasted or grilled whole. Ask the butcher to prepare it for you in the classic manner, or do this yourself at home. Cut down 5 cm /2 in between each chop bone and remove the intervening fat and meat. Cut the fat away from the top of the bone and scrape the bones clean of all meat. This will leave the ends of the bones sticking out with a comb effect. *Persillé* is the French for 'with parsley' and refers to the typically French coating of mixed buttered breadcrumbs, garlic and parsley which covers the lamb fat, giving it a crisp, crumbly exterior.

 2 hours standing, then 1 hour   Beaujolais

Harem pilaff

Serves 4–6
6 large, firm tomatoes
175 g /6 oz button mushrooms
½ Spanish onion, finely chopped
90 g /3½ oz butter
250 g /8 oz long-grain rice
60 ml /4 tbls dry white wine or cider
850 ml /1½ pt well-flavoured chicken stock, home-made or from a cube
salt and freshly ground black pepper
1 garlic clove, finely chopped
30 ml /2 tbls finely chopped parsley
1.5 ml /¼ tsp dried oregano
1 avocado pear, peeled and diced
75 g /3 oz chicken livers, trimmed and diced

1 Heat the oven to 180C /350F /gas 4. Drop the tomatoes into boiling water and leave for 1 minute. Remove with a slotted spoon and skin them at once. Remove all the seeds and juice with a teaspoon (reserve for another dish) and dice and reserve the flesh.
2 Slice or quarter the button mushrooms, according to size.
3 Sauté the finely chopped onion in 50 g /2 oz butter in a medium-sized flameproof casserole until golden. Add the rice and stir over the heat for 1–2 minutes. Pour the dry white wine or cider and chicken stock over the rice. Season with salt and freshly ground black pepper to taste. Bring to the boil. Cover the casserole and cook in the oven for 30–40 minutes or until tender. After about 10 minutes, stir once with a fork.
4 Meanwhile sauté the sliced button mushrooms in 25 g /1 oz butter in a frying-pan for 3 minutes. Add the finely chopped garlic, parsley, oregano, diced tomato flesh and season to taste with salt and freshly ground black pepper. Simmer for 2–3 minutes. Scatter with the peeled and diced avocado pear and keep warm.
5 In another pan, sauté the diced chicken livers in 15 g /½ oz butter for 2 minutes. Then stir the livers into the finished rice mixture with a fork.
6 Form the rice into a ring on a warmed serving plate and fill the centre with the avocado and mushroom mixture. Serve at once.

1 hour

Green beans à la grecque

Serves 4–6
450–550 g /1–1¼ lb green beans
150 g /5 oz tomato purée
60–90 ml /4–6 tbls olive oil
½ Spanish onion, finely chopped
¼–1 garlic clove, finely chopped
salt and freshly ground black pepper

1   Top and tail the green beans and slice them in half lengthways.
2   Mix the tomato purée with 425 ml /14 fl oz water, olive oil, finely chopped onion and garlic.
3   Put the beans in a saucepan, pour over the tomato-onion mixture and season to taste with salt and freshly ground black pepper. Bring to the boil. Lower the heat and simmer gently, stirring from time to time, for 35–45 minutes, or until the sauce has reduced and beans are tender.

● Green beans à la grecque are delicious hot or cold. Cold, they form a simple but sophisticated appetizer.

 50 minutes

Pineapple Bavarian cream

Serves 6
15 ml /1 tbls cornflour
600 ml /1 pt milk
6 medium-sized egg yolks
225 g /8 oz caster sugar
820 g /1 lb 13 oz canned
    pineapple slices in syrup
15 g /½ oz (1 envelope) gelatine
juice of 2 lemons

60 ml /4 tbls very cold milk
300 ml /10 fl oz thick cream
almond oil or a flavourless
    cooking oil for greasing
For the garnish
remaining pineapple slices
glacé cherries
sprigs of fresh mint leaves
whipped cream

1   Blend the cornflour with 60 ml /4 tbls of the milk. Bring the remaining milk to just below boiling point. Stir a little into the cornflour mixture, and return this to the pan.
2   Beat the egg yolks with the sugar in a large bowl until fluffy and lemon coloured.
3   Gradually add the scalded milk mixture to the egg yolks and sugar, beating constantly. Pour the mixture into the top of a double saucepan (or bowl over a pan of simmering water). Cook over simmering water, stirring constantly with a wooden spoon, until the mixture thickens and coats the back of the spoon. Do not let the mixture boil as the eggs will curdle.
4   Remove the mixture from the heat and plunge the base of the saucepan into cold water. This will stop the cooking process and prevent the cream separating.
5   Drain the pineapple slices and measure out 150 ml /5 fl oz pineapple syrup into a small bowl. Sprinkle the gelatine over the surface and leave to soften for a few minutes. Then stand the bowl in a pan containing a little hot water and stir until the gelatine has completely melted. Add this to the custard and mix well.
6   Cut 8 pineapple slices into thin shreds. Add to the custard, together with the lemon juice.
7   When the custard is cold, but not set, add the cold milk to the cream and whip until thick but light. Fold into the custard.
8   Brush a 1.75 L /3 pt mould with oil and pour the cream into the mould. Chill until ready to serve.
9   To serve, hold a cloth wrung out in hot water around the mould for a few seconds, then turn out carefully onto a serving dish. Decorate with remaining pineapple slices, cut into half rings or small pieces, glacé cherries, sprigs of mint and whipped cream.

50 minutes plus cooling and chilling

Turkish lamb stew with okra

Serves 4
1 kg /2 lb shoulder of lamb, cut into 25 mm /1 in cubes
olive oil
salt and freshly ground black pepper
3 large Spanish onions, coarsely chopped
500 g /1 lb fresh okra, stems removed, washed, drained and
    dried in a tea-towel
225 g /8 oz canned peeled tomatoes
300 ml /10 fl oz chicken stock, home-made or from a cube (optional)
generous pinch of cayenne pepper
45–60 ml /3–4 tbls tomato purée
30 ml /2 tbls finely chopped parsley

1   Heat 45 ml /3 tbls olive oil in a heavy-based sauté pan or frying-pan. Add the cubed lamb, in 2 batches if necessary, and sauté until golden brown on all sides. Season with salt and freshly ground black pepper to taste. Remove the lamb cubes with a slotted spoon and put into a flameproof casserole.
2   In the same pan, brown the coarsely chopped Spanish onions in 3 batches, then brown the okra in 3 batches, adding olive oil when necessary. Add the browned vegetables to the lamb.
3   In a saucepan, combine the canned peeled tomatoes with the stock or the same amount of water. Season to taste with salt and pepper and a generous pinch of cayenne pepper. Simmer for 2 minutes and stir in the tomato purée. Mix with the lamb and vegetables.
4   Simmer the stew very gently, over the lowest possible heat, for 50–60 minutes or until the lamb is well cooked but the okra are still whole. To ensure that the lamb is tender and moist – not hard and dry – the sauce must just bubble very gently in the casserole.
5   Transfer the stew to a heated, deep serving dish. Sprinkle with finely chopped parsley and serve immediately.

● Okra is a plant of the cotton family and is native to the West Indies. In Britain it is often known as ladies' fingers, and in Greece and Turkey it is known as bamia. It gives a rather jelly-like texture to a sauce. Be careful when removing the okra stems. Use a sharp knife to cut off the stem just before it joins the pod; if you pierce the pod, it will lose its shape during cooking and the seeds will spill out.

 1¾ hours

Lyonnaise potato cake with grilled kidneys

Serves 2
225–350 g /8–12 oz potatoes
freshly grated nutmeg
salt and freshly ground black pepper
50 g /2 oz butter
4 lambs' kidneys
25 g /1 oz melted butter
60–90 ml /4–6 tbls freshly grated Gruyère cheese
sprigs of parsley

1   Peel the potatoes and slice thinly on a mandolin or in a food processor. Drop the slices into cold water. Drain and then dry them thoroughly on absorbent paper. Season the potato slices with freshly grated nutmeg, salt and freshly ground black pepper to taste.
2   Heat 25 g /1 oz of the butter in an 18 cm /7 in frying-pan. Using half the potatoes, make 2 layers of potato slices in the pan, pressing them down into a 'cake' with a fish slice.
3   Cover the frying-pan with a lid and cook the potato cake for 2–3 minutes, or until the underside is browned. Reverse the potato cake onto the lid, return the cake to the pan and continue to cook for 2–3 minutes until the underside is done. Transfer to a heatproof plate and keep warm. Add another 25 g /1 oz butter to the pan and repeat the process to make a second potato cake.
4   Heat the grill to high. Meanwhile, skin the kidneys, cut in half and remove the core, season with salt and freshly ground black pepper. Place the kidneys cut-side down on the oiled grill rack and brush with half the melted butter. Cook the kidneys 7.5 cm /3 in from the heat for 2 minutes. Turn the kidneys over with a fish slice, brush with the remaining melted butter and cook for a further 1–2 minutes. Keep the kidneys warm.
5   To serve, sprinkle each potato cake with 30–45 ml /2–3 tbls freshly grated Gruyère cheese and cook under the grill, 7.5 cm /3 in from the heat, for 1–2 minutes, or until the cheese is just melted. Serve immediately, accompanying each cake with 2 grilled kidneys, and garnished with sprigs of parsley.

35 minutes

Boiled leg of lamb with caper sauce

Serves 6

1.8 kg /4 lb leg of lamb, shank
   bone removed
salt and ground black pepper
boiling water
1 bouquet garni
1 bay leaf
1 Spanish onion, quartered and
   stuck with 4 cloves
150 ml /5 fl oz chicken stock,
   home-made or from a cube
25 g /1 oz butter

24 small carrots
24 button onions
15 ml /1 tbls finely chopped
   parsley
For the caper sauce
40 g /1½ oz butter
45 ml /3 tbls flour
1 large egg yolk
75 ml /5 tbls thick cream
15 ml /1 tbls lemon juice
30 ml /2 tbls capers, drained

1   Trim most of the fat from the leg of lamb. Season generously with salt and freshly ground black pepper and wrap tightly in a piece of muslin, securing with string. Let it stand for 2 hours to come to room temperature.

2   Place the lamb in a large, deep, flameproof casserole or heavy saucepan and cover with boiling salted water. Boil for 10 minutes. Skim the surface and reduce to simmering. Add the bouquet garni, bay leaf and onion, cover and cook for 2 hours or until the meat is cooked but still a little pink in the centre.

3   Meanwhile, pour the chicken stock into a saucepan. Add the butter, carrots and button onions and simmer over a moderate heat for 10 minutes, or until tender. Stir in the parsley, season to taste and keep warm.

4   Drain the lamb. Strain the cooking liquid and reserve. Remove the muslin and put the meat on a heated platter. Keep warm.

5   To make the caper sauce, melt the butter in a saucepan. Blend in the flour and cook for 3–4 minutes, stirring constantly, until a pale roux forms. Pour 600 ml /1 pt reserved liquid onto the roux and beat vigorously with a whisk. Bring to the boil, then simmer for 2–3 minutes until thickened. Remove from the heat.

6   In a bowl, blend the egg yolk, thick cream and lemon juice. Pour a little sauce on to this mixture and blend. Return to the pan, stirring, and cook over a low heat for 1–2 minutes. Do not allow the sauce to come to the boil or it will curdle. Season to taste and stir in the drained capers.

7   Pour a little caper sauce over the lamb and arrange the vegetables on the platter. Serve the remaining sauce separately.

bringing to room temperature,
then 2½ hours

Lancashire hot pot

Serves 4

700 g /1½ lb best end neck of lamb, chined, with the rib bones
   trimmed
6 lambs' kidneys
700 g /1½ lb potatoes, thinly sliced
salt and freshly ground black pepper
1 Spanish onion, thinly sliced
300 ml /10 fl oz chicken stock, home-made or from a cube
25 g /1 oz butter, plus extra for greasing
sprigs of rosemary, to garnish

1   Heat the oven to 180C /350F /gas 4.

2   Cut the lamb into chops with a sharp knife, then cut away most of the fat, scraping the bones clean with the knife.

3   With a sharp knife, cut the lambs' kidneys in half. Remove the membrane, then snip away the centre core with scissors.

4   Cover the bottom of a medium-sized ovenproof casserole with a layer of overlapping potato slices, using one third of the potatoes. Season generously with salt and freshly ground black pepper. Arrange half the chops and prepared kidneys on top. Season generously with salt and freshly ground black pepper, then sprinkle over half the onion slices. Repeat the procedure, seasoning each layer with salt and freshly ground black pepper. Finish with a layer of overlapping potato slices.

5   Pour in the chicken stock. Cut a piece of greaseproof paper to fit the top of casserole, butter it and place it butter downward over the top layer of potatoes. Cover with a lid and bake for 1½ hours.

6   Remove the lid and buttered paper. Dot the potatoes with butter and return to the oven for a further 30 minutes, or until the potatoes are well browned and the meat is tender. Garnish with sprigs of rosemary and serve immediately.

30 minutes,
then 2 hours cooking

Lamb chops with rosemary

Serves 4
4 loin lamb chops, 25 mm /1 in thick
50 ml /2 fl oz olive oil
30 ml /2 tbls lemon juice
freshly ground black pepper
10 ml /2 tsp dried rosemary
1 garlic clove, crushed
For the garnish
1 lemon, quartered
4 sprigs of rosemary

1   In a medium-sized shallow mixing bowl, combine the olive oil, lemon juice, a generous sprinkling of freshly ground black pepper, the rosemary and crushed garlic.
2   Place the lamb chops in the marinade and baste them well. Set the chops aside in a cool place and leave them to marinate for 2 hours, basting frequently.
3   Heat the grill to high. Remove the chops from the marinade and reserve the marinade. Place the lamb chops on the grill rack 7.5 cm /3 in from heat. Grill the chops for 4–6 minutes on each side, basting with the marinade.
4   Remove the chops from the grill and place them on a warmed serving plate. Spoon the remaining marinade over the chops, garnish and serve immediately.

● Lamb chops marinated and cooked with olive oil, lemon juice, garlic and rosemary make a simple, yet delicious lunch or supper dish. Serve with a crisp green or tomato salad and crusty French bread and butter.

  2 hours marinating,
then 15 minutes

Kidneys in sherry sauce

Serves 4
8–10 lambs' kidneys
50 g /2 oz butter
1 medium-sized onion, finely chopped
6–8 button mushrooms, thinly sliced
25 g /1 oz flour
300 ml /10 fl oz hot chicken stock, home-made or from a cube
30–45 ml /2–3 tbls dry sherry
salt and freshly ground black pepper
4 slices of bread, crusts removed
olive oil for frying
15–30 ml /1–2 tbls freshly chopped parsley

1   Skin and halve the kidneys, removing the core. In a small frying-pan heat half the butter. Sauté the kidneys for 2–3 minutes. Remove with a slotted spoon and reserve.
2   Cook the finely chopped onion in the remaining butter until soft and lightly browned. Add the thinly sliced mushrooms and cook, stirring continuously, until lightly coloured. Remove from the heat.
3   Return the kidneys to the pan. Sprinkle with the flour and blend this in carefully. Stir in the hot chicken stock and return the pan to the heat. Bring to the boil, reduce the heat and simmer for 5 minutes. Do not continue to boil as this toughens the kidneys. Add the sherry, and season with salt and freshly ground black pepper to taste.
4   Meanwhile, cut the slices of bread into triangles. Heat the olive oil and fry the croûtons until golden brown. Remove from the oil, drain on absorbent paper and keep warm.
5   To serve, transfer the kidneys to a heated serving dish. Dip the edges of the croûtons in parsley and arrange around the edge of the dish, sprinkle the remaining chopped parsley over the kidneys and serve immediately.

35 minutes

Lamb and bacon kebabs

Serves 6
700 g /1½ lb boned leg of lamb
45 ml /3 tbls clear honey
30 ml /2 tbls olive oil
30 ml /2 tbls lemon juice
3 garlic cloves, crushed
15 ml /1 tbls soy sauce
12 button onions, peeled
1 large green pepper
450 g /1 lb streaky bacon slices
6 black olives, stoned
3 small tomatoes, halved

1   Cut the lamb into 30 × 25 mm /1 in cubes, discarding any fat and gristle. Put the meat into a large bowl.
2   Combine the clear honey, olive oil, lemon juice, crushed garlic and the soy sauce with 275 ml /10 fl oz hot, but not boiling, water. Pour over the lamb and marinate for at least 1 hour.
3   Put the button onions in a small saucepan, cover with water and bring to the boil, simmer for 2–3 minutes; drain well.
4   Halve, core and seed the pepper. Cut each half into 3 strips and each strip in half (12 pieces). Put the pepper into another small saucepan and cover with water, bring to the boil and simmer for 2–3 minutes. Drain well and refresh the peppers under cold, running water.
5   Prepare the barbecue and light the coals.
6   Remove the lamb from the marinade, reserving the marinade. Stretch each bacon slice out thinly with the back of a knife. Cut the bacon into 30 pieces. Wrap a length around each cube of lamb.
7   Assemble 6 × 25 cm /10 in long skewers as follows: bacon-wrapped lamb, button onion, followed by bacon-wrapped lamb, pepper, bacon-wrapped lamb, button onion, bacon-wrapped lamb, pepper, finishing with bacon-wrapped lamb and a black olive.
8   Barbecue the kebabs over the hot coals, turning occasionally and brushing with the reserved marinade. They will take 10–15 minutes, depending on the intensity of the heat. About 2–3 minutes before the end of cooking time, spear a piece of tomato onto the end of each skewer. Serve immediately.

 20 minutes, 1 hour marinating,
then 30 minutes

Lamb with prunes and raisins

Serves 4
1 kg /2 lb leg or shoulder of
   lamb, boned
30 ml /2 tbls flour
45 ml /3 tbls olive oil
1 Spanish onion, sliced
1 garlic clove, finely chopped
1.5 ml /¼ tsp powdered turmeric
1.5 ml /¼ tsp powdered saffron
1.5 ml /¼ tsp ground cinnamon
a large pinch of ground ginger
a large pinch of cayenne pepper
salt and freshly ground black
   pepper
375 ml /13 fl oz light chicken
   stock (made with 1 stock cube)
15 ml /1 tbls honey
225 g /8 oz dried prunes, soaked
   in water at least 2 hours and
   drained
75 g /3 oz raisins, soaked in
   water at least 2 hours and
   drained
boiled rice, to serve
thin lemon slices, to garnish
flat-leaved parsley, to garnish

1   Trim all the fat from the lamb and cut the meat into 4 cm /1½ in cubes. Toss the lamb in the flour.
2   In a large flameproof casserole heat the olive oil, and sauté the lamb, stirring occasionally, until it is brown on all sides. Remove with a slotted spoon and set aside.
3   Add the sliced onion to the casserole and sauté, stirring continuously, until it is golden brown. Then add the finely chopped garlic and spices, and season with salt and freshly ground black pepper to taste. Stir and sauté for 5 minutes before gradually adding the chicken stock. Bring to the boil.
4   Return the meat the the casserole; lower the heat and simmer the stew very gently, covered, for 40–50 minutes, or until the lamb is almost tender.
5   Stir in the honey, the soaked prunes, and the raisins, and cook covered for a further 10 minutes until the lamb is tender. Serve hot on a bed of plain boiled rice, garnished with lemon slices and flat-leaved parsley.

 2 hours soaking,
then 2 hours

Greek keftethes
with tomato sauce

Serves 4
750 g /1½ lb boned shoulder or leg of lamb
lamb fat made up to 225 g /8 oz with beef suet, if necessary
½ Spanish onion, finely chopped
100 g /4 oz fresh breadcrumbs
2 large eggs, beaten
6–8 mint leaves, finely chopped
6–8 sprigs of parsley, finely chopped
2.5 ml /½ tsp dried oregano or marjoram
1.5 ml /¼ tsp ground cinnamon
1.5 ml /¼ tsp ground ginger
1.5 ml /¼ tsp cayenne pepper
salt
olive oil for frying
For the tomato sauce
800 g /1¾ lb canned peeled tomatoes, coarsely chopped
½ Spanish onion, finely chopped
30 ml /2 tbls finely chopped parsley
1–2 garlic cloves, finely chopped
60 ml /4 tbls olive oil
1.5 ml /¼ tsp paprika pepper
1.5 ml /¼ tsp cayenne pepper
salt

1   Place all the ingredients for the sauce in a large saucepan. Add 300 ml /10 fl oz water and simmer gently, uncovered, for 1 hour.
2   Meanwhile put the lamb, fat and finely chopped Spanish onion through the finest blade of your mincer 3 times. In a large mixing bowl, combine the minced mixture, breadcrumbs, beaten eggs, finely chopped mint leaves and parsley, dried herb and spices. Season to taste with salt. Mix well.
3   Form the mixture into 48 little balls the size of large marbles. Heat the olive oil in a large frying-pan, add a batch of meat balls and fry until golden. Drain on absorbent paper. Continue frying the meat balls in this way until they are all cooked.
4   Add the meat balls to the tomato sauce and simmer for 15 minutes. To serve place 12 meat balls on each of 4 plates and coat them with the tomato sauce.

 1¼ hours

Pan-fried lamb chops
with wine

Serves 4
8 × 150 g /5 oz loin lamb chops, each 25 mm /1 in thick
salt and freshly ground black pepepr
75 g /3 oz butter
30 ml /2 tbls olive oil
60 ml /4 tbls finely chopped onion
150 ml /5 fl oz dry white wine
15 ml /1 tbls finely chopped fresh tarragon or chives, or a combination
30 ml /2 tbls finely chopped parsley
60 ml /4 tbls chicken stock, home-made or from a cube
finely chopped parsley, to garnish
sprig of parsley, to garnish

1   Trim the chops, leaving a small border of fat. Season the chops generously with freshly ground black pepper and leave to come to room temperature. Just before cooking, season with salt.
2   In a heavy frying-pan large enough to take the chops in one layer, heat 25 g /1 oz butter and the olive oil. When the foaming subsides, lay the chops side by side in the pan and brown them over a moderate heat for 3–4 minutes on each side, turning them with a spatula. Transfer the chops to a heated serving dish, using a slotted spoon, and keep them warm.
3   To make the sauce, pour off and discard the fat from the frying-pan and melt the remaining 50 g /2 oz butter. When the butter starts sizzling, add the finely chopped onion and cook for 2 minutes, stirring occasionally with a wooden spoon. Pour in the dry white wine and finely chopped herbs and simmer for 3–4 minutes, scraping the brown crusty bits from the sides of the pan into the sauce. Season with salt and freshly ground black pepper to taste.
4   Add the chicken stock to the frying-pan and boil rapidly for 5 minutes or until the sauce has thickened slightly. Strain the sauce and pour it around the chops. Sprinkle the onion from the pan and the finely chopped parsley over the chops, garnish with a sprig of parsley and serve immediately.

bringing to room temperature, then 30 minutes

Brittany lamb with haricots

Serves 6

1.8 kg /4 lb leg of lamb
350 g /12 oz dried haricot beans,
    soaked overnight
butter for greasing
1–2 garlic cloves, cut into thin
    slivers
salt and ground black pepper
30 ml /2 tbls melted butter

1 Spanish onion, coarsely
    chopped
90 ml /6 tbls olive oil
400 g /14 oz canned peeled
    tomatoes, coarsely chopped
60 ml /4 tbls finely chopped
    parsley
flat-leaved parsley, to garnish

1   Cook the soaked beans in unsalted water for 1½ hours or until
tender. Allow the lamb to come up to room temperature.
2   Heat the oven to 170C /325F /gas 3. Butter a shallow,
flameproof casserole or gratin dish just large enough to hold the leg
of lamb comfortably.
3   Prick the lamb all over with the point of a sharp knife and insert
a sliver of garlic in each incision. Season generously with salt and
freshly ground black pepper. Place the lamb in the greased baking
dish on a rack and sprinkle with the melted butter. Roast for 45
minutes.
4   Sauté the coarsely chopped onion in 30 ml /2 tbls olive oil until
transparent.
5   Remove the lamb from the rack. Spoon the drained cooked
beans, chopped tomatoes, sautéed onions, finely chopped parsley
and 60 ml /4 tbls olive oil into the dish in which the lamb was
cooked. Place the lamb on top and cook for a further 25 minutes.
Give the bean mixture a stir, then continue roasting for another 20
minutes, or until the lamb is tender and the juices run pink when
the meat is pierced.
6   When the lamb is cooked, place it on a heated serving dish and
leave to rest for 10–15 minutes in the turned-off oven, with the door
open. Keep the bean mixture hot and when the lamb has rested add
the bean mixture to the dish. Garnish with sprigs of flat-leaved
parsley and serve.

● Brittany is famous for its lamb – tender young animals that graze
on the salt marshes off the coast. Dried white beans are the
traditional garnish for this dish, and it is excellent served with tiny
new potatoes and carrots.

 soaking the beans, bringing to room temperature,
then 2¼ hours

Herb-breaded lamb cutlets

Serves 4

8 × 75 g /3 oz best end of neck lamb cutlets
freshly ground black pepper
75 g /3 oz fresh white breadcrumbs
15 ml /1 tbls finely chopped fresh parsley
5 ml /1 tsp finely chopped fresh thyme
5 ml /1 tsp finely chopped fresh marjoram
grated zest of ½ lemon
2 large eggs, beaten
salt
60 ml /4 tbls olive oil
For the garnish
sprigs of fresh thyme
sprigs of fresh marjoram

1   Trim most of the fat from the lamb cutlets, leaving only a
narrow layer to keep the meat moist. Season generously with freshly
ground black pepper and leave to come to room temperature.
2   In a shallow dish, mix together the breadcrumbs, finely chopped
parsley, thyme and marjoram, and grated lemon zest.
3   Place the beaten eggs in a separate shallow dish.
4   Season the cutlets with salt to taste and dip them into the beaten
eggs, then toss them in the herbed breadcrumbs, pressing the
coating on firmly.
5   In a frying-pan large enough to take the cutlets in 1 layer, heat
the olive oil. Sauté the cutlets for 3–4 minutes each side, turning
them over once with a spatula (they should be slightly pink inside).
6   Transfer the cooked cutlets to a heated serving platter. Arrange
them in pairs and garnish with sprigs of thyme and marjoram.

bringing to room temperature,
then 30 minutes

Lamb hash parmentier

Serves 6

500 g /1 lb cooked lamb, diced
12 medium-sized potatoes, peeled
salt and ground black pepper
150 g /5 oz butter
2 large eggs, beaten
60 ml /4 tbls olive oil
1 Spanish onion, finely chopped
60 ml /4 tbls freshly grated
    Parmesan cheese

For the tomato sauce

30 ml /2 tbls olive oil
60 ml /4 tbls finely chopped
    onion
800 g /1¾ lb canned, peeled
    tomatoes
2.5 ml /½ tsp dried basil
2.5 ml /½ tsp sugar
salt
freshly ground black pepper

1   For the tomato sauce, heat the olive oil in a small saucepan and
sauté the onion over moderate heat until it is soft and golden.
2   Add the canned tomatoes together with their juices, the dried
basil, sugar and a little salt and freshly ground black pepper to taste
– season lightly at this stage, bearing in mind that the sauce will
reduce as it simmers. Simmer for 20 minutes until the sauce has
thickened, stirring and mashing occasionally with a wooden spoon.
3   Rub the tomato sauce through a sieve and adjust the seasoning.
4   Meanwhile, reserve 4 of the potatoes in a bowl of cold water.
Place the remaining potatoes in a pan of boiling, salted water and
cook until tender. Drain well then return to the pan and mash with
75 g /3 oz butter until quite smooth. Beat in the eggs and season to
taste with salt and freshly ground black pepper. Leave to cool
slightly.
5   Using a piping bag fitted with a 10 mm /½ in nozzle pipe a
border of mashed potato round a large shallow flameproof dish.
6   For the lamb hash, cut the remaining potatoes into 5 mm /¼ in
dice. Blot well with absorbent paper. Heat 25 g /1 oz of butter with
half the oil in a large frying-pan and sauté the diced potatoes for
5–7 minutes or until they are golden brown, shaking the pan and
turning constantly with a spatula. Season with salt and pepper.
Transfer the potatoes to a plate with a slotted spoon and keep warm.
7   In a large, deep frying-pan, heat the remaining butter and oil.
Add the chopped onion and sauté for 5 minutes, stirring
occasionally, until the onions are soft. Add the diced lamb and sauté
for a further 5–7 minutes until the lamb is golden brown, stirring
constantly. Season to taste. Heat the grill to high.
8   Add the cooked, diced potatoes and tomato sauce to the lamb
and bring the mixture to a simmer. Correct the seasoning with salt
and pepper. Pour the mixture into the centre of the piped potato.
Sprinkle the lamb with Parmesan cheese and grill for 7–10 minutes
until golden brown. Serve immediately.

 1 hour

Marinated lamb chops with green butter

Serves 4–6

8–12 small, trimmed loin lamb
    chops
salt and freshly ground black
    pepper
2–3 bay leaves, crumbled
30–45 ml /2–3 tbls finely
    chopped onion
90 ml /6 tbls olive oil
90 ml /6 tbls dry white wine
lamb fat or oil for greasing

parsley sprigs, to garnish
matchstick potatoes, to serve
For the green butter
100 g /4 oz butter, softened
1–2 garlic cloves, crushed
90 ml /6 tbls freshly chopped
    parsley
15–30 ml /1–2 tbls lemon juice
salt and freshly ground black
    pepper

1   Arrange the chops in a large flat dish and season to taste with
freshly ground black pepper. Scatter over the crumbled bay leaves
and finely chopped onion, and pour over the olive oil and dry white
wine. Cover the dish. Leave in a cool place for at least 2 hours,
turning the chops once or twice in the marinade.
2   Meanwhile, prepare the green butter. Place the softened butter
in a mixing bowl, add the crushed garlic, 15–30 ml /1–2 tbls freshly
chopped parsley and beat vigorously with a wooden spoon until
smooth. Beat in the lemon juice and salt and pepper to taste.
3   Form the green butter into marble-sized rounds and chill in the
refrigerator until firm. Roll the chilled rounds of butter into smooth
balls, then roll one at a time in freshly chopped parsley until
completely coated. Arrange in a serving dish, cover loosely with
greaseproof paper and chill in the refrigerator until required.
4   Heat the grill without the grid to very hot 15–20 minutes before
cooking. Grease the grid (with pieces of lamb fat if possible) to
prevent sticking.
5   Drain the chops and arrange on the greased grid. Grill for about
2–3 minutes on each side, turning once. Transfer the chops to a
heated serving platter, garnish with parsley and serve immediately
with the green butter and matchstick potatoes.

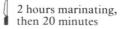 2 hours marinating,
then 20 minutes

Pork

ROASTING PORK

Pork makes some memorable roasts, whether it is simply roasted with a golden crisp crackling or stuffed and rolled to make a delicious and attractive main dish.

Pork is a relatively inexpensive meat, but because of its fat content, most cuts can be roasted. This versatile meat can be roasted on or off the bone, flavoured with a complementary topping or stuffing, or roasted plain and served with delicious accompaniments.

Pork should never be served rare, not only as it may be dangerous to your health, but also because it does not look or taste good like this. The maximum flavour of pork is attained when it is cooked slowly and thoroughly in an uncovered shallow casserole or roasting tin.

Choosing pork for roasting

Good pork will be pale pink, smooth in texture, with a fine grain and a fair proportion of very white fat. The skin should not be too thick. But above all there should be no unpleasant smell. In fact, a sweet smell and a pale pink colour are the best indications of top-quality pork. I have found that if the pork is too dark the meat tends to be dry and tough. If the pork fat is flabby and badly coloured, it is an indication that the pork is not fresh.

How much pork to buy

Allow 100–175 g /4–6 oz boned meat per person, or one chop if you are serving loin. For meat with an average amount of bone, allow 175–275 g /6–10 oz (uncooked weight) meat and bone per person. For meat with a large amount of bone, allow 275–350 g /10–12 oz (uncooked weight) meat and bone.

Cuts of pork for roasting

Leg is one of the most economical cuts of pork, ideal for large families. A half leg can be bought, if you prefer, and the fillet end will be meatier than the knuckle end.
Loin of pork makes a very acceptable roast, especially when the skin has been expertly scored to make the crackling easy to carve. Nowadays, butchers often remove the skin before the meat is sold in order to cut away some of the fat, so valuable for larding and barding meats and covering pâtés.

When buying a loin of pork, always ask your butcher to chine it for you by carving through the bone that runs along the length of the joint, so that when the meat has been cooked the bone can be removed, leaving a much easier job for the carver. Allow one thick chop per person.
Boned loin of pork is also sold for roasting. If you buy a boned loin, ask the butcher for the removed bones. Put them in the roasting tin with the joint, to add extra flavour to the meat. A boned loin of pork is easier to handle than an unboned loin, and makes a more elegant roast. I like to cut slits in a boned loin so that a forcemeat or stuffing can be pressed down between the slices before cooking.

Fillet, also known as tenderloin, is the best cut of pork. It has no fat at all, and is naturally the most expensive of all pork cuts. It is delicious partly cooked, then wrapped in puff pastry and baked until puffed and golden and thoroughly cooked.
Sparerib and shoulder joints are fairly lean, and moderately priced. They make excellent small roasting joints. Shoulder may be bought with the bone, or boned and rolled. This cut makes a delicious roast when filled with herb stuffing.
Blade is cut from behind the head, on top of the foreleg. It is an inexpensive joint which is delicious when roasted, especially when it has been boned and stuffed.
Hand and spring is an inexpensive, well-flavoured joint, cut from the foreleg. It can be boned and rolled for roasting.
Belly is often rather fatty, but it can be rolled and roasted for an inexpensive meal.

Roasting pork

Always take the joint out of the refrigerator in plenty of time to allow it to come to room temperature. Plainly roast joints of pork at 200C /400F /gas 6 for 1 hour per kg /30 minutes per lb allowing an extra 30 minutes for meat that is on the bone. For rolled and stuffed cuts of pork cook at 190C /375F /gas 5 allowing 1 hour per kg /30 minutes per lb plus 20–30 minutes extra for both. If using a meat thermometer cook to a temperature of 82C /180F. To check that pork is thoroughly cooked, pierce the thickest part of the meat with a fine skewer. If the juices are clear, the meat is done; if the juices are pink, the meat is not yet done, so continue cooking until they run clear.
Crackling, the crisply roasted rind or skin of a joint of pork, is an English speciality. (In French cooking the rind is always removed.) The rind of all cuts, except perhaps the belly, can make crisp crackling, but that of the loin and leg are best quality. When buying the joint, ask the butcher to score the rind closely – not more than 5 mm /¼ in apart, in the same direction that you will carve – and deeply, right through to the fat beneath (he has a special knife for this).

Before cooking, brush the rind lightly with oil and rub in salt and pepper. The rind will keep the meat moist; for crisp crackling don't cover or baste the joint. If necessary, increase the oven heat for the last 15 minutes to crisp it.

If the rind has been removed but you still want some crackling, prepare it as above. Cook on a rack, uncovered, in a separate tin.
Crisp crust for rindless joints: baste the joint gently while roasting, then increase the heat for the last 20 minutes of cooking and spread the fat side of the joint thinly with made mustard and thickly with dried breadcrumbs mixed with a little soft brown sugar – dark or light.

Flavouring roast pork

Many interesting flavours can be added to pork in a marinade, topping or stuffing. Try honey, sage, soy sauce, thyme, bay leaf, ginger, onion, garlic, leeks, apple, dried apricots or prunes. Your joint of pork can be moistened with cider, cream, dry wine, tomato sauce or pineapple, apple or orange juice. Or serve roast pork with pickled peaches, baked apples, apple sauce, brandied or pickled pears, fresh or canned pineapple, sauerkraut or a spicy chutney or pickle.

To give your joint of pork a golden glaze, increase the oven temperature to 220C /425F /gas 7 at the end of the cooking time, sprinkle the fat with 30–45 ml /2–3 tbls brown sugar and return the joint to the oven for a few minutes, to glaze.

Roast pork with mustard butter

4 hours marinating, then 2 hours

Serves 4–6
1 loin of pork, 4–6 cutlets
3 fat garlic cloves
½ Spanish onion, finely chopped and mixed with 30 ml /2 tbls olive oil
50 g /2 oz softened butter
5 ml /1 tsp crumbled fresh thyme or 2.5 ml / ½ tsp dried thyme
1 bay leaf, crumbled
15–30 ml /1–2 tbls Dijon mustard
salt and freshly ground black pepper
25 g /1 oz flour
25 g /1 oz butter
watercress, to garnish
puréed potatoes, to serve

1 Ask your butcher to remove the rind and half the thickness of fat from a loin of pork.
2 Remove the pork from the refrigerator 4 hours before you plan to cook it. Score the fat on the loin with a sharp knife in a criss-cross pattern. Cut each garlic clove into 4 slices. Pierce the pork loin in 12 places with a thick skewer and insert a garlic slice and a little chopped onion mixture into each hole.
3 Mix the softened butter, crumbled thyme, bay leaf and mustard to a smooth paste and rub this well into the pork. Sprinkle with salt and pepper, and let the meat stand at room temperature for 4 hours.
4 Heat the oven to 230C /450F /gas 8. Arrange the meat, fat side up, in a roasting tin and brown it for 15 minutes. Reduce the temperature to 180C /350F /gas 4 and continue to roast until the meat is done, about 1¼–1½ hours.
5 Remove as much fat as possible from the juices in the tin, blotting them with a strip of absorbent paper. Mash together the flour with the butter and add this a little at a time to the pan drippings. Stir constantly over a low heat until the sauce thickens. Pour this mustard butter into a small serving dish.
6 Garnish the pork with sprigs of watercress and serve with puréed potatoes and the mustard butter.

Roast pork with mustard butter

Tenderloin stuffed with gooseberries

|| 2 hours standing, then
   1½ hours

Serves 4–6
2 × 500 g /18 oz pork tenderloins
175 g /6 oz green gooseberries
25 g /1 oz butter
1 medium-sized onion, finely chopped
75 g /3 oz fresh wholemeal breadcrumbs
15 ml /1 tbls freshly chopped parsley
15 ml /1 tbls freshly chopped marjoram
a pinch of ground cloves
30 ml /2 tbls dry white wine
30 ml /2 tbls clear honey
For the gravy
150 ml /5 fl oz dry white wine
150 ml /5 fl oz stock

1   Remove the pork from the refrigerator about 2 hours before you intend to roast it. Heat the oven to 190C /375F /gas 5. Slit down one long edge of each tenderloin, leaving it uncut down one side. Open each tenderloin out flat, like a book. Beat the meat with a mallet or rolling pin until thin.
2   Top and tail the gooseberries and finely chop 125 g /4 oz of them. Cut the remaining 50 g /2 oz into half lengthways and reserve.
3   Melt the butter in a frying-pan over a low heat and cook the onion until it is just transparent. Stir in the finely chopped gooseberries and continue cooking until the onion is soft.
4   Remove the pan from the heat and stir the breadcrumbs, herbs, cloves and 30 ml /2 tbls wine into the onion mixture. Cool.
5   Spread the mixture on the open pork tenderloins, reshape each piece and tie up like a parcel with strong thread or cotton string. Lay the tenderloins side by side on a rack in a tin and roast for 45 minutes.
6   Take the tin out of the oven, remove the rack and put the pork in the bottom of the tin. Spoon the honey over each piece, and arrange the reserved gooseberries on top.
7   Mix together the wine and stock and pour into the tin around the meat. Cook in the oven for a further 15 minutes.
8   Transfer the pork to a serving platter and carefully remove the thread or string without dislodging the gooseberries. Remove any fat from the pan juices by blotting with absorbent paper, then strain into a sauce-boat and hand round separately with the pork. Cut the meat into slices at the table so that the topping is shown to best advantage.

Cantonese roast pork

|| 15 minutes, 4 hours marinating,
   then about 50 minutes

Serves 4; serves 8 with 3–4 other dishes
900 g–1.1 kg /2–2½ lb boneless, rindless
*   pork in one piece, such as leg, blade or*
*   neck cuts with a little fat on the outside*
about 30 ml /2 tbls thin honey

For the marinade
30 ml /2 tbls hoisin sauce
30 ml /2 tbls canned ground yellow bean
*   sauce*
60 ml /4 tbls thin soy sauce
90 ml /6 tbls sugar
15 ml /1 tbls Shaohsing wine or medium-dry
*   sherry*
5 ml /1 tsp salt

1   Cut the pork into 4 strips lengthways. Leave any fat on for added flavour.
2   Make 3–4 diagonal cuts across the width of each strip of pork, cutting only ¾ of the way through so as not to cut the strip into pieces. This allows the marinade to penetrate and is the traditional presentation.
3   Mix the ingredients for the marinade in a large bowl. Add the pork strips and coat them all over with the marinade, piercing them with a fork for better absorption. Leave the mixture at room temperature for 4 hours, turning the strips over every 30 minutes with a fork and repricking them.
4   Heat the oven to 190C /375F /gas 5. When hot, drain the strips of meat, reserving the marinade, and put them side by side on a rack in the top third of the oven. On the shelf below put a roasting tin filled with water to a depth of about 15 mm /½ in. Cook for 30 minutes, by which time the top of the meat will already be reddish brown.
5   Remove the rack from the oven, dip each strip of meat into the marinade and return them to the rack with their bottom sides up. Cook for another 10–15 minutes, then reduce the heat to 180C /350F /gas 4 and continue cooking for 15 minutes.
6   Transfer the slices to a rack. Brush them all over with the honey, making sure you don't miss the crevices.
7   Bring the reserved marinade to a boil in a small saucepan and pour it into a warmed sauce-boat. Slice the meat and serve.

● Hoisin sauce is available from specialist shops and Chinese supermarkets.

Roast loin of pork with apricots

Use plump, dried dessert apricots for this dish, not the very shrivelled ones which have too sharp and strong a flavour. Prepared with care, this roast is sensationally pretty.

|| 2 hours standing, 45 minutes,
   then 1¼–1½ hours roasting

Serves 6
1.4 kg /3 lb loin of pork, boned
225 g /8 oz plump dried apricots
50 g /2 oz sugar
freshly ground black pepper
salt
1.5 ml /¼ tsp dried thyme
30 ml /2 tbls softened butter

1   Remove the pork from the refrigerator about 2 hours before you intend to roast it. Remove the rind from the pork, and some of the fat, leaving just a thin layer. Leave the

joint to stand until it has lost its chill.
2   Meanwhile, put the apricots in a pan with the sugar and 600 ml /1 pt water. Bring to the boil, then cover the pan and simmer for 10 minutes. Remove the lid and simmer for a further 10 minutes, or until the apricots are soft but still firm. Drain.
3   Heat the oven to 200C /400F /gas 6. Make horizontal cuts in the pork at 25 mm / 1 in intervals, to a depth of 4 cm /1½ in. Season the joint all over with freshly ground black pepper. Sprinkle only the fat with salt. Push the apricots into the slits. The meat will contract during cooking and push the apricots towards the surface, so press them in as deeply as possible.
4   Line the roasting tin with foil. Tie the joint at intervals with string, then place it in the foil-lined tin. Sprinkle the thyme over the meat, then spread with the butter.
5   Roast the joint in the oven for 1¼–1½ hours, basting with the juices in the tin from time to time and covering the joint with foil half-way through the cooking time to prevent the apricots caramelizing. It may be necessary to add a spoonful or two of water to the roasting tin to prevent the juices in the tin drying out and burning.
6   Remove the strings from the joint and transfer it to a heated serving platter. Remove any fat from the pan juices by blotting with absorbent paper then use the juices to glaze the meat. Serve at once.

Roast loin of pork à la provençale

Ask the butcher to skin, chine and bone the loin of pork, so that it will be easier to carve when roasted. Your 1.4 kg /3 lb pork loin should consist of 6 chops so that it will serve 6 people easily.

🔪🔪 45 minutes, 2 hours standing,
🍴🍴 then 1½ hours

Serves 6
1.4 kg /3 lb loin of pork (6 large chops),
*   boned, skinned and chined*
6 dried mushrooms
2 large garlic cloves
freshly ground black pepper
salt
few sprigs of parsley, to garnish
For the stuffed vegetables
15 g /½ oz butter
45 ml /3 tbls finely chopped onion
225 g /8 oz pork sausage-meat
90 ml /6 tbls freshly grated Parmesan cheese
15 ml /1 tbls finely chopped fresh parsley
2.5 ml /½ tsp each finely chopped fresh
*   tarragon and chives*
6 large ripe tomatoes
175 g /6 oz large white mushrooms, stems
*   removed*

1   Soak the dried mushrooms in warm water for about 30 minutes. Pour the mushrooms and their soaking water into a small pan and simmer gently until the mushrooms are soft and swollen, and the water has almost evaporated. Drain off any remaining liquid and cut any hard ends off the mushroom stalks.

2   Reserve 3 of the mushrooms, then cut each remaining mushroom into 4 strips, making 12 strips in all. Cut 1 of the garlic cloves into 12 slivers. Reserve the other garlic clove for later use.

3   Make 12 deep slits in the pork fat with the point of a sharp knife and push a strip of mushroom and a sliver of garlic well down into each slit. Season the joint all over with freshly ground black pepper. Sprinkle only the fat with salt. Leave the pork to stand at room temperature for 2 hours, so that the meat absorbs the flavours and loses its chill. Towards the end of this time, heat the oven to 200C /400F /gas 6.

4   Transfer the pork to a roasting tin and roast for 1½ hours or until thoroughly cooked, basting the pork occasionally with the juices in the roasting tin. It may be necessary to add a spoonful or two of water from time to time to prevent the juices in the tin drying up and burning.

5   Meanwhile, prepare the stuffed vegetables. Finely chop the remaining garlic clove. Melt the butter in a small pan and

Roast loin of pork à la provençale

sauté the finely chopped onion and garlic for 3–4 minutes, until soft. Leave to cool. Finely chop the reserved cooked, dried mushrooms and place them in a bowl with the cooled onion mixture, sausage-meat, Parmesan cheese, parsley, tarragon and chives. Mix the ingredients together well and season to taste with salt and freshly ground black pepper.

6   Slice off the tops of the tomatoes and scoop out the seeds, taking care not to break the shells. Lightly sprinkle the insides of the tomatoes with salt, then leave them upside down on a rack for a few minutes, to drain. Wipe the large mushrooms clean. Stuff the tomatoes and mushrooms with the sausage-meat mixture, smoothing the top surfaces neatly.

7   About 30 minutes before the end of the cooking time for the pork, place the stuffed tomatoes around the joint; 10 minutes later, place the stuffed mushrooms around the joint. Complete the cooking.

8   Transfer the roast pork to a hot serving platter, surround it with the stuffed tomatoes and mushrooms and garnish with a few sprigs of parsley. Remove any excess fat from the roasting tin by blotting with absorbent paper, then moisten the pork and stuffed vegetables with the remaining juices. Serve the joint immediately.

Roast leg of pork

3 hours standing,
then 3½–4 hours

Serves 8–10
2.7–3.2 kg /6–7 lb leg of pork, rind scored
oil, for brushing
salt and freshly ground black pepper
425 ml /15 fl oz vegetable or chicken stock,
home-made or from a cube
30 ml /2 tbls flour
25 g /1 oz butter

1   Remove the leg of pork from the
refrigerator 3 hours before you plan to cook
it so it can come to room temperature.
2   Heat the oven to 200C /400F /gas 6.
Lightly brush the surface of the pork rind
with oil and rub in salt and pepper
3   Put the leg in a large roasting tray and
cook for 3¼–3¾ hours without basting to
make the crackling really crisp. Increase the
temperature for the last 15 minutes if
necessary. Test to check the pork is cooked
by piercing the thickest part with a fine
skewer: the juices should run clear.
4   Transfer the meat to a serving platter
and keep warm. Make the gravy: remove
any excess fat from the juices in the pan.
Add the stock and bring to the boil, scraping
to dislodge any crusty bits. Reduce the heat.
5   Mash the flour and butter together to
form a paste and add, a bit at a time, to the
gravy. Simmer for 2–3 minutes until
thickened and season with salt and pepper.

Roast fillet of pork in pastry

1 hour standing, 1¾ hours,
then 40 minutes cooking

Serves 4
400–450 g /14–16 oz fillet of pork
freshly ground black pepper
40 g /1½ oz butter
400 g /14 oz made weight puff pastry,
defrosted if frozen
50 g /2 oz Parma ham, sliced very thinly
1 small egg, beaten
For the mushroom duxelles
50 g /2 oz butter
1 Spanish onion, finely chopped
450 g /1 lb mushrooms, finely chopped
1.5 ml /¼ tsp powdered dried thyme
salt and freshly ground black pepper
30 ml /2 tbls finely chopped fresh parsley
60 ml /4 tbls fresh white breadcrumbs
2 medium-sized eggs, well beaten

1   Remove the pork from the refrigerator
about 1 hour before you intend to roast it.
Season it all over with freshly ground black
pepper. Leave to come to room temperature.
2   Meanwhile, begin preparing the
duxelles. Melt the 50 g /2 oz butter and
sauté the finely chopped onion for 3–4
minutes. Add the finely chopped mushrooms
and the powdered thyme, then season to
taste with salt and pepper. Cook the mixture
for 30–40 minutes, or until there is no liquid

left. Add the parsley and breadcrumbs to the
pan, mix in the beaten eggs and heat
through to lightly set the eggs. Leave to cool.
3   Heat the 40 g /1½ oz butter in a frying-
pan until it is foaming, and quickly sear the
fillet on all sides. Leave it to cool.
4   Heat the oven to 200C /400F /gas 6.
Roll out the puff pastry to 3 mm /⅛ in
thickness, and cut a rectangle, about 25 cm /
10 in wide, and 5 cm /2 in longer than the
fillet. Reserve the pastry trimmings.
5   Spread half the duxelles down the centre
of the pastry rectangle and place the fillet on
top. Spread the remaining duxelles on the
fillet and top with the Parma ham. Fold one
side of the pastry over the fillet. Brush the
upper surface with a little beaten egg, then
fold over the second side to overlap the first,
and press the edges together to seal. Roll the
pastry ends out flat taking care not to
stretch the pastry, brush the upper side of
the roll with beaten egg, fold over the ends
and press together to seal.
6   Place the pastry-wrapped fillet, joins
downwards, on a lightly dampened baking
sheet. Make 3 holes in the top to allow the
steam to escape, and decorate around the
holes with 'leaves' made from pastry trimmings, attaching them with a little beaten
egg. Brush the pastry all over with beaten
egg, and lightly score the top with a knife,
crossways, diagonally or in V-shapes.
7   Bake for 40 minutes, until the pork is
thoroughly cooked and the pastry is puffed
up and golden brown. Slice and serve.

Roast leg of pork

Carving a fillet end of leg

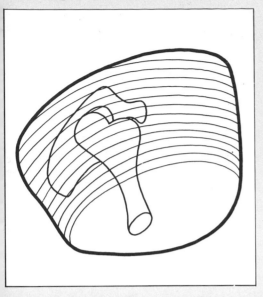

Carve down on the thick side towards the bone along the length of the joint.

Turn over and carve the other side in the same way.

Carving a hand and spring

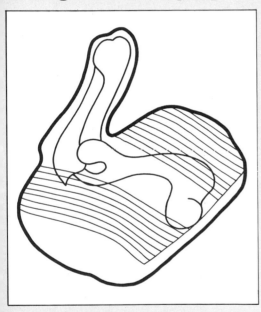

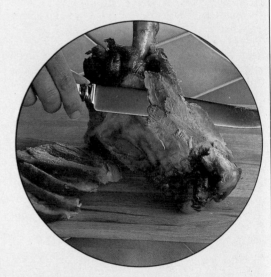

As the meat is fattier at one side, carve alternate slices, 5 mm /¼ in thick, from each side. Serve both lean and fatty meat.

When the bone is reached, turn the joint over and cut slices from each side of the bone, above and below it.

Carving a loin

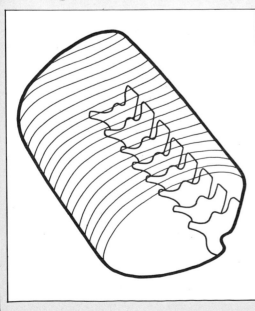

The loin is a better shape cooked with the chine bone (the butcher may remove it). Remove it with a knife after cooking.

Carve the loin across the grain vertically into slices. If the loin has crackling, remove a section, then carve this on the board.

GRILLING PORK

Succulent loin chops with a citrus stuffing, sweet and sour Chinese-style spareribs, tender fillet steaks wrapped round with bacon – all these delicious things are made by grilling pork.

I consider pork an ideal candidate for the grill – pork chops are at their best grilled until the meat is tender and tasty and the fat around the edge is crisp and crunchy, and if you're in an Oriental mood it's hard to beat a Polynesian saté – lean cubes of pork in a nutty, piquant marinade.

What pork to grill?

Always choose young, tender pork for grilling. Chops come from both the middle loin and the chump end. Some middle loin chops may contain a slice of kidney, while chops from the back of the chump are particularly meaty. These chops are lean; choose economical sparerib chops from the neck for meat marbled with a little fat.

The ribs themselves, cut Chinese style from the belly, can be separated for cooking,
but if cooked in rack form they will be easier to handle and more moist to eat.

The lean meat of the fillet end of the leg can be cut into steaks which take well to grilling, especially if they are marinated or served with a flavourful sauce.

Fillet of pork – sometimes called tenderloin – is a very lean, tender cut. Try using it as you would fillet of beef which is sliced into tournedos: make pork tournedos by cutting the fillet into neat chunks. Surround them with bacon to keep them moist and juicy while you grill them – they're delicious, and much cheaper than beef fillet!

For kebabs, any lean, boneless pork will do. Shoulder and fillet are probably the best as leg tends to be a little dryer, but all three are tender.

Preparing pork for grilling

Always trim off any excess fat from pork chops, leaving just a thin border of fat round the meat to help moisten it during cooking. Slash the fat at intervals with a sharp knife to prevent the meat from curling up while grilling.

Sometimes when you buy pork the rind is still on. This must be removed from the meat before cooking, but don't throw it away; it is a useful source of fat. Render the rinds down with any trimmings of fat that you cut from the meat, and use the resulting fat for frying.

Marinating: marinating for several hours or overnight is a good way to tenderize meat, and to add moistness and flavour. There are two kinds of marinade for pork – wet and dry. Wet marinades, which form a 'bath' for the meat, usually contain oil; an acidic liquid such as wine, vinegar or lemon juice, and aromatics – herbs, spices and vegetables, while the simplest dry marinade consists only of salt, spices and herbs rubbed into the meat.

If you marinate the meat in your refrigerator, remember to let it come up to room temperature before grilling it.

Seasoning: if you have not marinated your pork, season it with freshly ground black pepper when you take it from the refrigerator to bring it to room temperature; then, just before grilling it, sprinkle it with salt and more pepper and brush it with oil.

Grilling pork

Always heat the grill to maximum before starting to cook, but remember that the grid should be cold, so remove it from the grill until you are ready to cook. Brush the grid with oil and place the pork on it. Grill, with the grid 7.5 cm /3 in from the heat, until the meat is well done.

Very lean cuts of pork should be brushed with oil or a marinade during grilling to keep them moist. My pork tournedos are tied round with bacon to keep them juicy.

Pork should always be well done (it is dangerous to eat it underdone) but it should not be dry. To test that the pork is done, slip a knife into the meat beside the bone, where the meat takes longest to cook. It should be an even beige colour right through.

Polynesian pork saté and
Pork tournedos with grilled mushrooms

Polynesian pork saté

🍴🍴 10 minutes, at least 2 hours marinating, then 25 minutes

Serves 4
1 kg /2 lb lean, boneless shoulder of pork
6 Brazil nuts, grated
15 ml /1 tbls coriander seeds, crushed
2 garlic cloves, finely chopped
1 Spanish onion, grated
30 ml /2 tbls lemon juice
15–30 ml /1–2 tbls brown sugar
60 ml /4 tbls soy sauce
5 ml /1 tsp cracked black peppercorns
cayenne pepper
olive oil
For the garnish
lime wedges
sprigs of flat-leaved parsley
For the salad
1 lettuce
1 bunch of watercress, trimmed
1 avocado
1 garlic clove, halved
30 ml /2 tbls finely chopped chives
salt and freshly ground black pepper
60 ml /4 tbls olive oil
15 ml /1 tbls wine vinegar
about 20 ml /4 tsp lemon juice
8 whole, shelled Brazil nuts

1 Cut the pork into 32 × 25 mm /1 in cubes. Combine the remaining ingredients, except the oil, in a large bowl. Add the pork cubes, turn to coat, then leave to marinate for at least 2 hours, turning occasionally. Heat the grill without the grid to high.
2 Thread 8 cubes of pork onto each of 4 skewers. Brush the grill grid with olive oil and place the skewers on the grid. Grill, 7.5 cm /3 in from the heat, for 10 minutes or until cooked through, turning frequently.
3 While the pork is cooking, make the salad: rub a salad bowl with the cut garlic clove. Arrange the lettuce and watercress in the bowl. Chop the garlic and add with the chives and salt and pepper to taste. Dress with the olive oil and wine vinegar.
4 Peel and slice the avocado and sprinkle with lemon juice. Toss the salad and garnish with the avocado and Brazil nuts.
5 Arrange the skewers on a heated serving dish, garnish with lime wedges and parsley and serve once, accompanied by the salad.

Pork chops with grapefruit stuffing

🍴 standing, then 45 minutes

Serves 4
4 loin pork chops, trimmed
salt and freshly ground black pepper
50 g /2 oz butter
1 Spanish onion, finely chopped
2 celery stalks, finely chopped
grated zest of ½ grapefruit
30 ml /2 tbls grapefruit juice
60 ml /4 tbls fresh breadcrumbs
olive oil for greasing

1 Slice the pork chops horizontally through the width on the side opposite the bone to make a pocket, leaving a 25 mm /1 in border uncut all around the chops. Season with pepper, bring to room temperature, then season with salt and more pepper.
2 In a small saucepan heat 25 g /1 oz of the butter and sauté the finely chopped onion and celery for 5 minutes, or until soft, stirring constantly. Add the grated grapefruit zest, grapefruit juice and breadcrumbs and season with salt and pepper to taste. Leave to cool.
3 Heat the grill, without the grid to high. Stuff each pork chop with one quarter of the stuffing and sew up the cut side with strong thread.
4 When ready to grill, brush the grid of the grill pan with a little olive oil. Place the pork chops on the grid and grill 7.5 cm /3 in from the heat for 5–6 minutes on each side or until cooked through, basting constantly with the remaining butter.
5 Remove the thread from the pork chops and arrange on a heated serving platter. Serve immediately.

● Try substituting grated orange zest and orange juice for the grapefruit zest and juice in this recipe.

Pork tournedos with grilled mushrooms

🍴 10 minutes, standing, then 20 minutes

Serves 4
500 g /1 lb pork fillet
4 slices streaky bacon, rinds removed
freshly ground black pepper
salt
olive oil
250 g /8 oz button mushrooms, stalks removed
watercress sprigs, to garnish

1 Cut the pork fillet into 4 pieces – each will be about 6 cm /2½ in long. Stand each piece on end and flatten with the hand until it is 5 cm /2 in wide and 25 mm /1 in thick. Wrap a slice of bacon around each steak and tie in place with fine string. Season on both sides with freshly ground black pepper and allow to come to room temperature.
2 Heat the grill without the grid to high. Season the pork tournedos on both sides with salt and more freshly ground black pepper, and brush with olive oil.
3 Brush the grill grid with oil and place the pork tournedos on the grid. Grill, with the grid 7.5 cm /3 in from the heat, for 10 minutes, turning after 7 minutes and brushing again with olive oil.
4 Place the mushrooms on the grid with the tournedos and brush them with olive oil, then grill for a further 5 minutes, brushing the mushrooms with oil occasionally.
5 Remove the strings from the steaks, leaving the bacon in place surrounding the tournedos like a collar. Arrange the steaks on a heated serving platter. Garnish with the mushrooms and watercress and serve.

Grilled spareribs

Serve these sweet and tangy spareribs as a starter for 6–8 or, as part of a Chinese meal, a main course for 4.

⏱ 10 minutes, at least 2 hours marinating, then 10 minutes

Serves 4–8
700 g /1½ lb Chinese-cut pork spareribs
oil for greasing
flat-leaved parsley, to garnish
For the marinade
100 g /4 oz apricot jam
15 ml /1 tbls lemon juice
15 ml /1 tbls brown sugar
30 ml /2 tbls soy sauce

1 First prepare the marinade: heat the apricot jam with the lemon juice until the jam has melted. Add the brown sugar and soy sauce, then boil the marinade over a high heat for 5 minutes, until syrupy.
2 Lay the spareribs in a shallow dish, pour over the marinade and leave to marinate for at least 2 hours.
3 Heat the grill without the grid to high.
4 Brush the grill grid with oil and place the spareribs on the grid. Grill, with the grid 7.5 cm /3 in from the heat, for 10 minutes or until well done, turning frequently and brushing with the marinade. Serve immediately, garnished with parsley.

Pork chops in a cider marinade

Vintage cider, sweet and strong, is ideal for this unusual and tasty dish.

⏱ 10 minutes, then 4 hours marinating, then 20 minutes

Serves 4
4 pork loin chops, trimmed
7.5 ml /1½ tsp ground cinnamon
1 large garlic clove, finely chopped
pinch of salt
150 ml /5 fl oz vintage cider
30 ml /2 tbls cider vinegar
oil for greasing

1 Crush together the cinnamon, garlic and salt and spread this paste over both sides of the chops. Lay the chops in a flat dish. Pour over the cider and the cider vinegar and marinate at room temperature for 4 hours.
2 Heat the grill without the grid to high. Brush the grid with oil.
3 Remove the chops from their marinade and lay them on the grill rack. Grill them, turning once, until they are golden brown and cooked through, about 15 minutes.
4 Place the chops on a warmed serving dish and keep warm. Remove the grill rack and set the grill pan on top of the stove on a medium heat. Pour in the marinade and bring to the boil, stirring in the crusty bits from the bottom of the pan. Simmer for 2 minutes, then spoon the cider sauce over the chops and serve at once.

Pork and prune brochettes

The affinity of prunes for pork is well known, but you can vary these brochettes by substituting pineapple chunks or even chicken livers for the prunes. Or soak the prunes in red wine or strong black tea instead of water.

⏱ 15–20 minutes, 2 hours marinating, then 40 minutes

Serves 4
500 g /1 lb pork fillet
150 ml /5 fl oz olive oil
juice of 1 lemon
½ Spanish onion, finely chopped
30 ml /2 tbls pickling spice
5 ml /1 tsp dried sage
salt and freshly ground black pepper
24 prunes with stones
1 L /2 pt boiling water
12 thin slices streaky bacon, rinds removed
oil for greasing

1 Cut the pork into 20 cubes. In a large bowl, combine the olive oil, lemon juice, finely chopped onion, pickling spice and sage, adding salt and pepper to taste.
2 Marinate the pork cubes in this mixture for at least 2 hours, turning them

Grilled spareribs

occasionally to ensure that they remain evenly coated. At the same time, cover the prunes with the boiling water and leave to swell and soften for 2 hours.
3 Pour the prunes with their soaking liquid into a saucepan. Bring to the boil, then simmer for 10 minutes, or until the prunes are soft but not disintegrating. Meanwhile, cut the streaky bacon slices in half. Drain the pork cubes thoroughly, reserving the marinade, and brush off the spices.
4 Heat the grill without the grid to high and brush the grid with oil. Drain the prunes and, using a sharp knife, slit each one along one side and remove the stone. Wrap each prune in a half slice of bacon.
5 Thread the marinated pork cubes and bacon-wrapped prunes alternately onto 4 skewers, starting and ending each brochette with a prune.
6 Lay the brochettes on the grill grid and grill, with the grid 7.5 cm /3 in from the heat, for 10 minutes or until cooked through, turning the brochettes frequently and brushing with the marinade to keep them moist.
7 Season the brochettes with salt and freshly ground black pepper and arrange them on a heated serving platter. Pour over any juices from the grill pan and serve the brochettes immediately.

Grilled pork chops with orange slices

 15 minutes preparation, at least 4 hours marinating, then 20 minutes

Serves 4

4 × 25 mm /1 in thick loin pork chops, weighing 175 g /6 oz each
30–45 ml /2–3 tbls soy sauce
60 ml /4 tbls olive oil
5 ml /1 tsp ground ginger
5 ml /1 tsp dry mustard
30 ml /2 tbls brown sugar
2.5 ml /½ tsp salt
1.5 ml /¼ tsp cracked black peppercorns
olive oil for greasing

For the garnish

12 thin slices of unpeeled orange
watercress sprigs

1 Wipe each chop with absorbent paper and trim off the excess fat, leaving a narrow border only. Using a sharp knife, slash the fat at intervals to prevent the chops from curling up under the heat of the grill.
2 In a small bowl, combine the soy sauce, olive oil, ground ginger, dry mustard, brown sugar, salt and cracked peppercorns. Rub the mixture well into both sides of each chop, lay the chops in a shallow dish, cover and leave to marinate for at least 4 hours.
3 Heat the grill without the grid to high.
4 Brush the grill grid with olive oil and place the chops on the grid. Grill, with the grid 7.5 cm /3 in from the heat, for 8 minutes each side, or until cooked through, turning the chops once and brushing occasionally with the marinade.
5 Arrange the grilled chops on a heated serving dish and garnish with the orange slices and sprigs of watercress. Serve the chops immediately.

Sausage patties with spicy cucumber relish

🍴 50 minutes

Serves 4

500 g /1 lb lean boneless pork shoulder
4 shallots
5 ml /1 tsp ground coriander
2.5 ml /½ tsp ground ginger
30 ml /2 tbls finely chopped fresh parsley
salt and freshly ground black pepper
oil for frying and greasing

For the cucumber relish

½ cucumber, peeled
30 ml /2 tbls thinly sliced shallots
½ hot green chilli, very thinly sliced
30–45 ml /2–3 tbls lemon juice
20–30 ml /4–6 tsp sugar

1 First make the cucumber relish: cut the cucumber in half lengthways, then slice each half very thinly. Put the sliced cucumber in a bowl with the thinly sliced shallots and green chilli, lemon juice and sugar. Mix lightly, then chill until ready to serve.
2 Put the pork and shallots through the finest blade of your mincer, or blend them in a food processor. Add the coriander, ginger and finely chopped parsley and season with salt and freshly ground black pepper. To test the patty mixture for seasoning, heat 5 ml /1 tsp oil in a small frying-pan and cook a small piece of the patty mixture. Taste, then adjust the seasoning, if necessary.
3 Heat the grill without the grid to high. Mould the pork into 4 patties, each 5–7.5 cm /2–3 in wide and 25 mm /1 in thick.
4 Brush the grill grid with oil and place the patties on the grid. Grill, with the grid 7.5 cm /3 in from the heat, for 15 minutes, or until cooked through, turning once. Serve immediately, with the cucumber relish.

Grilled pork chops with orange slices

PAN FRYING PORK

Chops are not the only cut of pork that can be pan fried; try cooking fillet, belly and loin in the same way – served fresh from the pan, and cooked to perfection every time.

Meaty pork chops and tender pork from the fillet and loin, as well as lean belly, are all perfect for pan frying. Cheaper than the prime cuts of beef and veal, they are nonetheless tasty, succulent cuts that cook quickly.

Choosing pork for pan frying

Raw pork should be light, pale pink and slightly moist; avoid pork that looks wet. Although pork chops need a layer of fat when cooking to protect the meat from hardening, avoid excess fat. This probably indicates an older animal and the flesh will be over-rich to most tastes. Ask the butcher to trim off any protruding corners of bone.

Choose tender pork for pan frying. Tenderloin chops are the smallest, and probably the most tender. Loin chops are slightly larger and give a good portion of meat. Leg steaks are boneless as, often, are chump chops. These are meaty and very large – they will easily serve two.

Pork fillet, known in some areas as tenderloin, is an extremely delicate, tender cut with no fat at all. The whole piece usually weighs about 350 g /12 oz and can be used for escalopes or medallions.

Noisettes are similar to medallions except that they are surrounded with a thin border of fat. Make them from the 'eye' of the middle loin.

For a really economical family meal, choose thin slices of pork from the thick end of the belly – the slices should be as lean as possible.

Preparing pork for pan frying

Take the meat out of the refrigerator and wipe it dry with absorbent paper. Trim off some of the fat from chops, but leave a narrow border to keep the meat moist while cooking. It can always be cut off after cooking if someone doesn't like fat. Season the meat with freshly ground black pepper, then leave it to come to room temperature. Season with salt just before cooking. If you are coating the meat with egg and breadcrumbs, however, it's a good idea to chill the coated pork to let it firm up.

To make pork medallions, cut 25 mm /1 in thick slices from the fillet (tenderloin) and, if you wish, tie each one securely round the middle with fine string so that it holds its shape. Make noisettes from a skinned, boned and rolled loin in the same way.

Pan frying pork

Use a combination of butter and olive oil if you wish, but the tastiest fat to use is that trimmed from the outside of the chops. To render this, making it give up its fat, chop it, then fry it, with a little butter and olive oil if necessary, until the pieces shrivel and crisp up. Remove the pieces from the pan with a slotted spoon and use the remaining fat for frying. Lard is another alternative; it is, after all, rendered and clarified pork fat and will give the dish a true 'porky' flavour.

Heat the fat in a heavy frying-pan over a medium-high heat. Add the meat, making sure it is flat on the surface of the pan, and fry quickly for 2 minutes on each side to seal and brown. Then lower the heat to medium and cook until well done, turning once. For the cooking times for different cuts and weights of chops see the chart below.

Pork should always be served well cooked: moist and juicy but without a trace of pink in the flesh. To test the meat is thoroughly cooked through slip a knife blade down between the meat and the bone – where it takes longest to cook – and, if necessary, cook for a few minutes longer.

Pork escalopes, noisettes and medallions will cook more quickly, but should still be well done.

For the simplest sauce, deglaze the pan by adding 5–10 ml /1–2 tsp water, stock or wine; as it heats through stir well and scrape any sediment off the bottom of the pan. When the sauce is bubbling, stir in a small knob of butter to make it glossy, pour it over the chops and serve at once.

Pork chops with soured cream

standing,
then 25 minutes

Serves 4

4 loin pork chops
60 ml /4 tbls Moutarde de Meaux or any other coarse-grained mustard
2.5 ml /½ tsp ground ginger
1.5 ml /¼ tsp freshly ground black pepper
1.5 ml /¼ tsp salt
30 ml /2 tbls olive oil
150 ml /5 fl oz soured cream
parsley sprigs, to garnish

1 Trim any excess fat from the chops. Leave them to come to room temperature.
2 Mix together the mustard, ginger, pepper, salt and 1.5 ml /¼ tsp of the oil.
3 Spread one third of the mustard mixture

Cooking perfect pork chops

*Marinated chops will take about 1 minute longer on each side.

Cut	Weight	Thickness	Cooking time each side*	Result
Chump chop	450–550 g /1–1¼ lb	5–3 cm /1–1¼ in	12 minutes	well-done but juicy
Tenderloin chop	175 g /6 oz	15 mm /½ in	7–8 minutes	well-done but juicy
	300 g /11 oz	25 mm /1 in	10 minutes	well-done but juicy
Loin chop	275–300 g /10–11 oz	20 mm /¾ in	7 minutes	well-done but juicy
	350 g /12 oz	25 mm /1 in	8 minutes	well-done but juicy

*Including initial 2 minutes at high heat on each side.

over the chops on one side only. Heat the remaining oil in a large frying-pan over moderate heat and place the chops in the pan, *uncoated* side downwards. Cook for 7-10 minutes.

4 Turn the chops over and cook for another 7-10 minutes. Meanwhile spread the upturned cooked sides of the chops with another third of the mustard mixture.

5 Once cooked, remove the chops from the pan and keep warm on a heated serving dish. Stir the soured cream into the juices left in the pan. Mix in the remaining mustard mixture and heat through over a low heat for one minute, stirring well, then pour over the chops. Garnish and serve.

Pork chops with almonds

standing,
then 20 minutes

Serves 4
4 × 250 g /8 oz pork chops, about 15 mm /½ in thick
freshly ground black pepper
salt
20 ml /4 tsp curry paste (see note)
50 g /2 oz butter
30 ml /2 tbls olive oil
75 g /3 oz flaked almonds
1 lime, sliced, to garnish

1 Trim the excess fat from the pork chops, leaving a thin layer to protect the meat. Season with freshly ground black pepper and leave to come to room temperature. Just before cooking, season with salt.
2 Using a palette knife, spread 2.5 ml /½ tsp curry paste evenly on each side of each pork chop.
3 Heat the butter and olive oil in a frying-pan large enough to take the pork chops in one layer. When the foaming subsides, cook

Pork with soured cream

the pork chops over a moderate heat for 5–6 minutes on one side. Turn them with a spatula to avoid releasing the juices and cook for a further 5–6 minutes or until tender and cooked through.
4 Transfer the pork chops to a heated serving platter with a slotted spoon. Keep warm.
5 Add the flaked almonds to the frying-pan and sauté over a high heat for 1–2 minutes, stirring occasionally with a wooden spoon.
6 Remove the almonds with a slotted spoon and sprinkle them over the pork chops. Serve the chops immediately, garnished with the lime slices.

● Curry paste has a milder, less harsh taste than many commercial curry powders. You can find it in better supermarkets and delicatessens. Alternatively, mix a good-quality curry powder with a little water to make a smooth paste and use this instead.

Pork escalopes mimosa

30 minutes,
plus 30 minutes chilling (optional)

Serves 4
500 g /18 oz pork tenderloin, trimmed
well-seasoned flour for dusting
1 egg
75 g /3 oz dry white breadcrumbs
15 ml /1 tbls oil
25 g /1 oz butter
1 large lemon in 8 wedges
chives
flat-leaved parsley
For the mimosa garnish
1 egg, hard boiled, with the yolk sieved and the white finely chopped
5 ml /1 tsp finely grated lemon zest
15 ml /1 tbls snipped chives, spring onion tops or parsley

1 Using a sharp knife, cut the pork across into 10 mm /⅓ in slices. Lay each slice flat between 2 pieces of dampened greaseproof paper and beat gently with a rolling pin.
2 Dust each escalope lightly on both sides with seasoned flour. Beat the egg with 10 ml /2 tsp water, dip each escalope in the egg and then toss in the breadcrumbs until well coated. Lay flat on greaseproof paper and press on the coating with a palette knife. If possible, leave the meat in a cold place, lightly covered, for at least 30 minutes for the coating to firm up.
3 When ready to cook, heat the oil and butter in a large frying-pan. When sizzling, fry as many of the escalopes as the pan will hold for 3–4 minutes on each side, until golden and cooked through. Lift out, drain on absorbent paper and keep warm while you cook the remainder.
4 Meanwhile, combine the hard-boiled egg, lemon zest and chives, spring onion or parsley to make the mimosa garnish. When all the escalopes are cooked, pile them on a warmed serving platter, sprinkle with the garnish and arrange the lemon wedges in the centre with the chives and parsley.

Pork with juniper berries

🕒 15 minutes, standing,
then 30 minutes

Serves 4

12 thin slices of pork fillet
10 ml /2 tsp juniper berries, crushed
salt and freshly ground black pepper
100 g /4 oz butter
60 ml /4 tbls dry white wine
275 g /10 oz fresh green beans
350 g /12 oz canned pimentos, drained
10 ml /2 tsp sugar

1 Beat the pork slices between sheets of greaseproof paper with a meat bat or rolling pin until really thin. Season with juniper berries and pepper and bring to room temperature, then season with salt and more pepper.
2 Melt the butter in a large frying-pan over a low heat and add the white wine, letting it bubble for 1–2 minutes. Place 3–4 slices of pork in the pan, in one layer. Sauté

for 3–4 minutes each side, remove and keep warm. Repeat until all the slices are cooked.
3 Add the beans and cook for 5 minutes over medium-low heat Stir in the pimentos and sugar and cook for 4–5 minutes. Season and pile onto a serving platter.
4 Lay the slices of pork on top of the beans and pimentos, pour over the remaining pan juices and serve immediately.

Breaded pork chops with rosemary

🕒 1 hour,
including chilling

Serves 4

4 thick loin pork chops
5 ml /1 tsp grated onion
5 ml /1 tsp finely chopped fresh parsley
2.5 ml /½ tsp dried rosemary, crumbed
1 egg
salt and freshly ground black pepper
275 g /10 oz fresh white breadcrumbs
25 g /1 oz butter
30 ml /2 tbls olive oil

Pork with juniper berries

1 Mix the grated onion, finely chopped parsley, dried rosemary and egg in a wide, shallow dish. Beat well with a fork and season generously with salt and freshly ground black pepper. Put the breadcrumbs in another wide dish.
2 Trim the excess fat from the pork chops. Chop the fat and reserve it. Coat each chop first with the egg mixture, allowing the excess to drain back into the dish, and then in breadcrumbs, patting the coating on firmly. Put them on a plate and chill for at least 30 minutes to set the coating and allow the flavours to permeate the meat.
3 When you are ready to cook, fry the chopped fat trimmings in a heavy frying-pan with the butter and olive oil until they shrivel up and turn crisp. Remove the fat pieces with a slotted spoon and discard them. There should be a generous layer of melted fat in the pan.
4 Lay the pork chops in the hot fat, 2 at a time if necessary. The fat should be hot enough to foam when the chops come in contact with it. Fry over a high heat for 2 minutes on each side, reduce the heat to

medium and cook for a further 5–6 minutes on each side, until the chops are cooked through and crisp and golden on the outside. When the chops are cooked, the meat in contact with the bone should be quite beige, without a trace of pink. Remove the chops from the pan and drain on absorbent paper. Transfer to a heated dish and serve.

Pork medallions with mustard-cheese glaze

preparing medallions,
then 10 minutes

Serves 4

1 large fillet of pork, about 500 g /1 lb
salt and freshly ground black pepper
25 g /1 oz butter
olive oil
50 g /2 oz Gruyère cheese, finely grated
5–10 ml /1 2 tsp Dijon mustard

Wipe the pork and cut into 8 × 25–40 mm /1–1½ in thick medallions. Flatten each with the palm of your hand, and tie round with string. Season with black pepper and leave to come to room temperature. Just before cooking season with salt.

2 Heat 25 g /1 oz butter and 30 ml /2 tbls olive oil in a heavy frying-pan over medium heat and fry the medallions for 7 minutes, turning once. Heat the grill to high.

3 Mix the Gruyère cheese and Dijon mustard. Spread over the pork medallions.

4 Brush the grid of the grill pan with oil. Place the pork medallions on the grid and glaze under the hot grill for 1 minute, or until golden. Serve immediately.

Pork in oatmeal

20 minutes, standing,
then 15 minutes

Serves 4

500 g /1 lb lean belly pork, thinly sliced
15 ml /1 tbls lemon juice
salt and freshly ground black pepper
a pinch of cayenne pepper
1 egg
125 g /4 oz fine or medium oatmeal
grated zest of ½ orange
2.5 ml /½ tsp ground ginger
40 g /1½ oz lard

1 Beat each piece of thinly sliced belly pork individually between 2 pieces of wet greaseproof paper or cling film with a rolling pin or meat bat. Cut the pork into 5 cm /2 in squares. Brush with lemon juice; season with pepper and bring to room temperature, then season with salt, pepper and cayenne.

2 Break the egg into a bowl, season lightly with salt and pepper and beat lightly.

3 In another bowl mix the oatmeal, grated orange zest and ground ginger.

4 Dip each pork square into the beaten egg and then toss in the oatmeal mixture.

5 Melt the lard in a heavy frying-pan and fry the pork for about 5 minutes, turning once. Remove and serve immediately.

Pork noisettes with prunes

overnight soaking, standing,
then 1 hour 10 minutes

Serves 4–6

1.4 kg /3 lb loin of pork, skinned, boned and
    rolled
500 g /1 lb prunes, stoned
300 ml /10 fl oz red wine
salt and freshly ground black pepper
50 g /2 oz butter
30 ml /2 tbls olive oil
2 small onions, finely chopped
sprigs of watercress, to garnish

1 Soak the prunes overnight in the red wine.

2 Heat the oven to 170C /375F /gas 3. Cook the prunes, covered, in their soaking liquid in the oven for 1 hour. Remove from the oven and reserve, keeping the prunes warm.

3 Meanwhile, cut the loin of pork into noisettes approximately 25 mm /1 in thick. Season with pepper, bring to room temperature, then season with salt and more pepper.

4 In a large frying-pan heat half of the butter and the olive oil and sauté the noisettes for 7 minutes or until well done, turning them once. Remove from the pan and keep them warm. Pour off any excess fat from the pan and add 30 ml /2 tbls of the prune cooking liquid. Over a high heat, deglaze by stirring vigorously with a wooden spoon to remove any sediment from the base of the pan. Reserve.

5 While the noisettes are cooking, melt the remaining butter in a saucepan and cook the finely chopped onions, stirring occasionally, for 3–4 minutes or until transparent.

6 Blend the onions to a purée with 6 of the cooked prunes and 60–90 ml /4–6 tbls of the prune cooking liquid. Return to the saucepan and add the deglazing liquid and the remainder of the prune cooking liquid. Bring to the boil, then boil rapidly for 3–5 minutes, or until the liquid is reduced to about half its original quantity.

7 Arrange the pork noisettes and prunes on a heated serving dish. Pour the sauce over the pork, garnish with watercress sprigs and serve at once.

Pork noisettes with prunes

CASSEROLING & POT-ROASTING PORK

The full flavour of pork develops best with slow and thorough cooking, and it combines readily with a variety of ingredients, so there is virtually no end to possible combinations.

Pork is inclined to be more fatty than lamb but the medium and cheap quality cuts produce succulent pot-roasts, braises and casseroles. These three terms, however, are often used interchangeably and can cause confusion.

Casseroles, pot-roasts and braises

A casserole, as well as being the name of the cooking vessel, is food slowly cooked in it. There are two types of casseroles: cold start, in which the meat and other ingredients are all cooked from cold, and fry start, in which the meat is browned first in hot fat, then cooked very gently with the other ingredients. There should be only a moderate amount of liquid, so that the gravy or sauce becomes rich and full of flavour.

Braises are practically the same as fry start casseroles, though they usually contain slightly less liquid, while traditionally there is very little or no liquid in a pot-roast.

Only large cuts of meat are pot-roasted. Braises and casseroles can contain chunks of meat, chops or larger cuts.

Marinating the pork will flavour and tenderize the meat. Add the strained marinade or any meat juices to the cooking liquid, which can be beef or chicken stock, tomato juice or water. Add some wine, beer or cider for extra taste.

Flavourings that marry well with pork include tomato, apple and orange as well as mustard, juniper berries, coriander, cumin, ginger, soy sauce, rosemary, horseradish, sage, thyme and caraway.

Casseroling pork

Shoulder or hand and spring are suitable for cutting up for casseroles, while loin chops are excellent casseroled whole.

Pork is a valuable addition in casseroles with other meats, too. A few strips of belly pork (if it's salted, so much the better), pork rind, or a trotter added to a casserole will give extra flavour and add to the texture and richness of the sauce. The pork is often removed before serving.

Use the cold start method for tougher cuts such as hand and spring. Bring the ingredients slowly to simmering point, then reduce the heat and cook very gently, covered, on top of the cooker or in the oven at 150C /300F /gas 2.

Fry start cubes of shoulder meat or chops. Heat a small amount of butter, oil or dripping in a frying-pan, add the meat and fry over high heat for a few minutes until the meat is sealed. (The meat can be tossed in seasoned flour first, if wished.) Transfer to a casserole with a tightly fitting lid along with flavouring vegetables, herbs, spices and liquid, and cook very gently on the top of the cooker or in the oven at 150C /300F /gas 2 or 170C /325F /gas 3, according to the recipe, until the meat is tender.

Pot-roasting and braising pork

Any joint from the leg, loin, shoulder or hand and spring will make a good braising or pot-roasting joint. Sparerib is good, too, though slightly fattier. Leg and fore-leg can be boned and rolled as they are very large. Loin can be left on the bone if you prefer, but this will affect the cooking time. A joint on the bone will cook more quickly than one that is solid meat.

Although recipes vary, the meat is usually first browned on top of the cooker in hot fat. Remove the meat, add sliced vegetables and fry lightly. Pour off the excess fat and add sufficient liquid to almost cover the vegetables. Bring the liquid to the boil, then replace the meat on top of the vegetables. Cover tightly and simmer very gently on top of the cooker, or in the oven at 170C /325F / gas 3, for a minimum of 1½ hours, allowing 75 minutes per kg /35 minutes per 1 lb plus 35 minutes for joints. Check from time to time and add more liquid if needed.

To check that pork is thoroughly cooked – undercooked pork is unpleasant to eat and can be a potential health hazard – pierce the thickest part of the meat with a fine skewer. If the juices are clear, the meat is done; if the juices are pink, the meat is not yet done, so continue cooking until they run clear.

Loin of pork with red cabbage

standing,
then 2 hours

Serves 4
900 g /2 lb loin of pork, chined, rind scored
salt and freshly ground black pepper
2.5 ml /½ tsp dried oregano
450 g /1 lb red cabbage
25 g /1 oz butter
1 Spanish onion, thinly sliced
3 dessert apples, peeled, cored, quartered and sliced
30 ml /2 tbls red wine vinegar
finely chopped fresh parsley, to garnish

1 Bring the meat to room temperature.
2 Heat the oven to 170C /325F /gas 3. Remove the rind from the loin of pork. Season the pork with salt and freshly ground black pepper and sprinkle with dried oregano. Reserve.
3 Place the rind on a baking sheet, rub with a little salt and reserve.
4 Wash the red cabbage and cut it into quarters with a sharp knife. Remove the hard central core and shred the cabbage finely. Bring a saucepan of salted water to a boil and blanch the cabbage for 1 minute. Drain, rinse under cold running water and drain again.

5 In a large, flameproof casserole, heat the butter. Add the thinly sliced onion and sauté over a moderate heat for 7–10 minutes.
6 Remove from heat. Stir in the prepared apples, cabbage and vinegar. Season to taste with salt and freshly ground black pepper.
7 Place the loin of pork on top of the vegetables, cover tightly and cook in the oven for 30 minutes.
8 After the casserole has been in the oven for 30 minutes, place the pork rind on the top shelf of the oven. Continue cooking for a further hour, until the crackling is crisp and the meat is cooked: the juices should run clear when you insert a skewer into the thickest part.
9 Transfer the loin of pork to a board. Cut the crackling neatly into portions. Slice the meat neatly between the chop bones to make 4 chops. Arrange the cabbage and apple mixture in a large serving dish. Lay overlapping pork chops on top and arrange the crackling at either end. Garnish the chops and serve at once.

Casseroled chops in barbecue sauce

standing,
then 1½ hours

Serves 4
4 pork chops
salt and freshly ground black pepper
25 g /1 oz butter
30 ml /2 tbls olive oil
1 Spanish onion, sliced
45 ml /3 tbls wine vinegar
45 ml /3 tbls lemon juice
45 ml /3 tbls soft brown sugar
300 ml /10 fl oz tomato ketchup
30 ml /2 tbls Worcestershire sauce
15 ml /1 tbls Dijon mustard
1 green pepper, seeded and diced
2 stalks celery, diced

1 Trim the fat from the chops, leaving just a narrow border. Slash the remaining fat at intervals to prevent the chops curling. Season with pepper, bring to room temperature, then season with salt and more pepper.
2 In a large frying-pan, heat the butter and olive oil. When foaming subsides, brown the chops 2 at a time on both sides and transfer to a flameproof casserole.
3 Add the sliced onion to the frying-pan and sauté gently, stirring frequently, for 2–3 minutes until transparent.
4 Stir in the remaining ingredients, add 300 ml /10 fl oz water and season with salt and freshly ground black pepper. Bring to the boil, stir to remove the sediment from the base of the pan and pour over the chops. Reduce the heat, cover and simmer gently for 1 hour or until the chops are tender, turning them from time to time. Serve.

Loin of pork with red cabbage

Pork and chick-pea stew

overnight marinating, cooking
chick-peas, then 2–2¼ hours

Serves 4

800 g /1¾ lb shoulder of pork, cut into 25
  mm /1 in cubes
30–45 ml /2–3 tbls olive oil
2 medium-sized onions, halved and thinly
  sliced
100 ml /3½ fl oz red wine
3 medium-sized tomatoes, blanched,
  skinned, seeded and chopped
1 bay leaf
1 large red pepper, sliced
100 g /4 oz dried chick-peas, cooked and
  drained
sautéed aubergine slices, to serve
freshly chopped parsley, to garnish

For the marinade

7.5 ml /1½ tsp salt
freshly ground black pepper
a large pinch of ground allspice
1.5 ml /¼ tsp dried marjoram
2 large garlic cloves, crushed

1   Place the cubed pork in a bowl with the marinade ingredients and mix well with your hands, making sure the marinade is evenly distributed. Cover and refrigerate overnight, stirring once or twice, if convenient.
2   Dry the pork on absorbent paper, reserving any juices. Heat 15 ml /1 tbls oil in a large frying-pan over moderate heat. Add half the pork and fry, stirring, until it changes colour. Transfer the meat to a flameproof casserole, using a slotted spoon. Fry the second batch of pork cubes, adding more olive oil as needed.
3   Add more oil to the pan, if necessary, then add the onions and cook for a few minutes, until they are softened. Transfer them to the casserole. Deglaze the pan with the wine, stirring in the crusty bits.
4   Pour the wine into the casserole and add the tomatoes, bay leaf and reserved meat juices. Bring to simmering point, then lower the heat, cover and simmer gently for 30 minutes, stirring occasionally.
5   Add the sliced pepper and chick-peas. Continue to cook over gentle heat, stirring occasionally, for a further 1–1½ hours until the meat is very tender.
6   Transfer the meat and vegetables to a heated serving platter with a slotted spoon. Boil the remaining juices quickly until they thicken very slightly. Taste and adjust the seasoning, then pour the juices over the pork. Surround with the sautéed aubergine slices, sprinkle with freshly chopped parsley and serve at once.

● For sautéed aubergine slices, thinly slice a large aubergine and sprinkle generously with salt. Leave to drain for 45 minutes, rinse well and dry. Coat with seasoned flour and sauté quickly in olive oil until well browned and tender.

Pork with peppers

Chilli pork

45 minutes,
then 1¾ hours cooking

Serves 4

1 kg /2 lb boneless pork shoulder
60 ml /4 tbls flour
10 ml /2 tsp chilli powder
2 garlic cloves, very finely chopped
salt
50 g /2 oz butter
15 ml /1 tbls olive oil
500 g /1 lb ripe tomatoes, blanched, skinned,
  seeded and coarsely chopped
75 g /3 oz pine nuts
150 ml /5 fl oz soured cream
2 celery stalks, thinly sliced

1   Heat the oven to 170C /325F /gas 3.
2   In a bowl, combine the flour, chilli powder, very finely chopped garlic and a good pinch of salt.
3   Cut the pork into 25 mm /1 in cubes, discarding any excess fat or gristle. Add the pork to the spiced flour and toss to coat well.

Chilli pork

4   Heat 25 g /1 oz butter and the olive oil in a flameproof casserole. When foaming subsides, add enough pork cubes to cover the base of the casserole and brown thoroughly on all sides over a steady, moderate heat. Remove the browned pork to a plate and brown the remaining pork. When all the meat is browned, return it to the casserole.
5   Cover the pork with the chopped tomatoes and season with more salt if necessary. Cover the casserole and bake for about 1½ hours in the oven.
6   When the pork is tender, melt the remaining butter in a small frying-pan and sauté the pine nuts until golden.
7   Add the soured cream and the sliced celery to the pork. Heat gently, stirring, until well mixed. Add the pine nuts, correct the seasoning and serve immediately.

● Use the true, hot powdered chilli for this recipe; the soured cream tones down the heat a little. If this is too hot for your taste, use mild chilli seasoning and a little less soured cream.

Pork with peppers

 1 hour marinating,
then 1¼–1¾ hours

Serves 4–6
1 kg /2 lb shoulder of pork
3 garlic cloves
2.5 ml /½ tsp cumin seeds
2.5 ml /½ tsp coriander seeds
2.5 ml /½ tsp turmeric
2.5 ml /½ tsp chilli powder
1.5 ml /¼ tsp salt
75 ml /5 tbls olive oil
1½ Spanish onions, coarsely chopped
1 large green pepper, coarsely chopped
1 large red pepper, coarsely chopped
4 large tomatoes, blanched, skinned, seeded
   and coarsely chopped
freshly ground black pepper
flat-leaved parsley, to garnish
yellow rice, to serve

1 In a blender, combine the garlic, spices, salt and 45 ml /3 tbls oil. Mix well with the pork and marinate for at least 1 hour.
2 Heat the remaining oil in a large saucepan. Add the pork and marinade and fry quickly, in batches, until lightly browned on all sides. Remove to a plate with a slotted spoon and keep warm.
3 Add the chopped onion and cook for 5 minutes. Stir in the peppers, tomatoes and pork and season with salt and pepper.
4 Bring to the boil, then reduce the heat and simmer, uncovered, 1–1½ hours or until tender, stirring from time to time. Serve on a bed of yellow rice, garnished with parsley.

● Add 5 ml /1 tsp turmeric to the water when boiling rice for a bright yellow colour.

Pork chops with cider

🍴 1½ hours

Serves 4
4 pork chops
salt and freshly ground black pepper
50 g /2 oz butter
30 ml /2 tbls olive oil
1.5 ml /¼ tsp dried basil
1.5 ml /¼ tsp dried marjoram
1.5 ml /¼ tsp dried thyme
2 Spanish onions, finely chopped
150 ml /5 fl oz cider
150 ml /5 fl oz chicken stock, home-made or
   from a cube
1 dessert apple
5 ml /1 tsp arrowroot

1 Heat the oven to 170C /325F /gas 3.
2 Trim any excess fat from the pork chops, leaving just a narrow border. Slash the remaining fat at intervals to prevent the chops curling. Season the chops with salt and freshly ground black pepper.
3 In a large frying-pan heat 25 g /1 oz butter and the oil. When foaming subsides, brown the chops on both sides, 2 at a time.
4 Transfer the chops to a flameproof casserole and sprinkle them with dried basil, marjoram and thyme.
5 In the frying-pan, cook the finely chopped onions in the remaining fat for 2–3 minutes until transparent. Add to the chops.
6 Add the cider and stock to the frying-pan. Scrape the bottom and sides to remove any sediment and bring to the boil. Pour over the meat in the casserole and season with salt and freshly ground black pepper.
7 Cover and cook in the oven for 45–60 minutes or until tender.
8 About 10 minutes before the casserole is cooked, quarter and core the apple and slice thinly. Melt the remaining butter in a frying-pan and sauté the sliced apple until golden brown but still *al dente*.
9 Place the chops on a warmed serving plate. Blend the arrowroot with 10 ml /2 tsp cold water in a small bowl. Stir in 30 ml /2 tbls hot sauce, then blend into the sauce in the casserole; bring to the boil and simmer, stirring constantly, until the sauce thickens. Correct the seasoning and pour the sauce over the pork chops. Garnish with the sliced apple and serve immediately.

PORK SAUSAGES & OFFAL

Country people, pig farmers and cooks all agree that the only part of a pig which cannot be used is the squeal. Pork sausages and offal lend themselves to many delicious and unusual dishes.

Home-made and commercial sausages and pig's offal — liver, kidneys, heart, head and trotters — provide special-occasion dishes as well as economical family meals.

All offal is best cooked on the day of purchase. Store it, loosely covered, in the refrigerator until you are ready to cook it. Cased sausages can be stored, wrapped, in the refrigerator for up to 2 days, though sausage-meat mixtures should be cooked or put into casings on the day they are made.

Sausages

Sausages were first invented as a way to preserve small scraps of meat. The meat was either dried or smoked, to be kept for fairly long periods, or heavily spiced and eaten within a few days.

The sausages we buy today, whether all pork or pork and beef, vary greatly, though most contain a high proportion of cereal binder or filler, as well as sugar and chemical additives. More expensive ones usually have a higher meat content; some sausages are flavoured with herbs. All sausage-meat mixtures are fatty; although the proportions vary, an average mixture is 250 g /8 oz fat to 1 kg /2 lb lean meat.

Sausages are encased in skins or casings, which can be intestines or caul (the fat-veined belly lining) but are more often synthetic — long tubes of colourless cellulose.

'Bangers' or 'eights' come eight to 500 g / 1 lb; chipolatas (also called 'links' or 'thins') are smaller; cocktail sausages smaller still.

Making your own sausages: making your own sausage-meat is the best way to ensure high-quality ingredients, and it's easy if you have an electric mincer. You can use a hand mincer, but it will take much longer. If you are using natural casings, soak them in a bowl of tepid water while you make the sausage-meat. Mince the lean and fat meats together once or twice, depending on how finely textured you want the sausage to be. Add seasonings and other ingredients and mix well, then fry a little of the mixture so that you can taste it and adjust the seasonings if necessary. Let the mixture firm up in the refrigerator for 10–15 minutes, then put into casings or form into sausage shapes with your hands.

Filling the casings: rinse them in cold water, then open them out by fitting one end over the end of a running cold tap for a few seconds. Secure one end to the sausage-filling attachment of an electric mincer, pull up the casing over the tube and tie the spare end. Switch on the machine and the meat will be fed into the tube automatically.

Alternatively, fill the casings by hand: tie one end over the end of a large, wide-necked funnel. Pull the casing round the tube and tie the spare end. Then fill the bowl of the funnel half full with sausage-meat and push it through.

In both cases, make sure that the casing is filled evenly and not too tightly, and that the filling contains no air pockets, otherwise your sausages may burst.

When the casing has been filled, tie off both ends of the tube tightly, then moisten the casing, squeeze the sausage between two fingers at the point where you want to divide it, then twist to push the meat to either side.

Cooking sausages: instead of pricking them, moisten sausages with warm water to make their skins stretch and prevent bursting.

Shallow fry sausages in a little oil or fat, turning often, until well browned all over. Large sausages take about 12 minutes, chipolatas 8 minutes and cocktail sausages 7 minutes.

To grill, brush the grill rack with oil or fat, heat the grill to moderate, then grill the sausages, turning often. Large sausages take about 15 minutes, chipolatas 12 minutes and cocktail sausages 10 minutes.

To bake, heat the oven to 180C /350F / gas 4. Melt a small knob of fat in a shallow tin, put in the sausages in one layer and cook for 15 minutes or until well browned, turn and cook for 10 minutes. Cocktail sausages need only 15 minutes total cooking time.

Liver, kidney and heart

Pig's liver, kidneys and heart are all very rich in protein. They are less expensive than lamb's offal, but are prepared and cooked in similar ways. Pork liver and heart can be rather strongly flavoured, though this can be remedied by soaking them — liver in milk for one hour, heart in slightly salted water for 2 hours.

Pig's liver is the best liver to use for pâtés, faggots and stuffings. It is also good fried in the same way as lamb's liver, roasted, or braised in one piece.

Pig's kidneys are prepared like lamb's kidneys, and are excellent grilled, if firm and fresh. Softer, frozen kidneys can be casseroled, or fried and served in a pan sauce incorporating their juices. Allow one per person.

Heart is not easily available as it often disappears into manufactured brawns, pâtés and faggots. If you can find it, it is delicious braised (try substituting four pig's hearts for the lamb's hearts in the recipe for Orange and lemon hearts on *page 34*), grilled or roasted. One pig's heart will serve one or two people.

Heads and trotters

The average pig's head weighs about 8 kg / 16 lb and is usually sold whole, though you may be able to buy a half, with the tongue intact. Ask your butcher to split the head from the back to the front, leaving the skin joining the sides at the top. The pig's ears and cheeks may be sold separately.

The head should be washed thoroughly before cooking, and either parboiled in salted water for 5 minutes or salted (pickled). Your butcher will probably salt the head for you.

Pig's heads are usually made into head cheese or brawn, though they can be simmered with herbs and vegetables until very tender. The ears are best pickled, and may be cooked with the rest of the head or separately in the same way; long, slow cooking softens the cartilage. After poaching, they can be coated with breadcrumbs and grilled until crispy. Pickled, boiled and rolled pig's cheeks are known as Bath chaps; they are usually served cold with a piquant sauce.

Feet or trotters are sold whole or halved and sometimes you can find them already cooked. They do not have much meat on them; allow one or two per serving. Wash them well, then bring to the boil in salted water with herbs and vegetables for flavouring. Simmer them slowly until tender, up to 4 hours. Serve them hot or cold with vinaigrette or, for a crisp finish, brush them with melted butter, roll them in breadcrumbs and grill. Trotters are also used in brawn, for making aspics and for giving body to stews.

Breton sausages with mustard

Basic pork sausages

🍴 1 hour

Makes 12 × 50 g /2 oz sausages
450 /1 lb pork shoulder without rind or bone
225 g /8 oz hard back fat
25 g /1 oz soft white breadcrumbs
    (optional), plus milk to moisten
salt and freshly ground white pepper
2.5–5 ml /¼–1 tsp mixed grated nutmeg,
    gound mace and ground coriander
1.5–2.5 ml /¼–½ tsp dried sage
sausage casings (soaked if natural) or egg
    and breadcrumbs

1   Mince the pork and fat together once or
twice, then mix thoroughly with the
breadcrumbs (if using), salt and pepper,
spices and sage. If you are using
breadcrumbs, add a little milk to moisten.
2   Sauté a little of the sausage-meat
mixture until cooked, then taste it and
adjust the seasonings if necessary.
3   Refrigerate the mixture for 10–15
minutes to firm it up, then use it to fill
rinsed-out casings or mould into sausage
shapes with your hands. Egg-and-
breadcrumb the sausages before grilling or
frying if they are not cased.

Breton sausages with mustard

Breton sausages, which are made of pure
pork, fresh herbs and the usual sausage-
meat spices, are often served on a bed of
beans. You can use ordinary pork
sausages to make this version.

🔪 50 minutes

Serves 4
75 ml /3 fl oz dry white wine
3 shallots, finely chopped
120 ml /8 tbls concentrated canned
    consommé
30 ml /2 tbls Dijon mustard
30 ml /2 tbls English chive mustard
45 ml /3 tbls softened butter
450 g /1 lb pork sausages, 50 g /2 oz each
800 g /28 oz canned red kidney beans,
    drained
salt and freshly ground black pepper
butter for greasing

1   Heat the grill without the grid to
medium. In a small saucepan, bring the wine
and shallots to the boil over medium heat,
then reduce the heat and simmer until the
shallots are soft. Add 30 ml /2 tbls consommé, 5 ml /1 tsp of each mustard and the
softened butter. Stir; remove from the heat.
2   Smear the sausages with some of the
remaining mustard (it doesn't matter which
one). Place on the grill grid and cook,
turning frequently, for about 15 minutes or
until browned on all sides. Cut the sausages
into large chunks and keep warm. Heat the
oven to 200C /400F /gas 6.
3   Sieve or purée the drained beans with
the remaining consommé. Stir in the rest of
the mustard and season to taste.
4   Butter a shallow baking dish and pour in
the bean purée. Cover the dish with buttered
foil and place in the oven for 10 minutes.
5   Remove the foil and place the sausage
chunks on top of the beans. Pour the wine
and shallot mixture over them, cover loosely
with the foil and return to the oven for 3–4
minutes to heat through. Serve at once.

Greek sausages

These sausages, fried, then cooked in
tomato sauce, are called *soudzoukakia*.

🍴 mincing pork, then 1 hour

Serves 6–8
100 g /4 oz fresh white breadcrumbs
150 ml /5 fl oz milk
900 g /2 lb minced pork
30 ml /2 tbls grated onion
3 garlic cloves, finely chopped
salt and freshly ground black pepper
olive oil for brushing
flour for dusting
For the sauce
900 g /2 lb very ripe tomatoes, blanched,
    skinned and chopped, or drained canned
    tomatoes
10 ml /2 tsp sugar
2 bay leaves
a pinch of ground cumin
1 small onion, peeled
salt

1   First make the sauce: put all the
ingredients into a saucepan, leaving the
onion whole. Bring to the boil, then simmer
gently, uncovered, for 30 minutes.
2   Meanwhile, make the sausages: soak the
breadcrumbs in the milk for a few minutes,
then squeeze dry. Mix the breadcrumbs with
the minced pork, grated onion and garlic,
and season well with salt and pepper. For
smooth-textured sausages, pound the
mixture or process in a food processor.
3   Fry a little of the sausage-meat until
cooked; taste and adjust the seasonings.
4   Shape the mixture into about 32 fat little
sausages about 5 cm /2 in long. Roll them in
flour and place them in the refrigerator for
10–15 minutes to firm up.
5   Brush the sausages with the oil. Place
them in a frying-pan over medium heat and
cook, turning frequently, until evenly
browned. Drain on absorbent paper.
6   Remove the onion and bay leaves from
the sauce and sieve it to remove the seeds, if
you wish. Add the sausages and simmer for a
further 15 minutes. Serve hot.

Pork butcher's pâté

Pâté de foie du porc is typical of the rough-textured pâtés found in family-owned French charcuteries. The pig's liver and fat belly pork balance each other to provide a rich, moist texture enlivened by the characteristic flavourings of garlic, brandy and spices. This makes an ideal starter served with crusty French bread or hot toast.

3¾ hours, including standing, then overnight chilling

Serves 4–6
225 g /8 oz pig's liver, washed and dried
225 g /8 oz fat belly pork, rind removed
50 g /2 oz cooked gammon fat
1 garlic clove, crushed
4 juniper berries, crushed
a large pinch of powdered mace
salt and freshly ground black pepper
15 ml /1 tbls dry white wine
30 ml /2 tbls brandy
butter for sautéing
2 thin slices unsmoked streaky bacon
2 bay leaves

Pork butcher's pâté

1 Mince the liver and the pork together fairly coarsely, and put in a mixing bowl.
2 Add the gammon fat, cut in 5 mm /¼ in dice, the garlic, juniper berries, mace, a little salt and plenty of freshly ground black pepper, and the wine and brandy. Mix well.
3 Shape a spoonful of the mixture into a patty and sauté in a little butter until cooked. Adjust seasoning if necessary.
4 Turn the mixture into a deep 600 ml /1 pt ovenproof terrine and smooth the surface with a palette knife.
5 Cut the bacon slices across the grain into 5 mm /¼ in strips. Scatter these over the pâté surface and lay the bay leaves on top. Cover and leave to stand for about 2 hours so that the flavours can blend.
6 Heat the oven to 170C /325F /gas 3. Stand the terrine in a baking tin and pour in enough hot water to come halfway up the sides of the terrine.
7 Cook in the centre of the oven for 1 hour, then uncover and continue cooking for 15–20 minutes to dry the bacon.
8 Remove the terrine from the baking tin and, when quite cold, cover and refrigerate overnight before serving.
9 Serve the pâté from the terrine.

Crispy topped liver

1 hour

Serves 4
500 g /1 lb pig's liver, cut in 10 mm /½ in
thick slices
25 g /1 oz bacon fat or dripping
25 g /1 oz flour
salt and freshly ground black pepper
8–10 thin slices smoked streaky bacon, rinds
removed
For the topping
40 g /1½ oz butter
1 medium-sized onion, finely chopped
1 celery stalk, finely chopped
65 g /2½ oz fresh white breadcrumbs
5 ml /1 tsp finely grated lemon zest
2.5 ml /½ tsp dried oregano or sage
15 ml /1 tbls freshly chopped parsley
1 medium-sized egg, beaten
salt and freshly ground black pepper

1 Wash the liver under cold running water and pat dry with absorbent paper. Trim away any skin or large veins.
2 To prepare the topping, melt the butter in a saucepan and gently fry the onion and celery for 5 minutes. Off the heat stir in the breadcrumbs, lemon zest, oregano or sage, parsley, beaten egg and seasonings.
3 Heat the oven to 180C /350F /gas 4. Choose a shallow baking tin large enough for the liver slices to lie flat in a single layer and use the bacon fat or dripping to grease it well. Put it in the oven to heat.
4 Meanwhile, season the flour and toss the liver in it until it is well coated.
5 Remove the baking dish from the oven and arrange the liver slices on the base. Spoon the topping evenly over the liver, press lightly, then cover completely with the bacon slices. Bake in the centre of the oven for 30–35 minutes, until the liver is cooked.

Brawn

This beautiful mould has a better flavour when made with a pickled head, but a fresh one may be used if this is more convenient.

1 hour soaking, 3½–4 hours, then overnight chilling

Serves 6–8
½ pig's head with tongue, pickled, with the ear removed
salt
freshly ground black pepper
250 g /8 oz ox cheek or shin of beef
2 pig's trotters
2 medium-sized onions, sliced
1 small turnip, quartered
1 medium-sized carrot, roughly sliced
2 cloves
bouquet garni
10 peppercorns, slightly crushed
a blade of mace
a large pinch of freshly grated nutmeg
lettuce leaves and watercress, to garnish
For the vinaigrette
60 ml /4 tbls wine vinegar
10 ml /2 tsp Dijon mustard
salt
freshly ground black pepper
240 ml /16 tbls olive oil

1 Wash the pig's head and the ear thoroughly, making sure that the snout and ear are perfectly clean. Rinse well under cold running water, then place them in a large saucepan of salted water and allow to soak for about 1 hour.
2 Blanch the ear in boiling salted water.
3 Drain the soaking liquid from the pig's head, then return it to the saucepan with the ear, ox cheek or shin of beef, trotters, onions, turnip, carrot, cloves, bouquet garni, peppercorns and mace. Cover with cold water and bring slowly to the boil. Remove any scum, then simmer gently over a low heat until the meat is tender, about 2–2½ hours.
4 Strain the liquid and reserve. Remove the bones and gristle from the meat and reserve the bones. Trim and skin the tongue and cut it into slices. Cut the ear into strips. Chop the rest of the meat.
5 Skim the fat from the stock, add the bones and boil to reduce by at least half; strain, allow to cool and remove any remaining fat.
6 Mix the chopped meats well with salt, pepper and nutmeg to taste and arrange in layers in a 1 L/2 pt mould. Pack the meat down well and moisten with the reduced stock. Cover with foil or a plate and top with a heavy weight. Allow to cool overnight in a refrigerator or a cool larder.
7 Just before serving the brawn, make the vinaigrette: combine the wine vinegar, mustard and salt and pepper to taste in a bowl. Beat in the olive oil with a whisk until the dressing emulsifies.
8 Dip the brawn mould in warm water and turn out onto a serving plate. Garnish with lettuce leaves and watercress sprigs and serve with the vinaigrette.

Purée of peas with sausages

Serve pork sausages on a bed of puréed split and green peas for a delicious combination of flavours.

soaking the split peas, then about 1½ hours

Serves 4–6
500 g /1 lb dried split peas
1 Spanish onion, stuck with 2 cloves
bouquet garni
salt
350 g /12 oz frozen green peas
150 ml /5 fl oz hot milk
75 g /3 oz butter
freshly ground black pepper
15 ml /1 tbls olive oil
500 g /1 lb well-flavoured pork sausages
90 ml /6 tbls dry white wine

1 Place the split peas in a large pan. Cover with cold water and bring to the boil over a low heat. As soon as the water boils remove from the heat, cover and leave the peas to soak for 1 hour.
2 Drain the peas and cover with fresh water. Add the onion stuck with cloves and the bouquet garni. Bring to the boil over a high heat, then reduce the heat and simmer gently for 45–60 minutes, or until tender, depending on their age and quality.

Purée of peas with sausages

3 Meanwhile, bring another saucepan of salted water to the boil. Add the frozen green peas and simmer gently for 5 minutes, or until very tender. Drain.
4 Drain the split peas, discarding the onion and cloves and the bouquet garni. Combine the split peas and green peas.
5 Rub the mixture through a fine sieve with a wooden spoon into the top pan of a double boiler or a bowl which is then placed over a pan of simmering water. Blend the hot milk and 50 g /2 oz of the butter into the sieved pea mixture and cook over simmering water until the purée is smooth and thick. Season to taste with salt and freshly ground black pepper
6 Meanwhile, heat the remaining butter and the olive oil in a frying-pan large enough to take the sausages in one layer. Moisten the sausages with warm water and place them side by side in the pan. Fry the sausages for 5–6 minutes on each side or until browned and cooked through, turning with a spatula. Remove with a slotted spoon and keep warm.
7 Pour off the fat. Add the wine to the frying-pan and reduce to half the original quantity over a high heat, stirring with a wooden spoon and scraping the sediment from the bottom of the pan.
8 To serve, heap the pea purée in a heated serving dish. Arrange the cooked sausages on top and spoon over the wine-flavoured pan juices. Serve immediately.

PORK FOR THE FAMILY

From a quick and easy family filler to a special-occasion Sunday lunch, pork is the meat that will fit the bill. Roast or casserole, snack or starter, it will always be popular.

Pork is a very versatile meat. As well as the many joints, it gives us sausages and offal, gammon and bacon, all of which offer a great selection of recipes. It is a lean, good-value-for-money meat, especially if you experiment with some of the more unusual cuts. And pork combines so well with many other ingredients.

Sausage-stuffed baked marrow

🔪 1½ hours

Serves 4–6
1 large marrow, about 1.4 kg /3 lb
50 g /2 oz butter
1 large onion, finely chopped
2 garlic cloves, finely chopped
500 g /1 lb pork sausage-meat
30–60 ml /2–4 tbls tomato purée
2.5 ml /½ tsp dried oregano
30 ml /2 tbls finely chopped fresh basil
salt and freshly ground black pepper
50 g /2 oz Cheddar cheese, grated

1 Heat the oven to 180C /350F /gas 4. Use a sharp knife to slice off both ends of the marrow and peel it. With a sharp-edged metal spoon, scoop out the seeds, making a cavity right through the centre.

2 To prepare the stuffing: melt half the butter over moderate heat in a large thick-bottomed frying-pan; add the finely chopped onion and half the finely chopped garlic. Sauté, stirring occasionally, for 5–7 minutes or until the onions and garlic are soft and translucent.
3 Add the sausage-meat, tomato purée, oregano, finely chopped basil and salt and freshly ground black pepper to taste, and sauté, stirring frequently, for 10 minutes.
4 Remove the pan from the heat and stir in the grated Cheddar cheese; spoon the sausage-meat mixture into the prepared marrow, packing it in tightly. Using the remaining butter, grease a large piece of aluminium foil and the outside of the marrow. Place the marrow in the centre of the foil. Sprinkle the remaining finely chopped garlic, and salt and freshly ground black pepper, all over the marrow. Bring the edges of the foil up and over the marrow, securing them to make a neat parcel.
5 Place the parcel on a large baking sheet. Place the baking sheet in the oven and bake for 1 hour or until the marrow is very tender when pierced with the point of a sharp knife and the filling is cooked.
6 Remove the baking sheet from the oven. Transfer the marrow to a large, warmed serving dish. Remove and discard the foil and serve the marrow immediately.

Sausage-stuffed baked marrow

Loin of pork with orange

This joint, which is equally good served hot or cold, has a crisp, spicy crust.

🍴🍴 2 hours 25 minutes

Serves 8
1.4 kg /3 lb loin of pork, weighed after skinning and boning (keep skin and bones if possible)
salt
freshly ground black pepper
1–2 garlic cloves, finely chopped
30 ml /2 tbls freshly chopped parsley
5 ml /1 tsp freshly chopped marjoram or 2.5 ml /½ tsp dried marjoram
30 ml /2 tbls oil
200 ml /7 fl oz chicken stock, home-made or from a cube
juice of 1 large orange
45–60 ml /3–4 tbls orange liqueur
15 ml /1 tbls French mustard
45 ml /3 tbls dry white breadcrumbs
15 ml /1 tbls soft light brown sugar
2–3 seedless oranges separated into segments, to garnish
sprigs of watercress, to garnish

1 Heat the oven to 170C /325F /gas 3. Sprinkle the meaty side of the loin of pork with the salt, pepper, garlic, parsley and marjoram. Form it into a neat roll, fat side outwards, and tie in several places with string.
2 Heat the oil in a flameproof casserole into which the meat fits closely. When the oil sizzles, add the meat to the pan and brown it lightly on all sides.
3 Gently heat the chicken stock, then add it to the casserole. Tuck the bones and pieces of skin, if available, around the meat, cover the casserole, transfer it to the oven and cook for 1¾ hours.
4 Discard the bones and skin. Pour the orange juice and liqueur over the meat, spread the meat thinly with mustard and sprinkle with the breadcrumbs and sugar. Return to the oven and cook, uncovered, for 15 minutes or until the juices run clear and the topping is crisp and golden.
5 Take the meat out of the oven and remove the string. Carve the pork into slices and arrange neatly on a well-heated serving platter, and keep warm in the turned-off oven. Degrease the pan juices by blotting the liquid with strips of absorbent paper, add the orange sections and heat for 2 minutes. Using a slotted spoon, arrange the orange sections in groups around the meat and tuck sprigs of watercress between the groups of orange. Check the gravy for seasoning, pour into a sauce-boat and serve at once.

Terrine of pork and veal

🕐🍴🍴 3 hours, overnight cooling, then 8 hours chilling

Loin of pork with orange

Serves 8
500 g /1 lb lean pork, minced
500 g /1 lb pie veal, minced
250g /8 oz pork fat, minced
1 medium-sized onion, finely chopped
1 garlic clove, crushed
25 g /1 oz butter
150 ml /5 fl oz dry white wine
1 medium-sized egg, beaten
10 ml /2 tsp salt
1.5 ml /¼ tsp freshly ground black pepper
a pinch of allspice
2.5 ml /½ tsp dried thyme
500 g /1 lb streaky bacon slices

1 Combine the minced pork, veal and pork fat in a large mixing bowl. Heat the oven to 180C /350F /gas 4.
2 In a frying-pan, sauté the onion and garlic in the butter until soft. Remove the onion and add to the meat. Rinse the pan with wine and add to the meat and onion.
3 Mix in the egg. Season the meat mixture with salt, pepper, allspice and thyme and beat well.
4 Remove the rinds from the bacon slices. Use two-thirds of the slices to line a 1.5 L / 2½ pt mould or rectangular ovenproof container. Press the meat mixture into the bowl or tin and cover with the remaining bacon.
5 Cover the terrine tightly with foil and a lid. Stand the mould in a baking tin of water and bake in the oven for 2 hours. It is ready when a skewer comes out clean.
6 Remove the lid and place a weight on top of the foil. Leave to cool overnight, then chill for at least 8 hours.
7 Run a knife around the dish to loosen the bacon lining from the sides, if the pâté has not shrunk. Turn the terrine out onto a plate and slice to serve.

Saucisses en chemise

🔥 45 minutes
plus cooling

Serves 4–6
30 ml /2 tbls olive oil
450 g /1 lb chipolata sausages
225 g /8 oz made-weight flaky pastry, defrosted if frozen
flour
15–30 ml /1–2 tbls tarragon or Dijon mustard
milk or water for glazing

1 Heat to oven to 200C /400F /gas 6.
2 Heat the olive oil in a frying-pan large enough to take the sausages in one layer. Place them side by side in the pan and cook them over a moderate heat for 8 minutes or until an even golden brown, turning frequently. Transfer to a plate and drain on absorbent paper. Cool.
3 Lightly flour a board and roll out the flaky pastry 5 mm /¼ in thick to make a strip just a little wider than the sausages. Cut the strip into rectangles large enough to fold over each sausage.
4 With a palette knife, spread each rectangle of pastry with a little tarragon or Dijon mustard, leaving the edges free. Place a cold sausage on each rectangle and brush the edges with a little milk or water.
5 Roll up the pastry like a little package, sealing the edges firmly together. Brush the top of each with a little milk and transfer to a baking tray. Bake in the oven for about 15 minutes or until the pastry is golden brown.
6 Arrange the pastry packages on a heated serving platter and serve immediately.

Pork and bean casserole

🔥 soaking and cooking beans if necessary, then 2–2½ hours

Serves 6
1 kg /2 lb lean boneless shoulder of pork
40 g /1½ oz flour
5 ml /1 tsp curry powder
salt and freshly ground black pepper
30 ml /2 tbls oil
1 large onion, thinly sliced
30 ml /2 tbls black treacle
150 ml /5 fl oz boiling water
400 g /14 oz canned peeled tomatoes
1 bay leaf
275–350 g /10–12 oz drained haricot or butter beans, cooked or canned

1 Heat the oven to 170C /325F /gas 3. Trim the pork of excess fat and cut it into neat 25 mm /1 in cubes.
2 Mix together in a bowl the flour, curry powder and generous seasonings of salt and pepper. Add the pork cubes and toss until all the coating adheres to the meat.
3 Heat the oil in a deep flameproof casserole and fry the onion over gentle heat for 5 minutes, stirring occasionally. Raise the heat, add the pork and stir for 1–2 minutes, until the oil has been absorbed.
4 Dissolve the treacle in the boiling water and add to the casserole with the tomatoes and their juice and the bay leaf. Bring to simmering point, cover tightly and cook in the centre of the oven for 1–1½ hours.
5 Stir in the beans, cover and continue cooking for another 30 minutes. Adjust the seasoning if necessary, then serve at once, from the casserole.

COOKING BACON & GAMMON

Everybody knows how perfectly bacon slices go with fried eggs or liver, but there are many other delicious ways to use the wide range of other bacon and gammon cuts.

There is sometimes confusion over the use of the terms bacon, gammon and ham, so bear in mind the following simple guidelines. Bacon is the term used to describe a cured side of pork. Gammon (the best joint of meat) is the hind leg cut from the cured bacon side. Ham is the hind leg cut from a fresh pig carcass and then cured separately.

Bacon is cured by being immersed in brine for a specified period and then 'matured' by hanging in a cool, air-controlled atmosphere.
Unsmoked bacon (also known as green bacon) is matured for only about 1 week. It has a light-coloured rind, pale pink meat and a mild flavour.
Smoked bacon is matured bacon that has been smoked for up to 8 hours. It is slightly drier, with a richer flavour and deeper colour than unsmoked bacon.

Cuts of bacon and gammon
Sides of smoked and unsmoked bacon are cut into joints, chops, steaks and slices or rashers. Gammon is available as a whole leg, middle gammon, corner gammon, gammon hock and gammon steaks and slices. (Full details of the cuts of both bacon and gammon are shown on pages 110 and 111).

Soaking bacon and gammon joints
Today's bacon is less heavily brined than it used to be and a joint may not need soaking at all to rid it of excess salt. Generally speaking, sweet or mild cured bacon does not need soaking and unsmoked bacon needs less soaking than smoked. For small unsmoked or smoked joints, 2–3 hours soaking in cold water is usually sufficient. Soak a whole gammon or fore-end for about 8 hours or overnight.

For small bacon joints a quick alternative to soaking is blanching. Simply cover the joint with cold water, bring very slowly to the boil, then drain thoroughly and cook by whichever method you prefer (see below).

Cooking bacon and gammon joints
Boiling: this is one of the simplest ways of cooking bacon and gammon. Wash the joint and weigh it, then calculate the cooking time. Allow 44 minutes per kg /20 minutes per lb plus 20 minutes, up to 4.5 kg /10 lb. A whole gammon will need 33 minutes per kg / 15 minutes per lb. Put the joint in a large saucepan, cover with cold water and bring to simmering point.

Remove the pan from the heat and skim off any scum that has risen to the surface. Return the pan to the heat, cover tightly and simmer gently. Calculate the cooking time from this point.

Either remove the joint from the water when it is cooked or leave to cool to lukewarm in the water. (The first method is better for smaller joints, the latter for larger ones.) Strip the rind off the joint and serve it plain, coated with browned breadcrumbs or finished with one of the various glazes described below.

Baking in foil: This method preserves all the natural flavour in the joint, so pre-soaking is advisable.

Weigh the joint then calculate the cooking time and heat the oven according to the chart below. Wrap the joint loosely in a large piece of foil, sealing the edges over the top of the joint. Place the joint on a rack in a roasting tin and pour a cupful of water into the tin. Cook for the calculated cooking time, then open up foil and peel off all rind.

Parboiling and baking: this combination of boiling and baking is especially suitable for shoulder cuts and stuffed joints. Soaking before cooking is not necessary with this method of cooking.

Weigh the joint and calculate the cooking time as for baking in foil. Boil the joint, as previously described, for half the calculated time if it is a small joint, then drain it, stuff if wished, wrap in foil and complete the cooking. Bake a large gammon joint for the last hour of the cooking time.

Braising is a flavourful method for cooking a small joint. Soak or blanch the joint, then weigh it. Allow 77 minutes per kg /35 minutes per lb, plus 35 minutes. Heat the oven to 180C /350F /gas 4.

Melt about 25 g /1 oz of butter in a deep flameproof casserole and fry a mixture of diced onion, carrot, celery or leeks (enough to cover the base of the casserole to a depth of 4 cm /1½ in) until lightly browned. Add enough stock, cider or water to cover the vegetables and season with herbs and freshly ground black pepper. Put the joint on top, bring to simmering point, cover tightly and cook in the oven.

When the joint is cooked, remove from the casserole and strip off the rind. Serve the joint with the vegetables and use the stock to make a sauce.

Glazing ham and bacon joints
Cook the joint to within 30 minutes of the calculated cooking time by any of the four basic methods described. Increase the oven heat (or heat from cold) to 200C /400F /gas 6.

Peel the rind off the joint, leaving the fat surface exposed. If foil wrapped, leave the foil around the lean meat to keep it moist. Spread the fat with your chosen glaze and bake for the remaining calculated cooking time, basting from time to time, until the fat is crisp and golden.

The following quantities are suitable for a 1.4–1.8 kg /3–4 lb joint; double or treble for a whole ham.
Sugar and clove glaze: with a sharp knife score the exposed fat in a diamond pattern. Press 30–45 ml /2–3 tbls Demerara sugar evenly over the fat surface, stud each diamond (or intersection) with a whole clove, and bake.
Honey glaze: blend 30 ml /2 tbls clear honey with 30 ml /2 tbls soft brown sugar and 5 ml /1 tsp made mustard. Spread over the fat surface, and bake.
Apricot glaze: mix 30–45 ml /2–3 tbls sieved apricot jam with 5 ml /1 tsp ground cloves or dry mustard, 15 ml /1 tbls soft brown sugar and 10 ml /2 tsp lemon juice. Spread the glaze over the fat surface, and bake.
Crispy topping: mix 15 ml /1 tbls clear honey with 15 ml /1 tbls wine vinegar and spoon over the fat. Sprinkle with equal parts of mixed brown sugar and dry breadcrumbs, and bake till crisp.

Cooking bacon rashers and steaks
Best back or long back slices (rashers) should be used whenever lean bacon is required. Remove any rind and bones. Streaky bacon is ideal for adding extra flavour and succulence, for barding meat and poultry, for grilling in kebabs and frying with liver.

Steaks and chops make quick and substantial main course dishes. Grill or fry them. Remove any rind or bones and snip the fat around the edges at 25 mm /1 in

Baking bacon and gammon joints

Cut and weight	Oven temperature	Minutes per kg/lb	
Whole gammon on the bone			
7.5–7.7 kg /16–17 lb	180C /350F /gas 4	44+20+(plus 20)	
Gammon joints			
up to 1.4 kg /3 lb	190C /375F /gas 5	66	30
1.5–2.7 kg /3¼–6 lb		55	25
over 2.7 kg /6 lb		42	20
All other bacon and gammon joints			
up to 1.4 kg /3 lb	190C /375F /gas 5	77	35
1.5–2.7 kg /3¼–6 lb		66	30
over 2.7 kg /6 lb		55	25

*Meat thermometer check: when cooked the centre of the bacon joint should never be below 70C /160F.

intervals with sharp scissors to prevent the steaks or chops curling during cooking.

Grilling: heat the grill to medium. Brush lean steaks or chops with fat on both sides to prevent sticking and arrange flat on the grill rack. Overlap thin slices so the lean of one is covered and protected by the fat of the next. Grill 5 mm /¼ in thick steaks or chops for 8–10 minutes, turning once. Grill slices for 2–3 minutes, turning once.

Frying: use a lightly greased frying-pan over a medium heat. Lay steaks or chops flat in the pan. Fry 5 mm /¼ in steaks or chops for about 10 minutes, turning once. Overlap thin rashers and fry for 3–4 minutes, turning once, until the fat is transparent.

Gala gammon with spiced peaches

For a dinner party or celebration meal, choose a middle gammon joint with a large surface for glazing.

marinating peaches overnight, soaking gammon, then 1½ hours

Serves 8–12
1.5–1.8 kg /3–4 lb middle gammon joint
15 ml /1 tbls brown sugar
6 peppercorns
2 bay leaves
For the spiced peaches
425 g /15 oz canned peach halves in syrup
45 ml /3 tbls wine vinegar
30 ml /2 tbls brown sugar
a small piece of root ginger
6 cloves
2 allspice berries
25 mm /1 in piece of cinnamon stick
For the glaze and garnish
60 ml /4 tbls of the spiced peach syrup
30–45 ml /2–3 tbls Demerara sugar
whole cloves
30 ml /2 tbls redcurrant jelly
watercress sprigs

1   Prepare the spiced peaches. Drain the peach syrup into a small saucepan, add the vinegar, sugar and spices, cover and simmer very gently for 15–20 minutes, until well spiced. Put the peaches in a bowl, strain the syrup over, cover and leave overnight.
2   Next day, soak the gammon joint in cold water for 3 hours. Then drain, weigh the joint and calculate the cooking time, allowing 44 minutes per kg /20 minutes per lb, plus 20 minutes.
3   Put the joint in a deep saucepan, cover with cold water, and add the brown sugar, peppercorns and bay leaves. Bring slowly to the boil, cover and simmer for 30 minutes less than the calculated cooking time.
4   Heat the oven to 200C /400F /gas 6. Drain the joint and carefully peel off the rind. Score the fat into diamond shapes with a sharp knife.
5   Place the joint in a deep ovenproof casserole, fat side up, and spoon over 60 ml / 4 tbls of the spiced peach syrup. Press the Demerara sugar evenly over the surface and stud each diamond with a clove.
6   Bake the joint uncovered in the oven for the rest of the cooking time until the surface is richly golden, basting now and then. Heat the spiced peaches in the remaining syrup in a covered flameproof dish, in the oven.
7   Place the gammon on a heated serving dish. Surround with watercress and peach halves, cut side up, and spoon 5 ml /1 tsp redcurrant jelly into each peach.

Gala gammon with spiced peaches

Gammon with Madeira sauce

🔪 40 minutes

Serves 4

4 gammon steaks, 15 mm /½ in thick, with
*   the fat snipped*
25 g /1 oz butter
15 ml /1 tbls oil
1 small onion, finely chopped
100 g /4 oz button mushrooms, sliced
25 g /1 oz flour
175 ml /6 fl oz ham or beef stock, home-
*   made or from a cube*
150 ml /5 fl oz dry Madeira
15 ml /1 tbls tomato purée
salt and freshly ground black pepper
150 ml /5 fl oz thick cream
braised spinach, to serve

1   Heat the butter and oil in a heavy-based frying-pan over moderate heat. Add the gammon and fry each side for 4 minutes, until golden brown. Transfer the steaks with a slotted spoon to a plate and keep warm while making the sauce.
2   Add the chopped onion and mushrooms to the pan and cook until softened. Stir in the flour with a wooden spoon and cook for 2 minutes, stirring continuously.
3   Remove the pan from the heat and stir in the stock and Madeira. Stir in the tomato purée and season the sauce to taste with salt

Stuffed bacon roll

and freshly ground black pepper.
4   Return the pan to the heat and bring the sauce to simmering point, stirring continuously. Then add the cream. Simmer for 5 minutes, until the sauce has reduced slightly.
5   Return the gammon to the pan and simmer for 10 minutes until tender. Arrange the gammon on a bed of braised spinach and pour the sauce over the steaks.

Stuffed bacon roll

🔪🔪 3 hours soaking,
    then 2½ hours

Serves 8–12

1.5–1.8 kg /3–4 lb rolled middle cut bacon
*   joint (back and streaky)*
15 ml /1 tbls Demerara sugar
butter for greasing
For the stuffing
50 g /2 oz butter
1 celery stalk, finely chopped
175 g /6 oz mushrooms, coarsely chopped
30 ml /2 tbls freshly chopped parsley
finely grated zest of 1 lemon
5 ml /1 tsp dried mixed herbs
75 g /3 oz fresh white breadcrumbs
1 medium-sized egg, beaten
salt and freshly ground black pepper

1   Cover the bacon joint with cold water and soak for 3 hours. Then drain, weigh and

calculate cooking time as for baking in foil.
2   Put the joint in a large saucepan, cover with cold water, bring to the boil, cover and simmer gently for half the calculated cooking time.
3   Meanwhile, make the stuffing. Melt 25 g /1 oz of the butter in a frying-pan and fry the celery gently for 5 minutes. Add the mushrooms and fry for another 3 minutes. Off the heat, stir in the parsley, lemon zest, herbs, breadcrumbs, egg and salt and pepper to taste.
4   Heat the oven to 190C /375F /gas 5. Drain the joint, remove the string and peel off the rind.
5   Unroll the joint and lay it flat, spread the stuffing on the inside, then re-roll and tie with string.
6   Place the joint in a deep, lightly greased casserole and dot with the remaining butter. Cover, transfer to the centre of the oven and bake.
7   About 30 minutes before the end of the cooking time, uncover the casserole, sprinkle the top surface of the joint with sugar, and allow it to brown a little.
8   Remove the string and serve hot, or leave the string on while the joint cools and serve cold, carved in slices.

Glazed pineapple gammon steaks

🔪 20 minutes

Serves 4

4 smoked gammon steaks, weighing
*   100–150 g /4–5 oz each*
40 g /1½ oz butter, melted
22.5 ml /1½ tbls Dijon mustard
4 or 8 pineapple rings, fresh or canned,
*   drained*
22.5 ml /1½ tbls Demerara sugar
watercress sprigs, to garnish

1   With scissors, cut off the gammon rind if any, and snip around the edges of the steaks at 25 mm /1 in intervals, to prevent them from curling under the heat. Heat the grill without the grid to medium.
2   Brush both sides of each steak with melted butter, lay the steaks on the grill rack, and cook for 4 minutes. Turn the steaks over, spread with mustard and grill for a further 3 minutes.
3   Arrange 1 or 2 pineapple rings on each gammon steak and brush with the remaining melted butter. Sprinkle the sugar evenly over the fruit and gammon, and grill for another 2–3 minutes, increasing the heat if necessary, until the pineapple rings are slightly browned and glazed.
4   Serve immediately, garnished with sprigs of watercress.

Bacon rolls with cider

⏰🔪🔪 soaking prunes overnight,
        then about 40 minutes

Serves 4

12 lean slices smoked bacon
25 g /1 oz butter
1 medium-sized onion, finely chopped
50 g /2 oz prunes, soaked overnight
1 large cooking apple, peeled, cored and
*   grated*
25 g /1 oz grated suet
25 g /1 oz chopped walnuts
60 ml /4 tbls cooked rice
finely grated zest of ½ lemon
1 egg, beaten
salt and freshly ground black pepper
275 ml /10 fl oz dry cider
15 ml /1 tbls finely chopped fresh parsley

1 Cut the rinds off the bacon slices and discard. Using the back of a knife, stretch each slice, being careful to keep it in 1 piece.
2 In a small saucepan, melt half the butter and sauté the chopped onion over a gentle heat for 7 minutes, or until softened, stirring occasionally. Leave to cool a little.
3 Drain the prunes well and cut in half. Remove the stones and chop the prunes finely. In a bowl, combine the chopped prunes, grated apple and suet, chopped walnuts, cooked rice, grated lemon zest and cooled sautéed onion. Stir in the beaten egg and season with salt and freshly ground black pepper.
4 Divide the stuffing equally between the bacon slices. Spread it evenly. Roll up carefully, starting with the thinner end, to make a fat roll. Secure each roll with fine string.
5 In a frying-pan large enough to take the bacon rolls comfortably in a single layer, heat the remaining butter. Lay the bacon rolls side by side in the hot butter and sauté over a moderate heat until lightly and evenly browned, turning them with a spatula.
6 Remove with a slotted spoon to a flameproof casserole. Pour the cider over and bring to a simmer. Cover and simmer gently for 15 minutes.
7 Remove the bacon rolls with a slotted spoon. Arrange neatly on a heated serving dish. Remove the strings and keep warm.
8 Boil the sauce over a high heat to reduce it by half, stirring occasionally with a wooden spoon. Strain the sauce over the rolls. Sprinkle a fine line of parsley down the centre and serve immediately.

Gammon with whisky sauce

Whisky gives the sauce for this dish a delightful and distinct flavour, which combines admirably with gammon. Serve the gammon with French beans and glazed new potatoes.

about 2 hours

Serves 6

1.4 kg /3 lb corner of gammon
15 ml /1 tbls olive oil
15 ml /1 tbls dried thyme
salt and freshly ground black pepper
8 shallots, peeled
2 garlic cloves, crushed
75 ml /3 fl oz whisky

1 Heat the oven to 190C /375F /gas 5. Put the gammon on a large piece of foil, skin side down. Rub the cut surface of the meat with oil, then with thyme and salt and pepper.
2 Put the whole shallots and crushed garlic around the gammon. Pour 50 ml /2 fl oz whisky carefully around the joint, then bring together the edges of the foil and seal. Put the joint on a rack in a roasting tin and pour a cupful of water into the tin. Cook for the calculated time.
3 Remove the tin from the oven and transfer the gammon to a warmed carving platter, skin side up. Reserve the juices in the foil. Carefully peel off the skin, then slice the gammon. Arrange the slices neatly on a serving platter and place the shallots on top of the slices. Keep warm.
4 Pour the reserved juices from the foil into the roasting tin, stir in the remaining whisky and heat through over a gentle heat. Pour a little of the sauce over the gammon slices and serve the rest in a sauce-boat.

Gammon with whisky sauce

COOKING HAM

A beautiful cold cooked ham is a universal favourite for a buffet party, while wafer-thin slices of top-quality raw ham served with slices of sweet juicy melon or ripe figs make a delicious starter.

A ham is the hind leg of the pig which is cured separately from the rest of the carcass – the kind one used to see hanging from a hook up the chimney in a farmhouse kitchen. The leg may be cut on the curve round the bone or straight across, when it is called a short-cut ham. A gammon is the identical portion of the pig, but it is cured with the whole bacon side before butchering. The cooking method is identical and the two joints are interchangeable.

Many varieties of ham have to be cooked before they are palatable. Other hams are specially cured to be eaten raw, though some of them may be used in cooking.

Cooking ham

Whole hams present a special problem because of their size; you will need a large preserving pan or stock pot to boil the ham in. A whole ham will feed a large crowd: buy the knuckle end of the leg, which will serve about 20. This has much of the beautiful appearance of a whole ham, but is considerably easier to carve.

Hams are nearly always soaked overnight before cooking to remove the curing salt.
Boiling: this is one of the simplest ways of cooking ham. Wash and weigh the joint and calculate the cooking time allowing 44 minutes per kg /20 minutes per lb, plus 20

minutes up to 4.5 kg /10 lb. A whole ham will need 33 minutes per kg /15 minutes per lb. Cover with cold water and bring slowly to simmering point in a large pan.

Remove the pan from the heat and skim the scum from the surface of the water. If liked, add 15 ml /1 tbls Demerara sugar or black treacle, a few peppercorns and 2 bay leaves for extra flavour. Root vegetables to serve with the joint may be added. Return the pan to the heat and simmer gently, calculating the cooking time from this point. Ham joints should never boil.

When a small joint is cooked, lift it out and carefully peel off the rind, if any. Reserve the cooking liquid for use as stock for a soup. Leave a large ham in the cooking liquid until it can be easily handled, then strip off the rind. If it is to be served cold allow 12 hours for cooling.

If you wish the ham may be glazed. In this case cooking is completed in the oven, so

Cold ham and Parma ham

Carving a knuckle end of ham

Stand the ham on the flat end and carve a 'V' below the knuckle. Slice the meat horizontally towards the bone.

Remove the loosely attached small bone at the knuckle end of the gammon. Release the slices by cutting parallel to the bone.

Turn the ham on its side and carve parallel to the bone, cutting neat slices. Repeat on the other side.

---

simmering time must be reduced to allow for this. Remove the ham from the simmering water 45 minutes before the end of the cooking time. Cut off the rind, working with a sharp knife and leaving a covering of fat about 5 mm /¼ in thick, then glaze.

Baking in foil: this method preserves all the natural flavour in the joint.

Weigh the prepared ham, then calculate the cooking time and heat the oven according to the chart on page 82. Wrap the joint loosely in a large piece of foil, sealing the edges over the top of the joint. Place the joint on a rack in a baking tin and pour a cupful of water into the tin. When the calculated cooking time is up, remove the joint from the oven, open the foil and peel off any rind. Reserve the juices that will have collected in the foil for a sauce to serve with the ham.

Parboiling and baking: this requires more attention than plain boiling or baking, but the cooked ham has a particularly good flavour and texture. Parboiling and baking is especially suitable for joints to be stuffed and for shoulder cuts. Soaking is not normally necessary.

Weigh the joint and calculate the cooking time as for baking in foil. Simmer the joint for half the total calculated cooking time if the joint is small, drain, stuff if wished, wrap in foil, and bake. For a large ham, bake for the last hour of the calculated cooking time.

Braising: weigh the prepared joint and calculate the cooking time, allowing 77 minutes per kg /35 minutes per lb, plus 35 minutes. Heat the oven to 180C /350F /gas 4. Melt about 25 g /1 oz butter in a deep, flameproof casserole and lightly brown some diced flavouring vegetables. Add a bay leaf, a sprig of thyme, black pepper and enough stock, cider or water mixed with wine to barely cover the vegetables. Set the joint on top.

Bring to simmering point, cover tightly and cook in the centre of the oven. When the joint is cooked, remove from the casserole and strip off the rind. Discard the herbs.

Honey-glazed baked ham

 overnight soaking, then 3½ hours plus cooling

Serves 18-20
4.5 kg /10 lb knuckle end raw ham or
  gammon
225 g /8 oz clear honey
fresh herbs, to garnish

1   Soak the ham or gammon in cold water overnight to remove any excess salt.
2   Place the joint in a saucepan and cover with cold water. Bring slowly to boiling point. Skim off any scum that rises to the surface then simmer, covered, for 2½ hours. Do not allow the joint to boil as this toughens the meat. When cooked, the knuckle bone should be loose enough to pull out easily, leaving the joint intact.
3   Lift out the boiled joint and allow it to cool slightly. Cut off the rind neatly with a sharp knife, leaving a covering of fat about 5 mm /¼ in thick. Heat the oven to 220C / 425F /gas 7.
4   Place the joint in a roasting tin and cover the fat with the clear honey. Bake the joint in the oven, basting it twice with the pan juices, for 30-45 minutes or until the ham is glazed. Leave until cold, then garnish with fresh herbs and serve.

● If you prefer, use a fruit glaze instead of honey. For a pineapple glaze use 150 g /5 oz soft brown sugar, 12.5 ml /2½ tsp dry mustard and 65 ml /2½ fl oz pineapple juice. Combine the ingredients in a small bowl and pour over the skinned joint. Bake as above, basting once or twice with the pan juices during the cooking time.
● For a spiced apple glaze use 150 g /5 oz soft brown sugar, 65 ml /2½ fl oz apple juice and 1.5 ml /¼ tsp ground mixed spice. Use as for pineapple glaze.

Cheese and ham soufflé

1 hour

Serves 4-6
50 g /2 oz butter
50 g /2 oz flour
425 ml /15 fl oz milk
6 medium-sized eggs
1 extra egg white
5 ml /1 tsp Dijon mustard
100 g /4 oz ham, cubed
150 g /5 oz freshly grated Cheddar cheese
25 g /1 oz freshly grated Parmesan cheese
salt and freshly ground black pepper
butter for greasing

1   Heat the oven to 180C /350F /gas 4. Melt the butter in a medium pan. Off the heat stir in the flour until smooth. Very slowly add the milk, stirring constantly. Return to the heat and cook slowly until thick and smooth. Remove pan from heat.
2   Separate the eggs and add the extra white to the other 6. Lightly mix the egg yolks together then stir them quickly into the sauce with a wooden spoon.
3   Add the mustard, cubed ham and the grated cheeses, and salt and pepper to taste. Mix everything in well. Lightly butter a 2 L /3½ pt soufflé dish.
4   Whisk the egg whites until they are very stiff, then gently fold them into the cheese mixture with a metal spoon.
5   Turn the soufflé mixture into the prepared dish. With a knife mark a circle round the top of the soufflé about 25 mm /1 in from the edge. (The centre of the soufflé inside this line will rise higher than the edge.) Bake for 40 minutes.
6   Test the soufflé with a clean knife inserted into the centre to see if it is ready. If the mixture is still runny, cook for a few minutes more. Serve at once.

STAR MENUS & RECIPE FILE

A glamorous barbecue dinner party on the patio is a delightfully different way to entertain your friends. Easy to prepare and fun to cook – especially as your guests can join in with the barbecueing – this menu is a marvellous idea for summer.

Start your outdoor meal with a summer spectacular – a chilled seafood salad tossed in a well-flavoured vinaigrette. Prawns, lobster meat, sole and crabmeat are the choices here but you can make your own selection. You'll find the flavour improves if the salad ingredients are left to marinate. Tasty and refreshing, this salad is a good contrast to the sizzling brochettes and the Courgette and tomato pilaff which follow. The pilaff adds body to what otherwise might prove to be too light a meal and the Salad Carrier contrasts very well with it.

To end the meal I chose a lemony dessert that reminds me of my childhood and is loved by everyone – Lemon meringue pie.

Côte d'Azur seafood salad

Barbecued pork and green pepper brochettes
Courgette and tomato pilaff
Salad Carrier

Lemon meringue pie

Wine: Provençal rose or a white Rhône wine

Plan-ahead timetable

On the day before
Côte d'Azur seafood salad: marinate the seafood overnight.
Barbecued pork and green pepper brochettes: prepare the pork and pepper; marinate in the refrigerator overnight.
Lemon meringue pie: make the pie and refrigerate.

One and a half hours before the meal
Barbecued pork and green pepper brochettes: remove bowl from the refrigerator. Light the barbecue.
Salad Carrier: prepare the lettuce and vinaigrette. Chill.

One hour before the meal
Courgette and tomato pilaff: prepare and keep warm.

Thirty minutes before the meal
Barbecued pork and pepper brochettes: thread skewers; cook.

Just before the meal
Côte d'Azur seafood salad: assemble.
Salad Carrier: assemble and dress.

Côte d'Azur seafood salad

Serves 4–6
225 g /8 oz cooked lobster meat
225 g /8 oz cooked halibut or sole
225 g /8 oz cooked crabmeat
225 g /8 oz prawns, defrosted if frozen
1 round lettuce, washed and chilled
1 cos lettuce, washed and chilled
4 medium-sized ripe tomatoes
8 large black olives
1 tomato rose
finely chopped fresh parsley
For the vinaigrette
10 ml /2 tsp Dijon mustard
150 ml /5 fl oz wine vinegar
450 ml /16 fl oz olive oil
salt and freshly ground black pepper
2 garlic cloves, finely chopped
30 ml /2 tbls freshly chopped parsley

1 Using a fork, whisk all the ingredients for the vinaigrette together.
2 Dice the lobster meat and halibut or sole. Flake the crabmeat. Put the prawns, lobster meat, crabmeat and halibut or sole in individual bowls. Divide half of the vinaigrette between the bowls and leave the seafood to marinate, preferably overnight but for a minimum of 5 hours.
3 When ready to serve, line a platter with the inner leaves of the lettuces. Arrange the prawns, diced lobster, flaked crabmeat and halibut or sole separately on the bed of salad greens. Garnish with wedges of ripe tomato, black olives, a tomato rose and finely chopped parsley. Serve with additional vinaigrette.

 30 minutes, 5 hours or more marinating, then 10 minutes

Barbecued pork and green pepper brochettes

Serves 4
1 kg /2 lb pork, cut from the leg
2 large green peppers
1 Spanish onion, finely chopped
salt and freshly ground black pepper
90–120 ml /6–8 tbls olive oil

1 Trim the fat from the pork and cut the pork into 25 mm /1 in cubes (24 pieces in all). Core and seed the peppers, then cut into 24 squares, 25 mm /1 in in size.
2 Put the pork cubes and finely chopped onion in a bowl with salt and freshly ground black pepper and 90–120 ml /6–8 tbls olive oil. Add the green pepper squares. Toss well, cover the bowl with a plate and refrigerate overnight. Remove from the refrigerator 1–2 hours before cooking to allow the meat to come to room temperature.
3 When ready to cook, remove the meat and green peppers from the onion mixture and arrange alternately on 4 skewers. Brush with the olive oil and onion mixture. Season the brochettes with salt and freshly ground black pepper. Place on a grill over hot coals and cook for about 20 minutes or until tender, turning the skewers frequently and basting several times during cooking. Serve immediately.

● To serve these brochettes as a light first course in the Polynesian manner, simply cut the pork and pepper into 10 mm /½ in cubes and thread them onto bamboo skewers, then reduce the grilling time by about half. Served in this way, these tiny brochettes will feed 8 people.

🕐 🍴 15 minutes, then overnight marinating plus 30 minutes | 🍾 White Hermitage or a Provençal rosé

Courgette and tomato pilaff

Serves 4–6
350 g /12 oz long-grain rice
¼ Spanish onion, finely chopped
75 g /3 oz butter
425 ml /15 fl oz boiling, well-flavoured beef stock, home-made or from a cube
2.5 ml /½ tsp dried thyme
salt and freshly ground black pepper
2–4 small courgettes (according to size)
2 small tomatoes

1 Heat the oven to 180C /350F /gas 4. Wash the rice; drain and dry by wrapping it up in a cloth.
2 In a flameproof casserole, sauté the finely chopped onion in 25 g /1 oz butter until light golden in colour. Add the rice and continue to cook, stirring constantly, until it begins to colour. Then pour in the boiling stock, add the thyme and salt and freshly ground black pepper to taste.
3 Cover the casserole and place in the oven for 40 minutes, or until the liquid has been absorbed and the rice is tender, not mushy.
4 Meanwhile, wash the courgettes; trim the ends and slice thinly. Submerge the tomatoes in boiling water for 1 minute, then peel off the skins; remove the seeds and juice and cut the flesh into dice. Sauté the sliced courgettes in 25 g /1 oz butter, stirring constantly, until the courgettes are just tender. Add the diced tomatoes and continue to cook until the tomatoes are warmed through. Season generously with salt and freshly ground black pepper.
5 Just before serving, toss the cooked vegetables and the remaining butter into the cooked rice.

🍴 50 minutes

Salad Carrier

Serves 4
2 lettuces
1 hard-boiled egg
90–120 ml /6–8 tbls olive oil
30 ml /2 tbls wine vinegar
2.5–5 ml /½–1 tsp Dijon mustard
salt and freshly ground black pepper
a squeeze of lemon juice
30 ml /2 tbls finely chopped fresh parsley
60 ml /4 tbls finely chopped chives or green spring onion tops

1   Wash the lettuce leaves carefully under cold running water, then gently pat each leaf dry between the folds of a clean cloth. Make sure the leaves are perfectly dry. The dressing will not stick to wet leaves, and any excess moisture, in its turn, will dilute the flavour of the dressing. Lay the leaves out on a fresh cloth. Roll the cloth up loosely and chill in the vegetable compartment of the refrigerator for at least 1 hour, or until ready to serve.
2   To make the dressing, finely chop the hard-boiled egg and put in a bowl with the olive oil and wine vinegar. Season to taste with a little mustard, salt, freshly ground black pepper and a squeeze of lemon juice. Add the finely chopped fresh parsley and chives or spring onion tops.
3   Just before serving, arrange the lettuce leaves in a salad bowl and pour the dressing over the salad. Toss until each leaf is glistening with dressing.

● If you like a touch of the South of France in your cooking, just add one small clove of finely chopped garlic to the dressing.

20 minutes plus chilling

Lemon meringue pie

Serves 4–6
225g /8 oz made-weight shortcrust pastry, defrosted if frozen
60 ml /4 tbls cornflour
2.5 ml /½ tsp salt
275 g /10 oz sugar
425 ml /15 fl oz boiling water
3 lemons
15 ml /1 tbls butter
4 egg yolks, slightly beaten
For the meringue
3 egg whites
salt
175 g /6 oz caster sugar

1   Heat the oven to 200C /400F /gas 6. Roll the pastry out to a circle 5 mm /¼ in thick. Lift into a 20 cm /8 in flan case and press well into the sides. Trim off the top of the pastry and prick the base. Line the pastry case with foil and beans and bake for 10 minutes. Remove the foil and bake for a further 8-10 minutes.
2   Increase the heat to 220C /425F /gas 7. Mix the cornflour, salt, sugar and boiling water in the top pan of a double boiler. Put the pan over direct heat and cook, stirring continuously with a wooden spoon, until the mixture comes to the boil.
3   Turn down the heat and simmer gently for 15 minutes, stirring from time to time. Meanwhile grate the zest of 1 lemon and squeeze the juice of all 3.
4   Beat the butter, 90 ml /6 tbls lemon juice and the grated lemon zest into the sugar mixture. Stir in the egg yolks and put the pan on the top of a double boiler containing simmering water. Cook, stirring, until thick. Do not allow the mixture to come to the boil or the yolks will curdle. Cool briefly.
5   Fill the half-baked pastry shell with the mixture.
6   Using a wire whisk or rotary beater, whisk the egg whites with a pinch of salt until they are stiff. Continue to whisk, adding the caster sugar in 4 batches. Spoon the meringue onto the pie, fluffing up the surface into attractive peaks. Bake in the oven for 15 minutes until golden brown. Serve hot or cold.

defrosting the pastry,
then 1½ hours plus cooling if wished

STAR MENU 2

Italian spinach flan

Loin of pork boulangère
Glazed onions and carrots
Provençal salad with
garlic croûtons

French walnut roll

Wine: Vacqueyras or
another Côtes-du-Rhône

S haring good food with friends in a relaxed atmosphere is one of life's real pleasures. This menu is for an informal, country-style lunch, perfect for a relaxed Sunday afternoon. In fact, entertaining at lunch on Sundays is a growing fashion, especially informal entertaining, when both you and your guests have plenty of time to sit round the table enjoying good food, good drink and pleasant company. You will find this Continental, country-style menu for six is simplicity itself to prepare, and equally good for serving in a country kitchen, or in the more formal surroundings of a dining room.

Start off with an Italian spinach flan. It contains a creamy mixture, typical of northern Italy, of spinach, cottage cheese, eggs and cream, enlivened by a little freshly grated Parmesan cheese and nutmeg. It is served cold, garnished for the party with thin, perfect slices of hard-boiled egg, though it is equally delicious lukewarm or cold.

Our main course is Loin of pork boulangère. Cook the loin in one piece on the bone, then cut down between the chops to serve the meat. The chops will be especially succulent from being cooked on a bed of herb-flavoured sliced potatoes. Accompany it with a bowl of Glazed onions and carrots; using tiny button onions and tender young carrots adds a touch of luxury for party presentation.

Serve a tossed green salad after the rich dish of pork and potatoes. Thin croûtons of stale French bread, rubbed with a cut clove of garlic, sprinkled with a little oil and topped by a section of anchovy fillet, give it a rustic, Provençal touch guaranteed to refresh you and clear your palate.

French walnut roll makes a light end to the meal: a nutty-textured sponge roll, filled with chilled whipped cream. This can be prepared on the day before the party if necessary. Just before it is served, unroll it and fill with its airy cream filling and reroll. It's so delicious, why wait for a Sunday with guests? Why not spoil the family with one this coming weekend?

Plan-ahead timetable

On the day before
Italian spinach flan: make and bake flan; cool completely then cover with cling film and refrigerate. Hard boil the eggs.

Early on the day
French walnut roll: prepare and bake sponge; roll up with greaseproof paper inside; leave to cool.

Two and a half hours before the meal
Provençal salad with garlic croûtons: prepare salad leaves and chill. Make the croûtons, cover with cling film. Make dressing.

One and three quarter hours before the meal
Loin of pork boulangère: heat oven to 220C /425F /gas 7. Prepare meat and roast for 1 hour. Parboil potatoes; arrange with onion, parsley and butter in large baking dish.
Glazed onions and carrots: prepare the vegetables.

Italian spinach flan

Serves 6
225 g /8 oz made-weight shortcrust pastry, defrosted if frozen
For the filling
350 g /12 oz frozen spinach
25 g /1 oz butter
salt and freshly ground black pepper
225 g /8 oz cottage cheese
3 medium-sized eggs, lightly beaten
30–60 ml /2–4 tbls freshly grated Parmesan cheese
90 ml /6 tbls thick cream
a pinch of freshly grated nutmeg
For the garnish
2 hard-boiled eggs, cut into 6 slices each
30 ml /2 tbls melted butter

1   Heat the oven to 200C /400F /gas 6. Roll the pastry out to a
circle 5 mm /¼ in thick. Lift into a 22 cm /8½ in flan dish and press
well into the sides of the dish. Trim off the top of the pastry and
prick the base. Line the pastry with foil and beans and bake for 10
minutes. Remove the foil and bake for a further 8–10 minutes.
Leave the half-baked pastry case, still in its tin, on a baking sheet.
Reduce the heat to 180C /350F /gas 4.
2   Place the spinach with the butter in a heavy-based saucepan and
stir over a low heat until the spinach is cooked. Season to taste with
salt and freshly ground black pepper, then thoroughly drain the
spinach and turn into a mixing bowl. Add the cottage cheese, beaten
eggs, grated Parmesan and cream to the bowl with grated nutmeg to
taste. Using a wooden spoon, mix the ingredients thoroughly
together.
3   Turn the spinach mixture into the pastry case and spread
evenly. Bake the flan in the oven for 30 minutes, or until the
spinach filling has set.
4   Just before serving, garnish the flan with slices of hard-boiled
egg and brush each slice with melted butter. Serve the flan hot,
lukewarm or cold.

 defrosting the pastry,
then 1½ hours plus cooling if wished

Thirty minutes before the meal
Glazed onions and carrots: begin cooking onions and carrots.
Italian spinach flan: remove from refrigerator.
French walnut roll: unroll cake, add cream filling and re-roll.

Twenty minutes before the meal
Loin of pork boulangère: reduce oven to 200F /400C /gas 6.
Place meat on vegetables, add stock and return to oven.
Heat individual plates and vegetable dish.
Italian spinach flan: place on serving dish, garnish and glaze.
Glazed onions and carrots: turn into hot dish and keep warm.

Between the first and main courses
Provençal salad with garlic croûtons: toss, then garnish.

Between the main course and dessert
French walnut roll: garnish and serve.

Loin of pork boulangère

Serves 6

1.5 kg /3¼ lb loin of pork from the rib end, without rind, chined
salt and freshly ground black pepper
mixed fresh rosemary and thyme, crumbled
6–8 large potatoes
275 ml /10 fl oz milk
1 Spanish onion, finely chopped
30 ml /2 tbls finely chopped fresh parsley
50 g /2 oz butter, softened
225 ml /8 fl oz light chicken stock, home-made or from a cube, or
*   water*

1   Heat the oven to 220C /425F /gas 7. Wipe the meat with a clean
damp cloth, then generously sprinkle the surface with salt, freshly
ground black pepper and crumbled fresh rosemary and thyme and
rub in with your fingers. Place the meat, fat side up, on a rack in a
roasting tin. Roast in the oven for about 1 hour or until the pork is
half cooked, basting occasionally.
2   Meanwhile, peel and thinly slice the potatoes. Pour the milk into
a large, heavy-based saucepan, add 275 ml /10 fl oz water and bring
slowly to simmering point. Add the sliced potatoes to the pan and
simmer for 10 minutes or until half cooked, then drain.
3   Select a shallow oval or rectangular gratin dish (preferably
flameproof) which is large enough to hold the pork. Combine the
drained potatoes with the chopped onion and parsley and spread
over the base of the dish. Season to taste with salt and black pepper
and spread with the softened butter. Remove the pork from the oven
and reduce the oven temperature to 200C /400F /gas 6.
4   Place the pork on top of the vegetables in the gratin dish and
pour in the hot stock or water. Set the dish on a protective asbestos
mat over medium heat and bring the liquid to the boil. Then
carefully transfer the dish to the oven. Cook for a further 30–40
minutes, or until the meat juices run clear when the meat is pierced
with a skewer, almost all the liquid has cooked away and the
potatoes are tender. Garnish with cutlet frills and serve.

● This dish acquired its name from the time when the only oven in
the village would be the bakery oven. Villagers would send along
their dinners to be cooked in the hot oven after the bread had come
out. Being sensible people, they packed as much into the tin as they
could, potatoes sliced underneath and meat on top, so that the juices
dripped down onto the vegetables.

1¾ hours   Vacqueyras or another
                  Côtes-du-Rhône red

Glazed onions and carrots

Serves 6

350 g /12 oz button onions
350 g /12 oz small carrots
25 g /1 oz butter
60 ml /4 tbls chicken stock, home-made or from a cube
15 ml /1 tbls sugar
salt and freshly ground black pepper

1   Peel the onions but leave them whole. Scrape the carrots and cut
them evenly into thick slices.
2   Place the vegetables in a heavy-based saucepan and pour in cold
water to cover. Set the pan over a high heat and bring the water to
the boil, then remove the pan from the heat and drain the
vegetables.
3   Return the vegetables to the pan; add the butter and chicken
stock, then season with sugar, salt and freshly ground black pepper.
4   Set the pan on a moderate heat and bring the liquid to the boil.
Cover the pan, reduce the heat to low and simmer the vegetables
until they have absorbed all the liquid and are lightly browned.
Shake the pan frequently to prevent the vegetables sticking and
burning. Turn the glazed vegetables into a heated vegetable dish
and serve.

● Cooking time depends on the age of the carrots and the size of the
slices; this is an ideal way to cook old carrots, which can take as long
as 45 minutes. Add more stock, if necessary, and put the onions in
towards the end of the cooking time.

30 minutes

Provençal salad with garlic croûtons

Serves 6–8
8 thin slices stale French bread
1–2 garlic cloves, cut in half
about 135 ml /9 tbls olive oil
coarse salt
2 anchovy fillets, cut in half lengthways
30 ml /2 tbls wine vinegar
2.5 ml /½ tsp Dijon mustard
salt and freshly ground black pepper
1–2 heads chicory, curly endive or lettuce
30 ml /2 tbls finely chopped fresh parsley or chives

1   Rub each slice of bread with a piece of cut garlic, then sprinkle with a few drops of olive oil and a few grains of coarse salt. Cut each half anchovy fillet into 2 pieces and place 1 piece on each slice of bread. Set the croûtons aside.
2   Make a mustard-flavoured French dressing: place the wine vinegar in a small bowl or cup and, using a fork, whisk in the mustard. Then whisk in 90 ml /6 tbls olive oil and season to taste with salt and freshly ground black pepper. Reserve.
3   Separate the chicory, endive or lettuce into leaves. Trim, wash and thoroughly dry the leaves and chill until needed. Just before serving, place the leaves in a salad bowl. Whisk the mustard dressing, pour over the leaves, and toss until the leaves are evenly coated and glistening. Garnish the salad with the croûtons and sprinkle over the herbs. Serve the salad immediately.

 20 minutes

French walnut roll

Serves 6
butter for greasing
30 ml /2 tbls flour
pinch of salt
2.5 ml /½ tsp baking powder
6 eggs, separated
125 g /4 oz caster sugar
125 g /4 oz walnuts, coarsely ground
For the filling and decoration
caster sugar for sprinkling
425 ml /15 fl oz thick cream
75–100 ml /3–4 oz caster sugar
icing sugar for dredging
8 walnut halves

1   Grease a 23 × 35 cm /9 × 14 in Swiss roll tin. Line the tin with greaseproof paper and grease the lining paper. Heat the oven to 180C /350F /gas 4.
2   Sift the flour, salt and baking powder into a bowl and reserve.
3   Place the egg yolks and caster sugar in a large mixing bowl and whisk lightly together using a balloon or hand-held electric whisk. Set the bowl over a pan half full of hot water. (The bowl should sit snugly and should not touch the water.) Continue whisking until the mixture will hold the trail of the whisk for 3 seconds – about 15 minutes whisking by hand or 5 minutes using an electric whisk.
4   Remove the bowl from the heat and whisk until the mixture is cool. Using a large metal spoon, fold in the walnuts.
5   In a clean bowl and using a scrupulously dry whisk, whisk the egg whites until stiff but not dry. Fold the whites into the walnut mixture. Then gently but thoroughly fold in the sifted flour.
6   Pour the cake mixture into the prepared tin and smooth the surface with a spatula. Bake for 20–30 minutes, until the cake is well risen and springs back when lightly pressed.
7   While the cake is baking, cut 2 pieces of greaseproof paper slightly larger than the size of the tin. Lay one piece on a damp tea-towel and sprinkle with 15–30 ml /1–2 tbls caster sugar.
8   Turn out the baked cake onto the sugared paper and peel off the lining paper. Trim away the crusty edges, then lay the remaining piece of greaseproof paper over the cake. With the aid of the towel and paper, roll up the cake from one of the long ends with the top piece of paper inside. Place the cake, seam side down, on a wire rack, cover with the damp tea-towel and leave until completely cold.
9   Not more than an hour before serving, whisk the cream until it forms soft peaks and sweeten to taste with caster sugar. Carefully unroll the cold cake and remove the paper. Spread most of the cream evenly over the surface, then roll up the cake again. (This time without the paper inside!)
10   Place the cake on a long, flat serving plate, dredge thickly with sifted icing sugar and garnish with cream and walnut halves.

1–1¼ hours plus cooling

Gammon steaks with piquant sauce

Serves 4
4 × 200 g /7 oz gammon steaks, each 15 mm /¼ in thick
40 g /1½ oz butter
45 ml /3 tbls olive oil
10 ml /2 tsp finely snipped fresh chives
tarragon leaves, to garnish (optional)
For the piquant sauce
4 shallots, or ½ Spanish onion, finely chopped
150 ml /5 fl oz dry white wine
4–6 tarragon leaves, finely chopped
150 ml /5 fl oz beef stock, home-made or from a cube
60 ml /4 tbls tomato purée
150 ml /5 fl oz thick cream
25 g /1 oz butter, diced

1   To make the sauce, combine the shallots or onion, wine and tarragon leaves in a small saucepan. Cook over high heat until the wine has reduced to about 30 ml /2 tbls.
2   Pour in the beef stock and stir in the tomato purée. Cover the pan and simmer gently for 1 hour over very low heat, or until the liquid has reduced to 150 ml /5 fl oz. Add the thick cream to the reduced sauce and simmer for a further 15 minutes.
3   Meanwhile, remove the rind from the gammon steaks and snip the fat at frequent intervals, to prevent the steaks from curling up during cooking.
4   In a large frying-pan, heat the butter and olive oil. Fry the steaks over a low heat for 6–7 minutes on each side, or until cooked. Keep warm.
5   Strain the sauce through a fine sieve. Gradually whisk in the diced butter.
6   To serve, transfer the hot gammon steaks to a heated serving dish. Pour the sauce over the steaks, then sprinkle with the chives. Garnish with tarragon, if wished, and serve immediately.

 1 hour 45 minutes

Risotto with ham and mushrooms

Serves 4–6
30 ml /2 tbls olive oil
25 g /1 oz butter
1 Spanish onion, finely chopped
225 g /8 oz Italian medium-grain rice
225 g /8 oz prosciutto or another raw or smoked ham, diced
90 ml /6 tbls dry white wine
600 ml /1 pt hot chicken stock, home-made or from a cube
1.5 ml /¼ tsp powdered saffron
90 ml /6 tbls finely chopped mushrooms
salt and freshly ground black pepper
pinch of grated nutmeg
90 ml /6 tbls freshly grated Parmesan cheese
parsley sprigs, to garnish

1   Heat the olive oil and butter in a large, heavy-bottomed saucepan. Add the onion and cook over a medium heat for 7–10 minutes or until softened, stirring with a wooden spoon occasionally.
2   Stir in the rice and ham and cook for a further 5–7 minutes, or until the rice has lightly browned.
3   Pour in the dry white wine, bring to simmering point and simmer until the wine has been absorbed.
4   In a small bowl, combine 30 ml /2 tbls hot chicken stock and the powdered saffron. Blend with a wooden spoon to dissolve.
5   Add the remaining stock to the rice with the finely chopped mushrooms. Season to taste with salt and freshly ground black pepper and the grated nutmeg. Bring to simmering point, stirring constantly. Cover and simmer for a further 15 minutes.
6   Stir in the saffron and grated Parmesan cheese and correct the seasoning. Cook for a further 5 minutes, until the rice is tender.
7   Transfer the risotto to a heated serving dish. Fork up the rice grains, garnish with parsley and serve immediately.

● Prosciutto is the best ham to use in this distinctly Italian recipe, though it is expensive. For an economical supper dish for 4, you may want to use a less expensive ham.

 50 minutes

Braised pork with cabbage

Serves 4

1.4 kg /3 lb lean belly of pork, skinned and cut into 4 serving pieces
1 garlic clove
salt and freshly ground black pepper
50 g /2 oz butter
1 medium-sized firm white cabbage
6–8 black peppercorns
15 ml /1 tbls caraway seeds
celery leaves, to garnish

1   Peel the garlic clove and cut it into 4 lengthways. Make an incision in each piece of pork and push a sliver of garlic into each one. Season them all over with salt and freshly ground black pepper.
2   Melt the butter in a large flameproof casserole and brown the pork all over (if your pan is not large enough for the meat to brown in one layer, brown it in a roasting tin and then transfer to a casserole and pour the fat over).
3   Cut the cabbage in half with a sharp knife. Remove the hard central core and ribs and cut the cabbage into thin wedges. Add the black peppercorns, caraway seeds and salt to taste and pack around the pork in the casserole.
4   Cover the casserole tightly, place over a low heat and simmer very, very gently for 1½ hours, stirring from time to time to prevent the cabbage and pork from sticking to the bottom. Do not add any water unless absolutely necessary; the cabbage should cook in its own juices and those of the pork.
5   Ten minutes before the end of the cooking time heat a large, shallow serving dish. When the pork and cabbage are tender, arrange a bed of cabbage on the dish and place the pork on top. Skim any fat from the remaining pan juices and pour over the entire dish. Serve very hot, garnished with celery leaves.

● You can control the cost of this dish by the cut of pork you choose; pork chops could be used, but a very lean piece of pork belly, skinned, is ideal for a family meal in winter. Ask for the thick end of the belly, which is leaner. Serve the dish with floury potatoes or plain dumplings.

1¾ hours

Skewered sausages and bacon

Serves 4

12 small slices streaky bacon, rinded
24 small canned cocktail sausages, drained
freshly ground black pepper
olive oil
tomato wedges, to garnish
watercress, to garnish

1   Heat the grill without the grid to high.
2   Cut each bacon slice in half and wrap each piece around a cocktail sausage. Thread six sausages wrapped in bacon on to each of 4 skewers. Season with freshly ground black pepper.
3   Brush the grid of the grill pan with a little olive oil, place the skewered sausages and bacon on the grid and grill 7.5 cm /3 in from the heat for 5 minutes on each side.
4   Arrange the skewers on a heated platter and serve immediately, garnished with tomato wedges and watercress.

20 minutes

Braised pork loin with cream and caraway

Serves 8

2.3 kg /5 lb loin of pork, boned
  and rolled, rind removed
salt
freshly ground black pepper
75 g /3 oz butter
45 ml /3 tbls olive oil
3 Spanish onions, coarsely chopped
25 ml /1½ tbls paprika
350 ml /12 fl oz dry white wine

215 ml /7½ fl oz chicken stock,
  home-made or from a cube
25 ml /1½ tbls caraway seeds
25 ml /1½ tbls beurre manié,
  made by mashing 12 ml /¾ tbls
  butter with 12 ml /¾ tbls flour
350 ml /12 fl oz soured cream
25 ml /1½ tbls finely snipped
  chives
chives and parsley, to garnish

1   Heat the oven to 170C /325F /gas 3.
2   Pat the pork dry with absorbent paper and season to taste with salt and freshly ground black pepper. In a large flameproof casserole, heat the butter and olive oil. When the foaming subsides, brown the pork evenly on all sides. Remove from the pan.
3   Add the chopped onions to the fat remaining in the pan and cook, stirring occasionally with a wooden spoon, for 20 minutes or until golden brown.
4   Pour off the excess fat and stir in the paprika, dry white wine and chicken stock. Season with caraway seeds and salt and pepper to taste and bring to the boil, stirring occasionally with a wooden spoon.
5   Return the browned pork to the casserole. Cover and cook in the oven for 2 hours, or until tender.
6   Remove the pork from the casserole, reserving the sauce, and place it on a heated serving dish. Remove the string and keep warm.
7   Strain the sauce into a small saucepan and bring to the boil over a high heat. Boil rapidly for 3–4 minutes, or until the liquid has reduced by about a quarter.
8   Stir in the beurre manié, a piece at a time, and continue to boil, stirring constantly, until the sauce has thickened.
9   Stir in the soured cream and finely snipped chives. Warm through gently without boiling. Correct the seasoning and pour the sauce into a heated sauce-boat. Garnish the pork with chives and parsley. Serve immediately, accompanied by the sauce.

 2½ hours

Fried cabbage and chipolatas

Serves 4

450 g /1 lb firm white cabbage
salt
100 g /4 oz fat bacon, diced
olive oil for greasing
450 g /1 lb chipolata sausages
freshly ground black pepper
2 tomatoes, thinly sliced

1   Discard the outer leaves from the cabbage, cut it into quarters and remove the central core. Shred the cabbage finely.
2   Bring to the boil 25 mm /1 in salted water in a large saucepan. Add the shredded cabbage and boil for 1 minute. Drain the cabbage, rinse under cold running water; drain again.
3   Heat the grill without the grid to high.
4   In a small saucepan, heat the fat bacon over a moderate heat for 10 minutes or until it has released 60 ml /4 tbls melted fat.
5   When ready to grill, brush the grid of the grill with a little olive oil and grill the sausages for about 12 minutes or until evenly cooked and golden brown.
6   Meanwhile, pour the melted bacon fat into a large saucepan. Add the shredded cabbage and cook over a high heat for 8 minutes or until tinged with brown, stirring constantly with a wooden spoon. Season with salt and freshly ground black pepper to taste.
7   Arrange the cabbage on a heated rectangular serving platter. Lay the sausages side by side over the top and garnish with the sliced tomatoes. Serve immediately.

● The crisp bacon pieces remaining when all the fat has been sweated from the bacon can be crumbled into a soup or over the top of a salad as a garnish.

50 minutes

Thai pork satés

Serves 4 as an appetizer

550 g /1¼ lb fillet of pork
15 ml /1 tbls curry powder
1.5 ml /¼ tsp coriander powder
1.5 ml /¼ tsp turmeric powder
pinch of cayenne pepper
salt
45 ml /3 tbls peanut oil

For Thai peanut sauce
100 g /4 oz finely cut desiccated
   coconut
100 g /4 oz salted peanuts
2.5 ml /½ tsp turmeric powder

2.5 ml /½ tsp curry powder
1.5 ml /¼ tsp cayenne pepper
30 ml /2 tbls sugar
5 ml /1 tsp lemon juice
salt

For Thai cucumber relish
½ cucumber, peeled
30 ml /2 tbls thinly sliced
   shallots or spring onions
½ hot green chilli, very thinly sliced
30–45 ml /2–3 tbls lemon juice
20–30 ml /4–6 tsp sugar

1   Cut the pork into 5 mm /¼ in thick slices, then cut each slice into
25 mm × 5 cm /1 × 2 in rectangles. Place the pork strips in a bowl
and add the curry, coriander, turmeric, cayenne pepper and salt.
2   Wet your hands and gently knead the spices into the meat,
adding 5 ml /1 tsp each of peanut oil and water to help work in the
spice mixture. Knead again. Cover the bowl and leave for 2 hours.
3   To make Thai peanut sauce, put the desiccated coconut in a
bowl and add 300 ml /10 fl oz water. Knead for 3 minutes. Strain
the coconut through a fine sieve, pressing the coconut milk – about
250 ml /8 fl oz – into a bowl with a wooden spoon.
4   Grind the peanuts coarsely, using a clean electric coffee grinder.
Add the turmeric, curry, cayenne pepper and sugar to the coconut
milk and cook over a medium heat, stirring, until the sauce comes to
the boil. Reduce the heat to low and add the ground peanuts.
Continue to cook, stirring constantly, for 2 minutes. Add the lemon
juice and salt to taste. Remove the sauce from the heat and cool.
5   To make Thai cucumber relish, cut the cucumber in half
lengthways and then cut each half into very thin slices. Put the
sliced cucumber in a bowl. Add the thinly sliced shallots or spring
onions and green chilli, lemon juice and sugar. Chill until ready to
serve.
6   To grill the pork satés, thread 8 thin metal or bamboo skewers
with 4 pieces of pork each. The skewer enters the meat 2–3 times,
like a needle threading through cloth.
7   Heat the grill without the grid to high. Brush the grid and the
pork satés with peanut oil and grill 10 cm /4 in from the heat,
turning frequently, until the satés are cooked through – 4–6
minutes on each side. Serve 2 skewers per person. Garnish each
plate with Thai peanut sauce and cucumber relish.

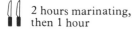 2 hours marinating,
then 1 hour

Bacon in beer

Serves 4–6

1 –1.4 kg /2–3 lb bacon collar joint
75 g /3 oz seedless raisins
8 cloves
10–15 ml /2–3 tsp dry mustard
30–45 ml /2–3 tbls dark brown sugar
275 ml /10 fl oz lager
15 ml /1 tbls cornflour
10 ml /2 tsp wine vinegar

1   Place the bacon joint in a large bowl and cover with cold water.
Leave to soak for at least 3 hours, or overnight if it is very salty.
2   Drain the bacon and place it in a large saucepan. Cover with
fresh cold water. Bring to the boil, then cover and simmer for 1–1½
hours, depending on size, until tender. Cover the raisins with 275
ml /10 fl oz lukewarm water and leave to soak for about 1 hour.
3   Heat the oven to 180C /350F /gas 4. Drain the raisins and
reserve the soaking liquid.
4   When the bacon is cooked, drain it well. When it is cool enough
to handle, remove and discard the skin. Using a sharp knife, score
the fat in a diamond pattern. Stud the diamonds with cloves.
5   Combine the mustard with the brown sugar, and spread this
evenly over the scored fat of the bacon. Place the joint in a roasting
tin, fat side up. Pour the lager into the pan and baste the lean sides
of the joint only. Bake in the oven for 25–35 minutes, basting the
lean meat of the joint occasionally with the pan juices.
6   Transfer the bacon to a heated serving dish. Skim the tin juices
of excess fat if necessary. Place the roasting tin over high heat and
boil it to reduce the juices by half. Add the reserved raisin soaking
liquid to the roasting tin and bring to the boil, stirring and scraping
the bottom and sides of the pan with a wooden spoon.
7   Dissolve the cornflour in 30 ml /2 tbls of cold water and stir into
the liquid in the roasting pan. Bring to the boil, stirring constantly,
and simmer until the sauce is thick and smooth. Add the wine
vinegar and raisins and mix well. Pour into a heated sauce-boat and
serve the sauce with the bacon.

● This is an unusual dish with a strong flavour. Serve it with a bowl
of floury boiled potatoes.

 soaking the bacon,
then 3 hours

Italian courgette and ham pie

Serves 6
900 g /2 lb courgettes
30 ml /2 tbls olive oil
25 g /1 oz butter
1 Spanish onion, finely chopped
salt and freshly ground black pepper
100 g /4 oz freshly grated Gruyère cheese
75 g /3 oz freshly grated Parmesan cheese
2 thin slices cooked ham, cut into strips
2 eggs, beaten
450 g /1 lb made-weight puff pastry, defrosted if frozen
flour for dusting
butter for greasing
1 egg yolk

1   Wipe the courgettes with a damp cloth. Trim them and slice in
half lengthways. Cut each halved courgette into 5 mm /¼ in slices.
2   In a heavy-based saucepan, heat the olive oil and butter. When
the foaming subsides, add the finely chopped onion and cook over a
moderate heat for 7–10 minutes or until soft, stirring occasionally
with a wooden spoon. Add the prepared courgettes, stir and season
to taste with salt and freshly ground black pepper. Cook over a
moderate heat for 10–15 minutes, or until just tender, stirring
occasionally.
3   Remove the pan from the heat and stir in the freshly grated
Gruyère and Parmesan cheeses and the ham strips. Leave the
mixture to cool slightly before stirring in the beaten eggs. Correct
the seasoning and leave to cool.
4   Heat the oven to 375F /190C /gas 5.
5   Roll out two-thirds of the pastry on a lightly floured surface and
use it to line a greased 25 cm /10 in loose-bottomed fluted flan tin.
Reserve the trimmings. Place it on a baking tray and fill it with the
cooled courgette and ham mixture.
6   Roll out the remaining pastry to fit the top of the pie. Brush the
edges with egg yolk, cover the pie and press down the edges lightly
to seal. Flute the edges attractively. Make decorations with the
pastry trimmings and stick to the pie with a little water. Using a
pastry brush, lightly glaze the surface with the remaining egg yolk.
7   Bake in the oven for 25 minutes, or until the pastry is golden
brown. Remove the pie from the tin and serve immediately.

 defrosting the pastry,
then 1¼ hours

Pot roast of pork with grapes

Serves 4–6
1.8 kg /4 lb lean loin of pork, skinned, boned and rolled (about 1.4 kg /3 lb weight after preparation)
salt and freshly ground black pepper
45 ml /3 tbls gin
150 ml /5 fl oz unsweetened grape juice
150 ml /5 fl oz dry white wine
25 g /1 oz butter
30 ml /2 tbls flour
For the marinade
8 juniper berries, crushed
2 cloves, crushed
1 garlic clove, crushed
45 ml /3 tbls olive oil
90 ml /6 tbls dry white wine
For the garnish
30 ml /2 tbls butter
450 g /1 lb seedless grapes

1   Place the pork in a deep dish. Combine the marinade ingredients
and pour over the meat. Cover and leave to marinate at the bottom
of the refrigerator for 24 hours, turning several times.
2   Heat the oven to 190C /375F /gas 5. Drain the pork, reserving
the marinade. Place the joint in a roasting tin and sprinkle with salt
and black pepper. Pour 150 ml /5 fl oz cold water around the meat.
Cover tightly and roast for about 1¾ hours, basting occasionally,
until the juices run clear when the pork is pierced with a skewer.
3   Ten minutes before the end of roasting time, prepare the
garnish. Melt the butter in a large, heavy-based frying-pan, add the
grapes and sauté for 4–5 minutes until golden brown. Reserve.
4   Transfer the cooked pork to a heated, deep flameproof serving
dish. Pour the gin into a heated metal ladle, set alight and quickly
pour all over the meat.
5   Skim the fat from juices left in the roasting tin. Pour back into
the tin any juices that have collected around the pork on the serving
dish. Cover the pork and keep hot.
6   Add the grape juice, white wine and reserved marinade to the
juices in the roasting tin. Bring to the boil, scraping the base and
sides of the tin with a wooden spoon to loosen any crusty morsels.
Reduce the heat and leave the sauce to simmer for 2–3 minutes.
7   Meanwhile, make a beurre manié by working together the
butter and flour to a smooth paste.
8   Strain the sauce over the sautéed grapes in the frying-pan. Set
over a low heat and stir in the beurre manié, a little at a time.
Continue stirring until the sauce comes to the boil, then simmer for
3–4 minutes longer to cook the flour. Season and spoon into a
heated sauce-boat. Serve with the pork, which should be very hot.

 24 hours marinating,
then about 2 hours

Boiled bacon hock and chicken with dumplings

Serves 8
800 g /1¾ lb bacon hock
1.1 kg /2½ lb chicken
6 medium-sized potatoes, quartered
2 Spanish onions, quartered
6 medium-sized carrots, cut into chunks
salt
freshly ground black pepper
1 small cabbage, cut into 8 wedges

30 ml /2 tbls finely chopped fresh parsley, to garnish
For the cornmeal dumplings
65 g /2½ oz cornmeal
65 g /2½ oz self-raising flour
1.5 ml /¼ tsp salt
15 g /½ oz butter
½ egg, beaten
60–75 ml /4–5 tbls milk

1   Put the hock and the chicken into a heavy 4.5 L /8 pt saucepan, cover with water and bring to the boil. Cover the pan, reduce the heat and simmer for 1 hour.
2   Add the potatoes and simmer for a further 10 minutes. Add the onions and carrots and season to taste with salt and freshly ground black pepper (the bacon may have made the stock already salty) and simmer for 15 minutes. Check the bacon and chicken; if they are cooked, remove them and keep them warm.
3   Meanwhile, prepare the dumplings. Sift the cornmeal, flour and salt into a bowl. Rub in the butter until the mixture resembles fine breadcrumbs. Stir in the beaten egg and milk to make a soft dough.
4   Add the cabbage wedges to the saucepan and push them down into the simmering stock.
5   Drop rounded teaspoons of dough into the simmering stock. Cover and cook gently for 10–15 minutes, or until the dumplings are fluffy and firm and the vegetables are tender.
6   Remove the bacon hock to a board. With a sharp knife, remove and discard the skin and fat and cut the meat into chunks. Place the chicken on the board, remove and discard the skin and cut into 8 portions. Divide the meat between 8 individual heated soup bowls.
7   Divide the vegetables, dumplings and broth between the bowls and sprinkle each one with finely chopped parsley. Serve immediately.

 about 2 hours

Pork chops à la flamande

Serves 4
4 large pork chops, trimmed of excess fat
salt and freshly ground black pepper
50 g /2 oz butter
60 ml /4 tbls olive oil
1 Spanish onion, finely chopped
4–5 tart dessert apples, peeled, cored and quartered
45–60 ml /3–4 tbls soft brown sugar
flat-leaved parsley, to garnish

1   Heat the oven to 140C /275F /gas 1. Bring the pork chops to room temperature.
2   Season the pork chops on both sides with salt and freshly ground black pepper to taste.
3   In a flameproof casserole, melt half the butter and 45 ml /3 tbls olive oil. When the foaming subsides, add 2 of the pork chops and sauté them for 2 minutes on each side or until they are golden brown. Transfer the chops to a plate and keep warm. Repeat with the remaining pork chops.
4   Return all the chops to the casserole, cover with a lid and bake in the oven for 15–20 minutes or until tender.
5   Meanwhile, melt the remaining butter with the oil in a saucepan. Add the finely chopped onion and fry over moderate heat for 5 minutes, stirring occasionally. Add the apples and cook for a further 10 minutes, or until the apples are soft and the onions are tender. Stir in the brown sugar and a little salt to taste.
6   Transfer the pork chops to a heated serving dish and pour the juices from the casserole over them. Garnish with the cooked apple and onion mixture and flat-leaved parsley, if wished. Serve immediately.

standing, then 45 minutes

Gammon in puff pastry with Cumberland sauce

Seves 6

1.6 kg /3½ lb middle or corner cut
  of gammon
1 bay leaf
1 onion studded with 3 cloves
450 g /1 lb made-weight frozen puff
  pastry, defrosted
flour for dusting
1 egg, beaten

parsley and orange slices,
  to garnish
For the Cumberland sauce
1 orange
1 lemon
225 g /8 oz redcurrant jelly
10 ml /2 tsp dry mustard
50 ml /2 fl oz port

1   Put the ham in a saucepan, cover with cold water and soak for 4 hours. Drain, add the bay leaf and onion and cover with cold water. Bring to the boil and simmer for 1½ hours. Remove the joint from the pan, cut away the string, if tied up, and peel off the rind. Press the joint between 2 boards, weighted down, and leave overnight.
2   Dust a work surface with flour.
3   If the joint is triangular, roll out the pastry to a rectangle. Lay the joint on the pastry, knuckle end close to one short edge. Bring up the second short edge to cover the fillet end and join the long edges. Trim off excess pastry from the seams, dampen them with beaten egg and seal. If the joint is round, roll out the pastry in 2 pieces, one larger than the other. Place the ham on the smaller piece, dampen the edge with beaten egg, then put the larger piece on top of the ham, trim off any excess and seal the edges.
4   Use the pastry trimmings to decorate the joint. Place the joint on a baking tray sprinkled with water and leave in the refrigerator for at least 30 minutes. Heat the oven to 220C /425F /gas 7.
5   Meanwhile, prepare the sauce. Pare the zest off the orange and lemon and cut into thin strips 25 mm /1 in long. Blanch for 5 minutes in boiling water and drain. Squeeze the orange and half the lemon and strain the juice.
6   Combine the redcurrant jelly and the strained juice in a pan and heat gently until the jelly is melted. Remove from the heat.
7   In a medium-sized bowl combine the dry mustard and a little of the redcurrant jelly mixture and stir until well blended. Gradually add the remaining mixture from the pan, the port and the zest strips. Transfer to a sauce-boat and leave to cool.
8   Brush the pastry with beaten egg to glaze. Bake for 20–30 minutes; cover the pastry with foil if it becomes too brown. Transfer to a warmed dish, garnish and serve with the Cumberland sauce.

 5½ hours, overnight pressing,
defrosting pastry, 2 hours

Rillettes of pork

Serves 6

500 g /1 lb pork fillet
salt and freshly ground black
  pepper
pinch of cayenne pepper

1.5 ml /¼ tsp ground nutmeg
225 g /8 oz clarified butter
150 ml /5 fl oz boiling water
2 bay leaves, plus extra to garnish
Melba toast, to serve

1   Cut the pork into 25 mm /1 in pieces. Put the pork in a bowl and season generously with salt and freshly ground black pepper. Add the cayenne pepper and ground nutmeg and mix well.
2   Place the pork in a heavy saucepan with the clarified butter, boiling water and bay leaves. Bring to the boil, then simmer gently for 45 minutes, until the pork is tender and the liquid reduced to half its original quantity.
3   Remove and discard the bay leaves. Lift out the pork with a slotted spoon. Strain the liquid fat and keep on one side.
4   Pass the pork through the finest blade of your mincer. Place the minced pork in a bowl and gradually beat in half of the reserved fat with a wooden spoon. Correct the seasoning and spoon the mixture into 6 individual ramekins, levelling the tops with a palette knife. Leave to cool.
5   If you are serving the rillettes the same day, chill in the refrigerator until ready to serve. If you are serving the rillettes later, pour the remaining fat over the pork mixture in the ramekins and chill. They will keep safely in the refrigerator up to 2 weeks.
6   To serve, remove the fat topping from each ramekin, if necessary, garnish with a bay leaf and serve with Melba toast.

Make Melba toast, named to honour the Australian opera singer Nellie Melba, to serve with the rillettes. Toast white bread of medium thickness on both sides under the grill. Lay each toast slice flat and slice through horizontally with a long sharp knife to make 2 very thin slices. Return these to the grill briefly to dry out the cut sides. Store in an airtight container for up to 1 day if necessary.

● To clarify the butter put it in a small, heavy-bottomed saucepan and melt it over a very low heat. The butter will foam and this foam then falls to the bottom of the pan, leaving the clarified butter in a layer on top. Pour this off gently so as not to disturb the sediment.

 1¼–1½ hours,
plus cooling and chilling

Noodles with ham and mushroom sauce

Serves 4–6

250 g /8 oz green noodles
250 g /8 oz egg noodles
salt
30 ml /2 tbls olive oil
freshly grated Parmesan cheese,
    to serve
For the sauce
175 g /6 oz cooked ham, cut into
    5 mm /¼ in dice

250 g /8 oz mushrooms, cut into
    5 mm /¼ in dice
50 g /2 oz butter
½ Spanish onion, finely chopped
25 ml /1½ tbls flour
150 ml /5 fl oz thick cream
15 ml /1 tbls brandy
salt and ground black pepper
a pinch of cayenne pepper

1 Bring a large saucepan of well-salted water to the boil. Add the green noodles and egg noodles and cook 8–10 minutes until *al dente* – that is, tender but still firm.
2 While the pasta is cooking, prepare the ham and mushroom sauce. Sauté the diced ham in 25 g /1 oz of the butter. As the ham begins to colour, add the diced mushrooms and cook until tender, about 3–4 minutes. Remove the ham and mushrooms from the pan with a slotted spoon.
3 Add 15 g /½ oz of the remaining butter to the pan and sauté the finely chopped onion until it is transparent. Remove from the pan with a slotted spoon and add to the reserved ham mixture.
4 In a clean pan melt the remaining butter, add the flour and cook, stirring constantly with a wooden spoon, for 1–2 minutes. Add the thick cream and stir until the sauce starts to thicken. Do not let the sauce boil, and once it has thickened remove the pan from the heat.
5 Add the ham mixture and brandy to the sauce, and season with salt, freshly ground black pepper and cayenne pepper to taste.
6 Drain the noodles and, while they are still very hot, toss them in a clean saucepan with the olive oil. Add the sauce to the noodles and heat through. Serve immediately with a generous amount of freshly grated Parmesan cheese.

 25 minutes

Spicy potato-topped pork pie

Serves 4

700 g /1½ lb lean boneless pork
salt and freshly ground black pepper
2.5 ml /½ tsp ground cumin
5 ml /1 tsp turmeric
225 g /8 oz drained canned tomatoes
75 ml /3 fl oz thick cream
40 g /1½ oz digestive biscuit crumbs
For the potato topping
900 g /2 lb potatoes
salt
40 g /1½ oz butter
125 ml /4 fl oz milk
freshly ground black pepper
flat-leaved parsley, to garnish

1 Heat the oven to 170C /325F /gas 3.
2 Cut the pork into bite-sized cubes, discarding any fat and gristle. Season generously with salt and freshly ground black pepper.
3 In a casserole, combine the pork with the ground cumin, turmeric, drained tomatoes, thick cream and the biscuit crumbs. Stir to blend and cover. Cook in the oven for 1¾–2 hours or until really tender. Correct the seasoning. Blot off any surface fat with absorbent paper.
4 Meanwhile, prepare the potato topping. Peel the potatoes and cut into even-sized pieces. Cook them in a saucepan of boiling salted water for 20 minutes or until tender. Drain.
5 Press the potatoes through a vegetable mill into a bowl, or sieve them, pressing with the back of a wooden spoon. Beat in the butter and milk and season with salt and freshly ground black pepper to taste. Spread the potato purée over the spiced pork and return to the oven for a further 15–20 minutes or until golden. Serve immediately, garnished with a sprig of flat-leaved parsley.

2¼ hours

Lamb: basic information

Economical and versatile, moist and tender lamb is suitable for most cooking methods. In the opening chapters we explained how to master the cooking techniques combined with a selection of recipes. Here we give you information on buying and storing lamb, and on buying lamb in bulk for the freezer.

When buying fresh lamb look for pink, firm and fine-grained flesh and dry, white fat. Freshly cut meat surfaces will have a slightly moist appearance. Legs and shoulders should look plump and rounded and have a thin covering of fat beneath a pliable outer skin. Avoid both very lean, rangy carcasses and very fat ones. As the lamb ages the flesh colour deepens and the meat acquires a more mature flavour. Once past its first birthday lamb is generally described as mutton.

Lamb produced in Europe and North America is available from March through to November, with supplies reaching their peak between August and November. New Zealand supplies are available from the beginning of the year.

Storing lamb

In the shops lamb is usually kept under refrigeration, so it should be transferred to your own refrigerator as soon as possible. Unwrap the meat, stand it on a plate and cover loosely with foil or cling film to prevent the surface drying. Place it on the shelf below the frozen food compartment where it should keep for up to 3 days. In fact keeping lamb for a few days before cooking helps to develop the full flavour and tenderness, especially if the lamb has not been hung in the butcher's cold store for at least 4 days. This applies to imported frozen lamb which the butcher has thawed before selling and even more so to imported lamb which is still frozen when you buy it. If no refrigerator is available, store the unwrapped lamb for up to 2 days inside a meat safe in a cool larder.

Store cooked meat for 1-2 days in a cool larder or 2-3 days in a refrigerator.

Lamb for the freezer

Lamb is a good buy for the freezer, especially if you are not used to buying meat in bulk for freezing, as it is not overwhelmingly large. The meat is tender and sweet and you can have it cut into plenty of chops, cutlets and steaks.

A whole lamb weighs anything from 12.7-18 kg /28-40 lb: English lamb is larger, New Zealand lamb is smaller. For every 16 kg /36

Identifying various cuts of lamb: 1 leg of lamb and lamb fillet; 2 tenderloin; 3 loin and loin chops; 4 shoulder of lamb and shoulder chops; 5 cutlets and a best end of neck; 6 breast of lamb; 7 middle neck; 8 butterfly or double chops

Buying and cooking guide to lamb

Cut and weight	Butchering	Cooking methods	Cut and weight	Butchering	Cooking methods
Leg very lean top-quality meat 1.2–2.3 kg/ 2¾–5 lb	Whole Halved, if large, into fillet and knuckle end From fillet end cut: 5 mm /¼ in or 25 mm /1 in slices; or 10 mm /½ in leg chops; or 4 cm/ 1 in cubes	Roast or braise Roast fillet; braise or slow roast knuckle end Fry or grill slices and chops; grill kebabs casserole cubes	**Loin** top-quality meat with fat cover. Chump end bonier than neck end 1.4–2.3 kg / 3–5 lb	Whole (ask butcher to chop the bone to help carving) Halved, if large, into best end and chump Boned out Chops, either loin or chump	Roast Roast Stuff, tie and roast, or braise Fry or grill
Shoulder sweet eating meat but fattier than leg 1.2–2.5 kg/ 2¾–5½ lb	Whole Halved, if large, into blade joint and knuckle joint Boned; use whole or cubed Minced	Roast Roast or braise Stuff, tie and roast or braise; cube for casseroles or kebabs Hamburgers	**Saddle** both loins still joined by the backbone 3.6–5 kg/ 8–11 lb	Whole (including tail which is usually split and curled)	Roast: cook fat side uppermost. Cover for first ⅔ of cooking time, then baste frequently and brown
Best end of neck versatile cut of sweet meat with covering of fat; consists of 6–8 cutlets joined by back (chine) bone 700 g–1 kg/ 1½–2¼ lb	Whole (ask butcher to chop joint to facilitate carving) Two best ends butchered to form a Guard of Honour or a Crown Roast Boned Noisettes Cutlets	Roast Roast Stuff, tie and roast Grill or fry Grill or fry; 2 each	**Middle neck** very bony but good flavour if slow cooked with moisture 1.2–2.5 kg/ 2¾–5½ lb **Breast** thin strip of meat including rib bones and fat 700 g–1 kg/ 1½–2¼ lb	Chopped with bones Neck fillet – tender strips of boneless meat (from large lambs only) Whole, if large enough to bone, stuff and roll Cut into riblets	Hot pots and stews Cube for kebabs or casseroles, add herbs and spices; the bones make good stock Stuff, tie and braise or slow roast Cook in barbecue sauce

lb lamb on the bone allow 43 L /1½ cu ft space in the freezer.

If you buy imported lamb remember that it is shipped frozen, so it can only be cut into joints, chops and steaks – see the Bandsaw method of cutting up a frozen carcass on *page 106*. You will have to do any boning and rolling when you have defrosted it. There will be no kidneys supplied with imported frozen lamb. It is important that you buy only lamb that is still frozen and has not been allowed to thaw out, as handling and re-freezing could involve the risk of contamination. Carcasses tend to be smaller than fresh lamb: 8–16 kg /18–36 lb. Frozen lamb is, of course, available all year round, but the new season's 'spring lamb' usually starts to arrive in January.

The New Zealand Meat Producers' Board carefully examines and grades all exported carcasses. 'PL' carcasses will give especially small joints. The larger 'PM' carcass is better for legs and shoulders large enough to divide into two joints each, or for cutting into chops and portions.

You can buy packs of ready-jointed lamb in whole, half or selection packs at freezer centres, but your own butcher will be able to prepare the meat to your personal requirements.

Give him plenty of time and make a written list of exactly what you want (see sample order on *page 106*). Tell him how you would like the meat prepared. The order should state the sizes you would like the joints cut; if you want any of them boned and rolled; what proportion you would like as chops, cutlets, steaks and stewing meat. The Buying and cooking chart lists all the cuts from lamb and suitable cooking methods for each one. Most butchers will package and freeze the meat.

Making a choice

When buying lamb you will get two of each cut if you buy a whole lamb and one each from half a lamb. The leg is an excellent roasting joint. It can be left whole or boned out and stuffed. If large, it can be divided into the fillet end (the broad meaty end) and the shank end. The shank end is suitable for braising. You can also have leg steaks cut across the fillet end which will give you large succulent pieces of lean meat for frying, grilling or braising.

The leg can also be cut into thin slices which can be either crumbed and fried like escalopes or left uncrumbed, fried and served in a cream sauce.

The loin is another good roasting joint. It can be cooked whole or boned, stuffed and rolled. A large loin can be divided into two, providing a loin roast and a chump roast. If preferred, the whole joint can be cut into loin and chump chops.

If you buy a whole lamb your butcher could cut a large party roasting joint called the saddle. This consists of the whole loin, from both sides of the lamb below the rib bones, still joined by the backbone.

Above the loin is the best end of neck, which can be roasted whole or boned, stuffed and rolled. It can also be cut into small chops known as cutlets, or boned, rolled, tied and cut into 25 mm /1 in thick rounds, called noisettes.

If you buy a whole lamb the two best ends can be made into impressive roasting joints. A crown roast consists of the best ends joined in a circle, bones outward. A guard of honour is the best ends facing each other in a row with the fat sides outward.

The shoulder is another good roasting joint, slightly fattier than the leg, but with sweet and succulent meat. It can either be left on the bone or boned and stuffed. Large joints can be divided into blade end and knuckle end. You could also cut the meat into cubes for stewing, or mince it.

The middle neck and scrag, above the shoulder, are usually sold as chops. They are bony but excellent for flavour in hot pots.

The breast can be boned, then stuffed and rolled to make a small roasting joint. Or you could sandwich two boned breasts together, with a stuffing between them. Boned breasts can also be cut up for stewing. If the bones are left in, cut the breast into riblets and cook with a barbecue sauce.

Butcher's order for a lamb

Ask your butcher to supply two of each of following cuts, bagged and labelled.

Shoulder, about 2 kg /4½ lb: leave one shoulder whole and bone out the other. Cut this into cubes for casseroling, then pack equal amounts into three bags.

Middle neck and scrag, about 700 g /1½ lb: cut all this into chops. Pack all the scrag (about 10 chops) in one bag and the middle neck chops (10) in another bag.

Best end, about 900 g /2 lb: bone and roll one best end and cut into 25 mm /1 in wide noisettes (6). Pack in twos. Divide the other joint into cutlets (8) and pack in fours.

Loin and chump, about 1.2 kg /2¾ lb: bone and roll one whole loin and chump into a roasting joint. Cut the other into loin chops (6) and chump chops (4). Bag the chops in sets of two.

Leg, about 2 kg /4½ lb: leave one leg whole and cut the other into two joints of fillet (about 900 g /2lb) and shank (1 kg /2½ lb).

Breast, about 700 g /1½ lb: remove skin, then cut both breasts into riblets about 25 mm /1 in wide. Cut off remaining boneless flap (225 g /8oz) and pack separately to be used for stewing. Divide the riblets between two bags (8 in each).

Kidneys: remove fat and bag together.

Bones: pack all these together in one bag.

Fat: pack the suet fat from the kidneys and any other trimmed fat into one bag and leave unfrozen to be melted down.

Packaging and freezing

You can ask your butcher to freeze the meat for you, or do it yourself.

Unless the meat is well protected from the intense cold of the freezer it will dehydrate and deteriorate. It should be wrapped closely in tough moisture-and-vapour-proof material. If the meat does become dehydrated (also known as freezer burn) it will have greyish white marks on the surface. When cooked this part of the meat is likely to be tough, dry and unpalatable.

At least two hours before you get the meat home, switch the freezer to 'fast freeze' and clear the freezing compartment or, in an upright model, the shelf used for freezing. In order not to raise the temperature of food already in the freezer, put in only one tenth of the freezer's total capacity in 24 hours. If meat has to be frozen over 2 or 3 days, keep it well chilled in the refrigerator meanwhile. If this is not possible arrange to collect it in batches from the butcher.

● Freeze kidneys, mince and cut-up meat first, then chops and finally joints.

● Pack mince and cubed meat in amounts convenient for your family's needs. Weigh straight into polythene bags and press into a neat shape. Expel as much air as possible.

● Wrap chops individually or in sets, interleaving with polythene and overwrapping with foil or polythene bags.

● Pad any sharp bones on a joint with foil so they cannot puncture the wrapping.

● Expel as much air as possible from all packages, seal and label them. Place each package in contact with the base and/or sides of a chest freezer or on a freezer shelf in an upright model. After 24 hours transfer to the storage area and freeze further packs.

Carcass cutting

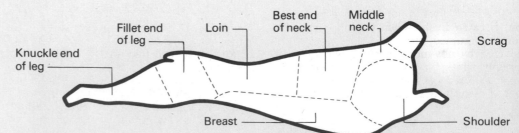

There is no standard way of cutting a lamb carcass, and methods differ from country to country and from district to district. This diagram shows the commonest British method. Even the British method varies from place to place in the United Kingdom. In Scotland the shoulder is not usually cut as a separate joint. Instead each side of the forequarter is boned, rolled and tied, then cut into smaller joints.

Bandsaw method for frozen lamb

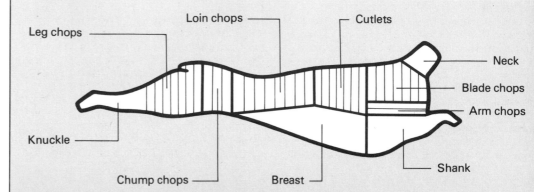

This is a way of cutting up a solidly frozen carcass to obtain the maximum number of individual portions for freezer storage, or for a large-scale barbecue. (It is not suitable for thawed carcasses.) Single chops and cutlet portions are obtained from a side of lamb, double cutlets or chops from a whole carcass.

Thawing times for frozen lamb

Cut	in a refrigerator	at room temperature
Large joint 1.6 kg /3½ lb or more	12-14 hours per kg 6-7 hours per lb	4-5 hours per kg /2-3 hours per lb
Small joints under 1.6 kg /3½ lb	6-8 hours per kg 3-4 hours per lb	2-4 hours per kg /1-2 hours per lb
Chops or slices	5-6 hours	2-4 hours

About 10 hours after the last batch of meat has been frozen, remember to switch the control back to normal.

Storage and thawing times

If it is stored at a constant temperature of −18C /0F or below, lamb has a reasonably long storage life with scarcely any deterioration in quality. Joints and chops will keep for up to 9 months in the freezer, offal and mince for up to 3 months. Meat kept longer than the recommended storage time does not become harmful, but its taste will deteriorate progressively the longer it is kept.

Whenever possible, thaw frozen lamb in the refrigerator rather than at room temperature and, once it is thawed, cook it as soon as possible.

Cooking from frozen

Most lamb can be cooked from frozen, but rolled joints like loin or breast must be thawed first to avoid a health risk. Roast lamb on the bone from frozen at 180C / 350F /gas 4, then make sure that joints are cooked through to the centre by using a meat thermometer. Towards the end of the estimated cooking time plunge the thermometer into the centre of the meat, as near the bone as possible, but not touching it. The thermometer must register a temperature of 82C /180F.

Small chops and slices of lamb can be grilled or fried from frozen. Start the cooking at a lower temperature, increasing it half-way through the cooking.

Cut-up lamb for stewing can be cooked from frozen, allowing an extra 30 minutes.

Pork: basic information

Unlike lamb, pork is not improved by ageing but is eaten fresh. When buying pork, look for fine-grained, firm and pale pink flesh, covered by not more than 15 mm /½ in of creamy white fat and a thin, supple outer rind. Avoid over-fat pork which is wasteful (or at least ensure that the butcher trims it before weighing).

Modern refrigeration has made pork an all-year-round meat, but prices fluctuate a little according to supply and demand. There is also a considerable price difference between the prime cuts in high demand and those that need more time to prepare.

When buying, allow 100–175 g /4–6 oz boneless pork per person or, depending on the amount of bone it contains, 175–275 g / 6–10 oz pork on the bone.

Pork for the freezer

A side of pork is an excellent buy for the freezer. It is not too large, the meat is tender and succulent and most cuts can be roasted, if you wish. The economy of bulk buying is considerable, while it is highly convenient to have your own meat stored, so you can cut down on shopping trips.

Pork is available all the year round though prices fluctuate. As demand tends to fall in hot weather, the summer is a good time to buy for the freezer. The weight range of a side of a pig is between 18–27 kg / 40–60 lb, so it is not a purchase to make without some thought. The average size of 22 kg /50 lb will take up 57 L /2 cu ft of freezer space.

If you have the choice, buy young pig, which is fairly lean. Half a pig will usually include half a head, two trotters and perhaps the tail. There will be no offal except one kidney, and about 275 g /10 oz fat (used in sausages).

On the whole the butcher will be your best source of supply, as he can cut the meat to your individual requirements. Give him plenty of time to prepare the order and make a written list of exactly what you want (see sample order on *page 108*). Your order should state the sizes you would like the joints cut; if you want any of them boned and rolled; what proportion you would like as chops, cutlets or escalopes; and how much of the meat is to be cubed, minced, or even made into sausages. The chart on *page 108* lists all the cuts from a pig and suitable cooking methods for each. Most butchers will package and freeze the meat for you.

Making a choice

The leg is prime quality roasting meat. It can be cut into joints to provide a rather bony knuckle end, a lean, meaty fillet end with just the central bone and, from a large leg, a middle cut. The leg produces the best crackling, and this is not impaired by freezing. If freezer space is short, or you plan to stuff the leg, it can be boned out, then cut and tied. If you prefer, however, the fillet end can be thinly sliced to fry.

The loin also produces prime roasting joints, but you have the option of having all or part of it as convenient chops. There are three different types. From the fore end come long chops which look like lamb cutlets, but are much larger. From the middle loin come shorter chops, which may include a portion of kidney. Chump chops are cut from the leg end.

Beneath the loin in heavy pigs there is a long strip of tender meat called the tenderloin. This is often sold as pork fillet, but should not be confused with the fillet end of leg. This can be roasted or made into escalopes. In small pigs, however, it is too small to separate from the loin chops.

The whole shoulder can be rinded and boned, then rolled and cut into joints. Alternatively, a compact roasting joint can be cut from the blade end of the shoulder and the

From the shoulder: 1 blade end joint; 2 spare rib chops. Belly: 3 whole belly including spareribs; 4 streaky end belly. From the loin: 5 tenderloin; 6 chump end of loin; 7 loin chops. From the leg: 8 chump chops; 9 leg escalopes; 10 leg steaks

Buying and cooking guide to pork

Cut and weight	Butchering	Cooking	Cut and weight	Butchering	Cooking
Leg Very lean; thin covering of fat and rind; makes good crackling 4-5.4 kg /9-12 lb	Whole Joints: lean fillet end; bonier knuckle end; Leg steaks Escalopes	Roast – can be boned and rolled or stuffed Roast or braise; knuckle end can be boned and stuffed Grill, braise or fry Sauté	**Chump end** Prime meat with good crackling; fairly high proportion of bone 1.4-1.6 kg /3-3½ lb **Loin** Finest roasting pork; makes excellent crackling 2.5-4.5 kg /5½-10 lb	Whole Chops Whole–ask the butcher to chine the joint French-style joint – without rind, fat or bones; meat tied Tenderloin	Roast – can be boned and rolled Braise or fry Roast Roast or braise, plain or stuffed Stuff and braise, bake en croûte, make into escalopes; cube for kebabs
Shoulder Fat and lean meat but good flavour 2.3-3.6 kg /5-8 lb	Boned and rolled joint Blade joint Sparerib joint or chops	Pot-roast or braise Roast – can be boned and stuffed Grill or bake in sauce; cube for stew or kebabs; mince		Loin chops– large and meaty Rib chops with long bone	Grill, fry or bake Grill, fry or bake
Belly An economical cut with high proportion of fat 2-3.9 kg /4½-8½ lb	Streaky end Thick end Thin slices Thick slices Chinese spareribs	Good pickled or boned and stuffed Roast Grill, bake or fry Cube for casseroles, mince for pâtés Barbecue or bake	**Hand and spring** Good value cut; ideal for pickling 2.3-3.6 kg /5-8 lb	Whole; hand can be boned and tied	Long slow cooking– pot-roast, braise or simmer

rest divided into spare rib cutlets. If you like fricassees, kebabs and casseroled pork, order this portion of pig cubed.

The hand and spring can be supplied as one large joint, but it is more useful to have the hand rinded, boned and rolled for slow roasting or braising and the shank end cubed for casseroling.

The belly is layered with fat, the thick end being the leanest. Joints can be slow roasted, braised, or pickled and boiled. The whole belly can be boned for stuffing and rolling and then divided into joints. Or you can ask for the bones as a complete set for Chinese spareribs and have the remaining meat cubed for casseroling. The streaky end makes an excellent fatty mince for mixing with leaner meats for pâtés and meat loaves.

Buy the half head if you plan to make brawn, and the trotters for enriching sauces. The bones make a rather sweet stock without other meat bones, but a few may be useful for adding to other meat stocks.

If you are ordering the loin without the rind, ask your butcher to leave only a thin layer of fat round the joints and to supply you with the back fat in a sheet: this will be useful for pâtés and for larding. Ask him to bag excess fat trimmed from other parts of the pig and let you have it fresh. When you get it home, cut it in small pieces, put in a baking tin and render it down in a cool oven. Pour off the liquid fat at frequent intervals. When cold and solid, package the resultant lard and freeze it.

Do not salt or pickle pork for the freezer as its storage life is very unpredictable. However, if you intend to marinate any of the cuts and you are freezing the meat at home, you can freeze it in the marinade.

Butcher's order for half a pig
Whole order to be bagged and labelled.

Leg, about 5.4 kg /12 lb: cut into three joints and score the rind well on all joints. The knuckle joint should be 2-2.3 kg /4½-5 lb in weight. Cut the remaining fillet end into two equal-sized joints (about 1.6 kg /3½ lb each).

Loin, about 5.9 kg /13 lb: cut two joints, one from the neck end, one from the loin end, each weighing about 1.6 kg /3½ lb; remove the rind, and all but a 15 mm /½ in layer of fat; bone, roll and tie them. Skin and halve the kidney and lay it on the centre of the rear end joint. The rest of the loin and the chump should be cut into chops and bagged in fours (or family numbers), interleaving each chop (2.7 kg /6 lb will make about 12 chops). Remove the rind.

Belly, about 3.4 kg /7½ lb: cut a 1.1 kg /2½ lb joint from the thick end. Remove bone from the rest of belly in one piece and bag. Mince 450 g /1 lb of the streaky end and bag separately. Cut the rest (about 1.4 kg /3 lb) into slices 10 mm /½ in thick and pack in fours, interleaving the slices (about 12).

Shoulder: Shoulder, about 2.5 kg /5½ lb: cut off 1.1 kg /2½ lb blade end (leaving bone in) as a roasting joint. Divide the rest of the shoulder (about 1.4 kg /3 lb) into sparerib chops about 25 mm /1 in wide, pack in fours, interleaving them (about 8).

Hand and spring, about 2.3 kg /5 lb: bone out, cube, then pack as three equal bags.

Trotters, about 450 g /1 lb: split both trotters into two and bag together.

Half head, about 2.3 kg /5 lb: please supply sausages of equivalent value.

Back fat: remove the rind from the fat, but leave in large flat pieces. Pack interleaved.

Fat: bag any trimmed-off fat together and leave unfrozen to melt down.
Bones: discard them.

Packaging
For large unwieldy shapes mould heavy duty foil closely around the meat. This will not need special sealing. For compact joints, chops, sausages, mince or cubed meat use extra-thick polythene bags (120–150 gauge). Cling film or a sheet of polythene is useful to interleave chops.

You will also need wire ties and labels. Plastic and card labels with incorporated wire ties are useful for packs with uneven surfaces, on which it is difficult to write or stick an adhesive label. Make sure everything is well labelled, as it is surprising how difficult it is to identify the contents of an unlabelled frosted package.

Freezing the meat
At least two hours before you get the meat home, switch the freezer to 'fast freeze' and clear the freezing compartment or, in an upright model, the shelf used for freezing. In order not to raise the temperature of food already in the freezer, put in only one tenth of the freezer's total capacity in 24 hours. If this means that the meat has to be frozen over 2 or 3 days, it is important to keep it chilled in the refrigerator meanwhile. If this is not possible arrange to collect it in batches from the butcher.

● Freeze kidneys, mince, sausages and cut-up meat first, then chops and finally joints.
● Pack mince and cubed meat in amounts convenient for your family's needs. Weigh straight into polythene bags and press into a neat shape. Expel as much air as possible.

- Wrap chops individually or in sets of a convenient number, interleaving with polythene and overwrapping with foil or polythene bags.
- Pad any sharp bones on a joint with foil so they cannot puncture the wrapping. Then pack in polythene bags or wrap in foil.
- Expel as much air as possible from all packages, seal and label them. Place each package in contact with the base and/or sides of a chest freezer or on the freezer shelf in an upright model. After 24 hours transfer to the storage area and freeze further packs. About 10 hours after the last batch of meat has been frozen, remember to switch the control back to normal.

Cooking from frozen

Most pork can be cooked from frozen, but all boneless pork joints, irrespective of weight, and joints on the bone over 1.8 kg /4 lb should be thawed first. Cook frozen pork on the bone under 1.8 kg /4 lb at 180C / 350F /gas 4 allowing 1 hour 15 minutes per kg /35 minutes per 1 lb plus 35 minutes extra. Make sure that joints are cooked through to the centre by using a meat thermometer. Towards the end of cooking time push it into the thickest part of the joint, making sure it is not touching a bone. The pork is cooked when the thermometer registers 88C /190F. Expect frozen small chops and slices of pork to take 10-15 minutes longer than when cooking from thawed. Allow 30 minutes longer than usual for frozen casseroles. It is a good idea to line casserole dishes with heavy duty foil before cooking. The whole dish can then be frozen and, when solid, the foil-wrapped food can be removed from the casserole for storage. To cook the dish from frozen, peel away the foil and replace the food in the casserole and heat through gently, turning occasionally and carefully.

Carcass cutting

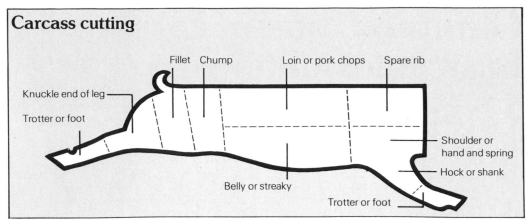

Thawing times for frozen pork

Cut	In a refrigerator	At room temperature
Large joint 1.5 kg /3¼ lb or more	8–14 hours per kg 4–7 hours per lb	4–8 hours per kg 2–4 hours per lb
Small joint under 1.5 kg /3¼ lb	6–8 hours per kg 3–4 hours per lb	4–6 hours per kg 2–3 hours per lb
Chops or steaks 25 mm /1 in thick	5–6 hours	2–4 hours

Storage and thawing times

Pork has a relatively short freezer life. Meat kept beyond the recommended storage time (see chart) does not become harmful, but suffers a slow deterioration in taste and texture.

It is better to slowly thaw pork in the refrigerator (see chart) than at room temperature. Once thawed, cook the meat as soon as possible, as you would fresh cuts of pork.

Batch cooking for the freezer makes long-term meal planning easy and provides a variety of menus

Pork freezer facts

Weight range of sides: 20–30 kg /44–66 lb.
Freezer space needed: for every 25 kg /55 lb pork on the bone allow 56 L /2 cu ft.
How supplied: usually jointed and on the bone as: whole side, which may include half the head and two trotters;
hind end (loin and leg) or fore-end (shoulder, hand and belly);
individual portions or joints.
Maximum storage times at −18C /0F:
joints and portions – up to 6 months;
offal, mince, sausages – up to 3 months.

Gammon, bacon & ham: basic information

Different kinds of traditional ham have acquired their individuality from variations in their preparation. The cure, which is basically a dry-salting, brining or sweet pickling process, may be followed by an extended drying and maturing period to give additional flavour. The hams may be smoked over different types of aromatic wood.

Hams eaten cooked: York ham, originally from the North of England, is a cure known all over the world. The ham is mild and pale pink, darker near the bone. It is considered the best ham for eating cold, though it is also delicious served hot. It is always made with a dry-salt cure, but may be lightly or heavily smoked.

Another famous British ham is Suffolk ham which is sweet-treacle-cured and then smoked. Bradenham ham is cured in molasses and spices according to an 18th century recipe and is easily recognizable by its black rind. Irish hams are usually dry-salted and then boned, before being smoked.

American hams are dry-salted with a secret cure and then smoked over apple and hickory wood. Virginia hams, and in particular Smithfield hams, are known all over the world. The true Virginian ham comes from pigs fed on peanuts and peaches. Pigs for Kentucky hams are grain-fattened after a diet of acorns, beans and clover.

Paris ham, which is also called *jambon blanc* (white ham), is actually very pale, delicate pink. It is only very lightly cured in brine and is either very lightly smoked or not smoked at all. Paris ham is always boiled – usually to eat cold.

The finest ham for serving hot is the Prague ham, *Pragerschinken*, from Czechoslovakia. This is brined for several months and then smoked over beech sawdust. Serve it baked, boiled or raw.

Hams eaten raw: *prosciutto*, Italian for ham (pronounced proshooto), is used almost synonymously with 'raw ham', because the most famous raw ham comes from Parma in Italy. It is dark salmon in colour, and semi-opaque, not unlike smoked salmon in appearance. Traditionally it is obtained from 8-week-old pigs which are cured by dry-salting, but not smoked.

Spanish *serrano* (mountain ham) is perhaps the nearest ham to prosciutto. It comes from the black-coated Iberian pig which runs free in the forests, and as a result the meat is rather tougher. The best hams come from the Huelva region.

Bayonne is the best-known French raw ham. It is wine-cured and, unlike the raw hams of Spain and Italy, it is smoked, wrapped up in straw. *Jambon de Bayonne* is usually eaten raw as a first course, but may also be used in cooking in a variety of ways. *Jambon de Toulouse* is another famous French ham that is eaten raw and may also be included in cooked dishes: it is merely salted and dried, not smoked. From Belgium comes the delicately smoked Ardennes ham.

Germany is renowned for strongly smoked hams. Best-known is Westphalian ham, which is cured with juniper berries and smoked over ash or beech.

Buying and storing ham

Ham for eating raw: this can be bought freshly sliced from delicatessens or in vacuum packs from supermarkets. It should be sliced paper thin and there should be no sign of the meat drying out. Allow 40–50 g / 1½–2 oz per person.

Raw ham for cooking: whole raw hams are ideal for buffet parties but may be difficult to buy, even from specialist suppliers.

A whole raw ham weighs 7–8 kg /15½–18 lb (half hams are sometimes available). About one fifth of raw ham will be the weight of the bone. Remember that the cooking will also shrink the final weight of the meat by another fifth. If raw ham has a slight bluish bloom on it from the cure, scrape this off after soaking.

Ready-cooked ham: whole hams, or half a ham, may be obtained from a specialist delicatessen or supplier. Sometimes they are available with the knuckle bone in, but the shank bone removed.

In some delicatessens ham may be carved or sliced to order, but cooked ham is widely available, vacuum-packed, from supermarket chilled cabinets. With the ham you will also find a cooked meat which may be described as 'picnic ham' or 'ham shoulder'. This may be cured in the same way as ham, but it is from the shoulder of the pig, rather than being the finer meat from the hind leg and, therefore, is not legally ham. Its texture and quality are inferior to real ham but it, nevertheless, supplies a cheaper substitute. Allow about 50 g /2 oz ham per person when serving for a salad.

Canned hams are ready-cooked and are widely sold and exported. Danish, Polish and Dutch are the best-known. Buy a small one to keep in your store cupboard: a 1 kg /2 lb sterilized or pasteurized ham can be kept in a cool place for up to 6 months.

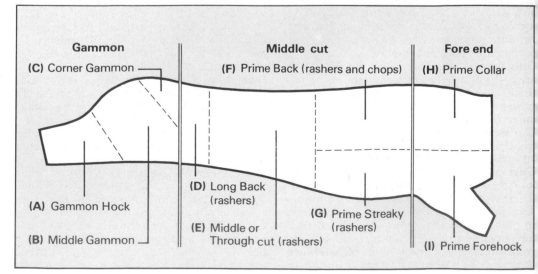

Fore end

Storing: in theory a whole, uncooked ham can be hung until ready for use. In practice it is difficult to find a dry, airy place between 1–15C /34–60F. Refrigerate bought slices of cooked ham in cling film or foil for 1–2 days. Store joints for up to 5 days, wrapped in cling film or foil.

Freezing: Heavily smoked ham will keep longer in the freezer than unsmoked or lightly smoked ham. A portion of a home-cooked ham will freeze only for 3–4 weeks. A vacuum-packed ham, however, can be frozen for 4 months. Dishes with cooked ham in them should not be kept frozen for longer than a few weeks.

Gammon	Middle cut	Fore end
(C) Corner Gammon	(F) Prime Back (rashers and chops)	(H) Prime Collar
(A) Gammon Hock	(D) Long Back (rashers)	(G) Prime Streaky (rashers)
(B) Middle Gammon	(E) Middle or Through cut (rashers)	(I) Prime Forehock

Gammon

Cuts of bacon and gammon

Sides of both smoked and unsmoked bacon are cut into joints, slices and thin slices known as 'rashers' in Britain. The diagram illustrates the main divisions and shows where the different cuts come from.

Gammon: this is the most expensive part of the bacon side and consists of prime quality solid meat with a thin covering of fat. It weighs up to 8 kg /17 lb and can be bought whole, on the bone or boned out, and is often cooked and sold sliced by specialist grocers. For home use it is usually cut into smaller joints, as follows:

Middle gammon (B): the prime cut from the centre of the gammon, with a high ratio of lean to fat. It weighs up to 3.5 kg /8 lb whole and is usually sold boned and tied and cut into smaller joints. Bake in foil, boil, parboil and bake, or braise.

Gammon steaks and slices: steaks, which are 5–10 mm /¼–½ in thick, and 5 mm /¼ in thick slices are cut from the middle gammon. They are prime lean cuts for grilling or frying.

Corner gammon (C): is a small, triangular, boneless cut weighing up to 1.4 kg /3 lb. Cook as for middle gammon.

Gammon hock (A): this cut from the shank (or knuckle) end can vary in size from half the gammon to a small, bony, shank end. The meat at the shank end is rather sinewy, so short cut joints are best boiled and used for stock or soup. However, a half-leg gammon hock is a meaty joint of handsome shape with plenty of surface area for glazing. Boil, parboil and bake, or braise.

Middle cut: the whole of this central area is usually sliced into bacon slices. Middle cut joints, which may need to be ordered specially, have a fairly high ratio of fat to lean meat, and are often rolled and tied.

Back bacon (F) is a prime lean meat with a fine flavour and a thin covering of fat, which provides thin slices, chops or a joint suitable for baking or braising.

Streaky bacon (G) is an economical cut consisting of alternate layers of fat and lean meat. It may be sold thinly sliced to grill or fry or as a joint which can be either boiled or braised.

Middle cut or Through cut (E) provides very long thin slices of bacon with lean meat from the back at one end and streaky bacon at the other. The joint is a similar mixture of lean meat and streaky; it is very suitable for stuffing as it can be rolled so easily.

Long back (D) provides large, substantial slices of bacon to grill or fry; when thickly cut they can be cubed and used for either casseroles or pies.

Fore end is the neck and shoulder and contains a mixture of lean and fat. The meat is coarser and cheaper than gammon. It absorbs a lot of salt during curing and needs more soaking than other cuts before cooking. Fore end is usually cut into economically priced joints as follows:

Collar (H) is the better part of the fore end and weighs up to 4 kg /9 lb. It is usually boned and tied and divided into smaller joints suitable for boiling or braising.

Alternatively, collar bacon is sometimes available sliced.

Forehock (I) contains the knuckle bone, but is often sold boned and rolled into small joints which are suitable for either boiling or braising.

Buying bacon and gammon

Bacon will keep longer than uncured meat, but is nevertheless perishable, with a very limited shelf life, so when choosing it is important to look for signs of freshness. Fresh bacon has very firm, white fat and moist, pink (but not 'wet'-looking) meat. It should smell mild and pleasant, never stale or strong, and bacon rashers should not be curling at the edges.

Cut to order: this traditional service is now rare, but still available in some first-class grocers or delicatessens where sides of bacon or whole gammons are on display. These shops will cut joints, and slices of specified thickness, as required. Small bacon scraps are sometimes available at a lower cost, and these are excellent for use in quiches and stews.

Film wrapped: ready-cut joints or slices wrapped in transparent plastic film are normally marked with the cut, weight and price. Vacuum-packed joints and slices are pre-packed in thick polythene. The vacuum packing extends the shelf life of the bacon considerably: note the 'sell-by' or 'open by' date and any cooking instructions.

Boil-in-the-bag: small joints are packed in a special transparent film able to withstand boiling water. Follow the label instructions and do not attempt to boil-in-the-bag any joint not so labelled.

Storing bacon and gammon

Treat vacuum-packed bacon as fresh once opened. Wrap joints or slices closely in cling film or foil and store in the refrigerator for up to 5 days or as directed. Refrigerate home-cooked bacon joints for 3–4 days, and bought, sliced cooked gammon for 24 hours.

Freezing: Closely wrap fresh bacon in foil, heavy-duty cling film or polythene, excluding as much air as possible. Layering slices or chops with film makes them easier to separate for cooking. Seal and label.

Because of its salt content, bacon has a shorter storage life in the freezer than other meat, for the salt acts as a pro-oxidant in freezing conditions, making the bacon taste rancid if kept too long. Smoke is an antioxidant, so smoked bacon keeps longer than unsmoked. Raw smoked joints will keep for up to 8 weeks, slices and chops for up to 4 weeks. Unsmoked joints will keep for up to 5 weeks, slices and chops for up to 2 weeks. Vacuum-packed joints, smoked and unsmoked, will keep up to 4 months in the freezer; vacuum-packed slices and chops up to 3 months. Home-cooked bacon joints will keep for not more than 3–4 weeks in the freezer.

A little chopped bacon is often fried with the onions when a base is being prepared for a casserole. If, however, you are preparing a casserole to freeze, it is wiser to leave the bacon out, as cooked dishes containing bacon are liable to develop an 'off' flavour if kept frozen longer than a few weeks.